Performative Linguistic Space

Anthropological Linguistics

Edited by
Svenja Völkel and Nico Nassenstein

Volume 3

Performative Linguistic Space

Ethnographies of Spatial Politics
and Dynamic Linguistic Practices

Edited by
Neriko Musha Doerr and Jennifer M. McGuire

DE GRUYTER
MOUTON

ISBN 978-3-11-221387-2
e-ISBN (PDF) 978-3-11-074478-1
e-ISBN (EPUB) 978-3-11-074484-2
ISSN 2701-987X

Library of Congress Control Number: 2023937082

Bibliographic information published by the Deutsche Nationalbibliothek
The Deutsche Nationalbibliothek lists this publication in the Deutsche Nationalbibliografie;
detailed bibliographic data are available on the internet at http://dnb.dnb.de.

© 2025 Walter de Gruyter GmbH, Berlin/Boston
This volume is text- and page-identical with the hardback published in 2023.
Cover image: _jure/iStock/Getty Images Plus
Typesetting: Integra Software Services Pvt. Ltd.
Printing and binding: CPI books GmbH, Leck

www.degruyter.com

Preface

The seed of this book was sown at a small cafe in Kyoto, where Doerr and McGuire discussed how space works when communicating in sign languages as opposed to spoken ones. What first struck Doerr was that, when signing, you can communicate with someone at a distance as long as you can see them clearly but cannot do so with someone right next to you if the view is obstructed. We further discussed communication in the "signing space," an area for producing language created around the signer's body (Klima and Bellugi 1979: 51)—though space created by signing is not limited to this three-dimensional zone of articulation. Signing and signers can produce fluid, temporal, and metaphorical unbounded deaf spaces. More permanent DeafSpace can also be constructed through architectural designers informed by "deaf collectivist social sensibilities" that are conducive to signing (Bauman 2014: 377). As we moved in our discussion between two types of space-language linkages (albeit simplified at the time of discussion)—of spoken languages and of sign languages—our taken-for-granted views of space-language relationships were put in relief: Doerr's understanding, which was derived from normalized oral communication, was challenged; McGuire (who has been doing intersectional research within the fields of anthropology and Deaf Studies)[1] was, in turn, surprised to see how fresh this realization was for Doerr.

Doerr's lack of familiarity with signing space is not uncommon for scholars in the social sciences and humanities. Insights and epistemologies from Deaf Studies have been overlooked across the disciplines even though they have been shown to enrich scholarship in the humanities by revealing new layers of interpretation (e.g., Sanchez 2017) which can push us to "consider new ways of listening, new ways of thinking, new ways of seeing the world through Deaf eyes" (Bauman 2008: 3).

This conversation heightened our awareness about the space as linguistic space and of the spaces we had occupied, as researchers and educators, prior to our meeting. Moving between two "academic spaces" challenged taken-for-granted assumptions about language and communication and ultimately sparked this collaboration. Going beyond the differences between Deaf Studies and anthropology, we considered other cases of moving between various spaces—physically and metaphorically—and their effects. We further pondered how exploring such processes could be a fruitful academic endeavor that opens new angles in analyzing linguistic practices in any

---

[1] Deaf Studies is influenced by and draws upon disciplines including anthropology, geography, sociology and political theory yet it rarely directly engages or intersects in these fields (Kusters et al. 2017: 3).

https://doi.org/10.1515/9783110744781-202

situation. Throughout this volume, contributors take different approaches in diverse research contexts to examine the very questions that arose during our initial conversation: How does space shape linguistic practices? How is that highlighted and complicated when individuals move between different types of space? And how are such spaces traversed by the linguistic politics that mobile individuals bring into them, creating complex performative linguistic spaces? By addressing these questions, this volume seeks to open up a new area of research: performative linguistic space that incorporates language, space, and mobility.

References

Bauman, Hansel. 2014. DeafSpace: An architecture toward a more livable and sustainable world. In Joseph J. Murray & H-Dirksen L. Baumann (eds.), *Deaf gain: Raising the stakes for human diversity*, 375–401. Minneapolis, MN. and London: University of Minneapolis Press.

Bauman, H-Dirksen L. 2008. Introduction: Listening to deaf studies. In H-Dirksen L. Bauman. (ed.), *Open your eyes: Deaf studies talking*, 1–32. Minneapolis, MN: The University of Minnesota Press.

Klima, Edward S. & Ursula Bellugi. 1979. *The signs of language*. Cambridge: Harvard University Press.

Kusters, Annelies, Maartje De Meulder & Dai O'Brien (eds.). Innovations in deaf studies: Critically mapping the field. 2017. In Annelies Kusters, Maartje De Meulder & Dai O'Brien (eds.), *Innovations in deaf studies: The role of deaf scholars*, 1–53. New York and Oxford: Oxford University Press.

Sanchez, Rebecca. 2017. Rejecting the talkies: Charlie Chaplin's language politics and the future of deaf studies in the humanities. In Annelies Kusters, Maartje De Meulder & Dai O'Brien (eds.), *Innovations in deaf studies: The role of deaf scholars*, 151–166. New York and Oxford: Oxford University Press.

Contents

Neriko Musha Doerr, Jennifer M. McGuire

Introduction: Performative linguistic spaces that make utterances and signs (not) happen

1 Introduction

Words not only describe but also make things happen. Words can start a class or unite people in "holy matrimony." This is the "performative" aspect of language, effective when the convention is invoked and the appropriate circumstances exist (Austin 1961/1979). In this volume, we apply this "performative" notion to space to investigate the ways space pushes us to produce linguistic acts. We call this productive aspect of space "performative linguistic space," and trace how individuals activate a performative aspect of space, reflecting their own linguistic trajectories through physical and metaphorical movement.

Researchers have illustrated that space produces perceptions and actions while being produced by them, though not necessarily with the notion of performativity. City and regional planning—e.g., redlining or the gap of investment between highways and public mass transit (Aalbers 2014; Soja 2010)—shapes our daily actions as well as our life chances, while also prompting us to challenge them. Individuals' movement and dwelling in space also affect, if not guide, others' actions and perceptions (de Certeau 1984; Egan 2021; Castañeda 2020). This volume adds a linguistic dimension to the notion of performativity of space.

Just as linguistic interactions are temporal and contextual (Voloshinov 1973), so is performativity of space. As will be explained, this performativity is shaped by temporal and contextual interactions not only between the dynamics of the space and interlocutors' subject positions but also by the ideologies that are being activated. Ideologies are also brought in from the spatial politics of other spaces that interlocutors have inhabited, just like Doerr's and McGuire's respective assumptions about space in spoken and sign language mentioned in the preface were imported from their respective ethnographic, disciplinary, and institutional spaces into a new space of comparison. Chapters in this volume explore divergent perspectives and frameworks as they investigate the performative linguistic space that emerges as individuals move between spaces.

Accordingly, this volume examines the ways in which contrasting spatial politics brought in by individuals from other spaces illuminate the taken-for-granted as well as highlight alternative linguistic practices. It demonstrates that linguistic practices are shaped by the language politics "dragged" from various spaces

https://doi.org/10.1515/9783110744781-001

participating individuals traverse. Interlocutors' past and current mobility must be understood to comprehend their linguistic transactions in a specific space. For instance, as Doerr's chapter illustrates, analyzing the way a Guatemalan American student spoke Spanish to a Spaniard in Spain can show the traces of language politics across different contours of performative linguistic spaces: (1) the legacy of Spanish colonialism in Guatemala that made Spanish its official language hence the student's proficiency in it as people were forced to use Spanish, (2) US immigration politics that hinder Spanish speech in mainstream US spaces which, in turn, made speaking Spanish in the study abroad space comforting, and (3) the legacy of Spanish colonialism in Spain that devalued the colonial variant of Spanish in Guatemala, thus discouraging its use. Traces of the language politics from these spaces this Guatemalan American carried with her turned Spain into a performative linguistic space that demanded a specific kind of utterance or lack thereof. In this way, every individual becomes involved in the dynamic spacing process.

That is, performative linguistic space is not a static space but a point of convergence. In performative linguistic space, heterogeneous spatial politics carried over by interlocutors activate new dynamics of linguistic practices. Chapters in this volume investigate such movements between spaces, including colonial spaces, immigrant spaces, and study abroad spaces (Doerr), monolingualist space and "translanguaging" space (Đỗ and Poole), in-person and virtual zoom spaces of language learning (Kumagai), deaf signing and hearing oral communication spaces (McGuire), and uninitiated and experienced voluntourism spaces (Jakubiak). Rather than perceiving language as a bounded unit corresponding to a linguistic community and space, as formulated by the nation-state ideology, we focus on space and linguistic practices that emerge or are inhibited in that specific space in context.

The main contributions of this volume, as will be discussed further in this chapter, are threefold. First, through ethnographic data, we explore the concept of "performative linguistic space" in which space ushers, coaxes, hinders, or silences utterances or signs. Second, we show that the space is not performative on its own. Instead, it becomes performative as a result of the specific intersections of linguistic politics brought by individuals from the various spaces they have traversed. This is because individuals carry with them linguistic politics they experienced in other spaces. Third, by focusing on specific utterances and signs in space linked to individuals' subject positions, we move away from assuming/reinscribing association of the linguistic community to the space, which allows us to avoid notions of stable and discernible units of language that would reinforce arbitrary scaling practices that assign more importance to a certain scale. This involves us in the discussion of the nation-state ideology as well as debates around "globalization" and scaling, which will be discussed later in the chapter.

In the following sections, we first provide an overview of the notion of place, space and spacing, before introducing this volume's core concept, "performative linguistic space." We then question the assumed connection between space and language constructed through the nation-state ideology and its (failed) subversion by ethnic movements and the globalist discussions, as well as the nation-state ideology's relationship to academic discussions that backgrounds this research. Next, we offer a brief review of some of the existing research on space and language, before ending with an introduction to each chapter.

2 Place, space, and spacing

Contestation of definitions, Bourdieu (1989) argues, is nothing but a contestation of who gets to impose their vision (and division) of the world onto others. This volume primarily focuses on "space" and spacing rather than "place," and authors use the term "space" variably and do not focus on space and place as a dichotomy. Nonetheless, to loosely position this volume in the ongoing "space" versus "place" debate with Bourdieu's argument above in mind, we provide a very brief review of how researchers have used these notions variously, followed by the contributors' usage. We then turn to the key concepts that underpin this volume: space and spacing.

"Space" and "place" are said to be constructs with roots in geography and have spurred extensive theorization in the social sciences and humanities (see summary in Low 2009). De Certeau (1984), for example, views place as meaningful with history, whereas space emerges through people's actions. Place for him is "fragmentary and inward-turning histories . . . accumulated times that can be unfolded but like stories held in reserve, remaining in an enigmatic state, symbolizations" (1984: 108). Space, in contrast, is activated by pedestrians' footsteps and intertwined paths which give shape to spaces by weaving places together. That is, "space is a practiced place . . . the street geometrically . . . is transformed into a space by walkers" (1984: 117). In discussing mobility as the dynamic equivalent of place, Cresswell (2006) summarizes "place" as meaningful segments of space. A place is "a center of meaning—we become attached to it, we fight over it and exclude people from it" (Cresswell 2006: 3). It is argued that spaces are not meaningless but have "their own grammar which can direct or limit mobility" and are "also actively produced by the act of moving" (Creswell and Merriman 2011: 15).

Some scholars, such as Low (2009) find it more fruitful and theoretically important to explore space and place as reproductions of human agency rather than "resolving the space/place dichotomy" (p. 23). Allowing the concepts to co-exist has also been advocated. For instance, Agnew (2005: 82) argues that "as conceptual twins, [space and place] offer more together than use of either does separately."

In this volume, two of the five chapters explicitly address space versus place. For Đỗ and Poole, space and place (as well as landscape) are concepts that should be used as verbs rather than nouns. Kumagai draws upon scholarship to give an overview of the contested distinction between place and space, determining that the online classroom is an abstract, conceptual space and that only physical locations will be referred to as "places." Keeping these diverging perspectives intact, we now turn to our discussion of space.

This volume contributes a new understanding of linguistic practices to the discussion of spacing. Space is constructed by a series of ongoing processes of "spacing" (Cresswell and Merriman 2011: 15) that are imbued with personal and collective meanings and marked by the trajectory of people's movement and dwelling in time. Space also enables or limits—i.e., directs—mobility and actively produces the act of moving (Cresswell 2006; Cresswell and Merriman 2011; de Certeau 1984). Chapters in this volume investigate various factors that affect spacing processes: the legacy of colonial language politics that create hierarchies among linguistic varieties and perceptions about immigrants as to what language they should speak (Doerr), discourses of study abroad and language education that dictate what language should be used or how language should be used in certain space (Doerr; Đỗ and Poole; Kumagai), educational trends, linguistic ideologies, and socialization into language habitus (McGuire), and competing understandings of humanitarianism (Jakubiak).

To understand the various kinds of forces that have affected spacing processes throughout history, we briefly review some significant ones, namely, labor relations, technological developments, maps, city and regional planning, legal measures, as well as constructed images and commercial, educational, and informal daily practices. The examples below are mainly drawn from the US context and are by no means exhaustive. We include them to illustrate diverse discussions of the ways our practices and perceptions of the world are intertwined with our spacing practices, in which our volume's discussions on performative linguistic space can be positioned.

Labor relations, such as post-Fordist capitalism in the latter half of the twentieth century—i.e., shortening of turn-around time and flexible accumulation of capital—as well as new technologies in communication and transportation altered the characteristics of space and the time. This is what David Harvey (1990) called the "time-space compression," which is often linked to the emerging perception of "globalization" in the late twentieth century.

Technological developments have affected the ways we experience space, as shown in Kumagai's exploration of online learning environments. Long before the creation of virtual classrooms, advances in technology were inextricably linked to a new engagement with space. For instance, shortened travel times via the introduction of airplanes reduced the distinctiveness and thus the aura of far-away places (Cresswell 2006), but also aroused interest in such faraway places by increased accessibility through a reduction in time commitment (Picard and DiGiovine 2014). Linking of computer technologies to automobiles, backgrounded by environmental concerns and/or changing priorities and economic conditions, created "carsharing" in some cities. There, individuals pay a fee to use an available car from the network of shared cars using a phone app, shifting the view of the automobile from "commodity" to "service" while also creating "collaborative consumption" and "networked subjectivity" as opposed to private ownership (associated with car ownership), which was then connected to the notions of freedom, autonomy, and progress (Dowling and Simpson 2013).

Maps are performative because they not only affect how we perceive and experience space but also produce actions. For example, the invention of the birds-eye-view map helped visualize territories with clear boundaries, playing a role in creating "imagined communities" of nations linked to specific bounded territory (Winichakul 1990; see also Anderson 1991). More recently, GPS navigation systems introduced a map that is designed to guide, thus pushing the viewer to act in a certain way, following the path suggested. Although GPS-generated maps resemble how we experience daily space, it is generative in that this is a way to suggest the path we should be taking next—performative. This is clearly shown in the augmented reality game based on the GPS technology in which a fantasy map is laid atop the physical world. For example, in augmented reality games like Pokémon GO, the mapping affects the flow and dwelling of its players by creating certain spots to visit and linger as well as pushing them to move to earn mileage for the game (Doerr 2019). Here, the GPS map of the game is not only a device of spacing but also performative in generating the players' actions.

City and regional planning policies work as major spacing processes. Legal measures, such as redlining in the US, color-coded neighborhoods ostensibly based on economic conditions, though frequently racially determined, resulted in uneven opportunities for attaining mortgages, thus opportunities for home ownership. It was designed to encourage mortgage lending in wealthier neighborhoods and to discourage it in red-coded low-income areas, often those with higher populations of African-Americans. This type of legally-determined uneven distribution of life opportunities continues to have an effect despite the end of legal segregation in the 1960s and of redlining in 1968 (Aalbars 2014; Coates 2014).

The investment gap between the building and maintenance of freeways and the construction of public mass transit provides another example of a discriminatory spacing practice. It creates what Edward Soja (2010: x) calls an "unjust metropolitan transit geography" that impacts the inner-city and largely minority working poor populations who rely on public transportation (also, see Henderson 2006). Contestation over public space can spur grassroots activism, such as the Bus Riders' Union in Los Angeles, which formed wider coalitions to fight for improvement in mass transit (Soja 2010), and the collective actions by "colectivos" or "biketivists" whose nightly collective rides in various parts of the city, including uncharted areas like the airport and wetland, playfully subverted urban planners' top-down design of space (Castañeda 2020).

Historical constructions of images about racialized space continue to affect current spacing practices. For example, images of nature in relation to US cities were constructed in two contradictory ways: non-whites as part of the "premodern" nature that white men sought to explore on the one hand, and nature being seen as an escape for "old stock" white Americans living in industrialized cities "crowded" with non-whites, on the other (Braun 2003). The legacy of these imaginings of the space, Braun (2003) argues, make "non-white outdoor adventurer" an oxymoron. It resulted in mainstream media's portrayal of outdoor activities as white male activities, discouraging non-white people, but especially African Americans, from participating (Finney 2014; Floyd and Stodolska 2014; Martin 2004). The racialized imagining of space, however, has at times been obscured as dominant discourses seek to portray the outdoors as a place of universal allure—as Eden (as Henry David Thoreau suggested) (Martin 2004)—or as a space for wholesome experiences for city children (The Fresh Air Fund 2017). These dominant portrayals serve to silence the non-white viewpoints for which "wilderness places may be tied more to the history of domination, enslavement, and lynching at the hands of Whites" (Martin 2004: 517).

Commercial practices also affect spacing processes. For example, Eisenhauer (2021) shows how the Asbury Park boardwalk, an emerging coastal vacation destination in the late nineteenth century, initiated racial segregation by framing it in commercial terms—as a way to draw white vacationers—in New Jersey where segregation was illegal. More recently, gated residential communities "intensify social segregation, racism, and exclusionary land practices" (Low 2003: 11) by feeding into the white middle-class's assumption regarding race/class-coded criminality.

Various spacing practices mutually affect educational practices. Gulson and Symes (2007) categorize the analyses in the field of education into three types: (1) Foucauldian analysis of space as the technology of surveillance and normalization that divides students; (2) examination of effects of neoliberal education reform in which school's spatial arrangement became part of its marketing strategies as well as the issue of access as schools are closed and students are forced to attend faraway schools; and (3) incorporation of space in critical pedagogy, literacy, curriculum, and geography of disability (Gulson and Symes 2007). For example, Critical Pedagogy of Place (CPP) encourages students to learn from and nurture places and related communities through decolonization (i.e., identifying and changing ways of thinking related to the place and people there) and rehabilitation (i.e., identifying, recovering, and creating material space/places to live better). This can then be further applied to indigenous studies and engaging with the aspect of reclaiming one's own history and turning a place into a space of resistance and hope, activating healing through engagement with the well-being of the place (Trinidad 2011).

Finally, informal daily practices also function as spacing practices. For example, bicycle riders claim their legitimacy over motorists as users of public space by employing diverse strategies, such as accentuating their presence to alert others and indicating the motorists' transgression through confrontational gestures (Egan 2021). Another example of such informal acts—albeit ones that engage formal institutions of power—is the policing of the white middle-class neighborhood by the residents, including calling authorities on the presence of African American individuals with the clear understanding of the possible excessive use of police force (American Anthropological Association 2020).

Our discussions of performative linguistic space are situated in these examinations of spacing, as will be detailed in the next section.

3 Performative linguistic space

As mentioned earlier, John Langshaw Austin (1961/1979) discussed how the act of saying something makes things happen, rather than merely describing what is happening, with the notion of "performativity." For example, "I name the ship the Queen Elizabeth" performs a christening and naming of the ship rather than describing the christening ceremony or stating the name of the ship. In order for that utterance to be performative—i.e., to make things happen—however, the convention invoked must exist and the circumstances have to be appropriate (Austin 1961/1979).

Building on this concept of performativity, Judith Butler (1993: 3) uses it "not as the act by which a subject brings into being what she/he names, but rather, as that reiterative power of discourse to produce the phenomena that it regulates and constrains." With the notion of citationality, Butler suggests that by being cited as the norm, certain matrices of difference become naturalized and materialized as meaningful sets of categories in which to classify people.

Many researchers have followed Butler's theorization in discussing performativity in terms of space (Smitheram 2011), though some merge it with the notion of more active human agency—what Butler critiques—modeled after Erving Goffman's dramaturgy (see Gregson and Rose 2000 for its critique). For example, Gregson and Rose (2000) examine subtle slippage of citational practices in community art workers citing hegemonic media and art institutions' discourse to obtain funding while critiquing it as inappropriate, superficial, or temporary, hence not reproducing by citing their importance. They also point out intersections of performative acts based on multiple subject positions at a transitory, temporary, and performative space of a car-boot sale, in which buyers perform their knowledge of the items they want to buy, which subvert conventional retail practices but reinforce the male-female binary because such items are often framed in gendered terms. While this volume's focus on the intersection of multiple subject positions bears some similarity to the approaches above, it focuses specifically on linguistic practices.

Butler's work has been expanded to include more specificity such as how each individual's lived experience intersected with other subject positions embedded in historical and geographical specificities (Nelson 1999; Tyler and Cohen 2010). Unlike the analyses of "queer migration" that tie coming out with physical movement in search of "home" even though it is often an ongoing journey with diverse paths, detours, and returns (Gorman-Murray 2007; Lewis 2012), Centner and Neto (2021) examine performative practices through which gay expatriates in officially homophobic Dubai temporarily created specific "Western gay" spaces at night clubs by publicly acting a heterosexual masculinity on the surface, and at home through specific gay habitus that nonetheless excluded those queer individuals who did not share their habitus. Our concept of performative linguistic space also considers an unstable, temporal and performative nature of space. However, our primary focus is not embodiment via habitus but of linguistic habitus (McGuire) and the linguistic actions and narratives about them.

The notion of performativity has been used variously regarding language. Fairclough (2014: 379) discusses effects that are produced by texts "on non-semiotic elements of the material, social and mental worlds" and Johnson (2010) suggests the effectiveness of macro-level policy in relation to teacher agency. Notions of performativity and language have also been used in "confused, misleading, and limited" ways (Cabantous et al. 2016: 199), such as in Critical Performativity Theory (CPT), which outlines intervention in managerial discourses and practices that encourage managers to provide space to activate "performative language" to create behavioral change and even political change in organizations (Cabantous et al. 2016; also see Spicer et al. 2009; Wickert and Schaefer 2015).

Regarding performativity in language and space, Qin (2020) discusses the role of performative acts in language learning—the sentence-starter language practice—that were used by immigrant students to subvert racialized, gendered, and schooled subjectivities, although the focus is on the curriculum despite classroom space providing the context. Concentrating more on the space itself, Hedman and Magnusson (2022) call "performative" the effect of space to build up the confidence of students. "Space for multilingualism" in Swedish as a second language classrooms empower students by valorizing their "multilingualism," though such spatial power remains limited and contextual. "Translanguaging Space" introduced by Li Wei (2018) discusses conceptualizations of space as open to new ways of thinking, including "mixing languages." However, as will be argued later, it is important to focus on specific exchanges of utterances (or signs) in context without imposing the researchers' perceptions of language boundaries or linguistic communities. It is because, depending on the intention of the speaker, not the researcher, even when the utterance is exactly the same, the same space can be considered a "regular space" or a Translanguaging Space (Doerr 2022). Therefore, our notion of performative linguistic space suggests paying attention to the interlocutors themselves and how they view the interaction—without assuming a sense of belonging (i.e., linguistic communities) or determining a "language" they are adhering to or "mixing."

Every space can be a performative linguistic space because space gives cues as to what kind of utterances or signs can occur. However, as this section has aimed to briefly demonstrate, how that happens has not been theorized rigorously. This volume identifies how and why this work needs to be done ethnographically, deciphering the interlocutor's intentions and reflections through participant observation and qualitative interviews. Assuming why certain linguistic practices occur in space—i.e., how space performatively encourages individuals' utterances or signs—can risk scaling practices on the part of the researcher through their determination of a hierarchy of scale of categories (of "language") or linguistic communities, a citational practice (Butler 1993).

In this volume, through ethnographic explorations, we delve into "performative linguistic space" as the site(s) where space via individuals initiates, encourages, discourages, or limits utterances and signs. The chapters demonstrate that the space is not performative on its own; rather the space becomes performative as a result of the specific intersections of linguistic politics carried from the various spaces that individuals have traversed. By focusing on specific linguistic practices in space that are linked to individuals' subject positions, we move away from assuming/reinscribing association of the linguistic community to the space. This, in turn, allows us to avoid notions of stable and discernible units of language(s)—what Doerr (2022) has called "unit thinking"—that are linked to individuals and space.

In the following section, in order to describe the perception of language and space that this volume challenges, we briefly review the historical development of this unit thinking of language. We look at its correspondence to space through the nation-state ideology and its failed subversions through ethnic movements and "globalization" as well as the academic notion of language.

4 Language, nation-states, ethnic movements, and globalist developments

One of the most influential backdrops that affect our current perception of language and its relationship to space—thus shaping the notion of performative linguistic space—is the emergence of the nation-state with its specific ideology in the eighteenth century. Though the ideology of nation-states—one nation, one people, one language, one territory—has been challenged by minority ethnic movements since the 1960s and the era of "globalization" since the 1990s, its legacy remains framed in academic discussions of language, with the perception of language as a discrete, internally homogeneous, bounded unit—"unit thinking" (Doerr 2022)—associated with a certain space.

4.1 The nation-state and language

The nation-state ideology encouraged the perception of language as an internally homogeneous bounded unit through various technologies and mapped such a unit of language on top of the perception of space specific to the nation-state. The nation is an "imagined community" that shares a sense of belonging, which was, itself, developed through several "technologies," that connected people, language, and space (Anderson 1991). As mentioned above, the bird's-eye-view map offers a visual framework to imagine the nation in territorial terms with clear borderlines and internal homogeneity. It contrasts with other "narrative of spaces," such as "a tour" that takes an individual's viewpoint (de Certeau 1984).

Researchers have formulated different arguments to explain how language came to be connected to the nation: from the discourse that asserted that shared language is the touchstone of a people or Volk (Johann Gottfried von Herder; see Balibar 1994), which creates an "internal border" within people that separates nations (Johann Gottlieb Fichte 1968) to the shared literacy via mass education which produced an interchangeable labor force within the national border (Gellner 1983) to the use of language as part of the totemic consciousness (Comaroff 1987) of the linguistic community that symbolizes nation as an autonomous unit with continuous existence (Balibar 1988).

In all these theorizations, language imagined as homologous to the nation-state is seen as internally homogeneous, despite this never having been the case. Even when diverse linguistic practices have been acknowledged, standardization was supposed to solve the "issue." Through standardization, the state chooses and imposes an official language on its citizens through a unified education system and establishes a "linguistic community" that (mis)recognizes the legitimacy of the standard with symbolic capital of social qualities like moral rectitude (Bourdieu 1991; see also Bauman and Briggs 2000; Milroy and Milroy 1991). These standardization processes led people to be simultaneously homogenized (by creating a shared criterion—the set "standard"—by which to measure the difference in language uses) and differentiated (by measuring gaps to rank them) (Foucault 1977; also, see Pennycook 1994). That is, despite standardization, diversity has remained, if not been highlighted (Doerr 2015). These linguistic situations background discussions of linguistic practices throughout this volume.

4.2 Ethnicity and globalism: Challenging the nation-state ideology?

Various ethnic movements revealed diversity within nations, and ideologies of globalization suggested the breakdown of national barriers. However, because of the ways such diversity was perceived, and the ways globalization was discussed, the perception of the world as consisting of discrete, bounded, internally homogeneous units—unit thinking (Doerr 2022)—has survived, if not been strengthened. These developments provide a significant background to the chapters in this volume.

Ethnic movements centered those at the periphery of a society with different linguistic and cultural practices from the dominant group. Marginalized groups globally were frustrated by continued discrimination despite their "successful" assimilation. In response, they shifted strategies to launch political movements demanding the end of discrimination and recognition of their cultural and linguistic distinctness (Kymlicka 1995; May 2001). Although this challenged the idea of the nation as being linguistically (if not culturally) homogeneous, the view of language as internally homogeneous bounded units persisted, merely moving the scale from the nation-state to ethnic groups.

Post-Cold War developments in the early 1990s have been variously theorized under the label of "globalization," which also appeared to challenge the nation-state ideology and yet ironically perpetuated it by reinforcing the unit thinking. Researchers began theorizing "globalization" in diverse ways, from the new sensibility of "global connectivity" (Tomlinson 1999) and global "disjunctive flows" (Appadurai 1990) or their channeling (Broad and Orlove 2007) and frictions (Tsing 2005) to the emergence of globally shared structures and systems of governmentality (Bayart 2007) and ways to measure "cultural differences" (Wilk 1995) and the construction of things and phenomena through "global assemblage" (Collier and Ong 2005).

Wimmer and Glick Schiller (2002) critique such research as an approach that prioritizes crossing and overcoming of "national" borders as an object of research even when crossing and overcoming regional borders may be more meaningful to the research participants (Wimmer and Glick Schiller 2011). As a result, the focus on the global perpetuates the meaningfulness of the national border based on the nation-state ideology, which they call "methodological nationalism."

Also, Anna Tsing (2000) critiques these debates on globalization as focusing only on specific aspects of post-Cold War developments, highlighting and assuming that the breaking down of national barriers are automatically good and new phenomena, ignoring a double standard in such processes, as will be discussed. She argues that such an approach is based on the ideology of globalism. Jonathan Friedman (2003) contends that the flow of people, ideas, and things have been happening throughout history at one end of the pendulum shifting between two poles—centralization on a global scale that forces cultural and linguistic "homogeneity" on the world versus decentralization that stresses cultural and linguistic diversity across the globe (Friedman 2003). Discussions of globalization also reveal a problematic double standard, which Glick Schiller and Salazar (2013: 189) call "regimes of mobility": wealthy, often white, individuals moving across national borders are viewed positively as "global citizens" (e.g., study abroad students), whereas poor, often non-white, individuals moving across national borders (e.g., immigrants and refugees) are viewed with suspicion and their movements are hindered through border walls and detention centers as well as long wait-times for visas and other necessary documentation.

In short, through the discussions of "globalization," the nation-state ideology, ironically, dies hard, and with it, the notion of language as a bounded unit that corresponds to the nation-state—"people" and "culture." Before we review this perpetuation of unit thinking of language in academic discussions in the next subsection, we will briefly review the effects of "globalization" in language, especially the rise of English as the "global language," in order to outline the wider language politics that frame the discussions in this volume.

Although various "languages" became linguae francae throughout history— Arabic, Spanish, Russian, French, to name a few—English has come to be viewed as the "global language" since the latter half of the twentieth century via explicit strategic foreign policies of the United Kingdom and later the United States (Phillipson 1992). At the turn of the century, Abram de Swaan (2001) put English at the top of the "linguistic galaxy" made up of "peripheral" languages (languages of conversation), "central" languages ("national" languages), "supercentral" languages (languages for international communication, which is often linked to colonial powers), and the "hypercentral" language (English). In the metaphor of central versus peripheral, relations of power are highlighted with the link to space weakening as the language becomes increasingly "central." English has also been framed as being the "global language" in terms of "ownership" of the language: "[English] is only international [global] to the extent that it is not their [native speakers'] language. It is not a possession which they lease to others, while still retaining the freehold. Other people actually own it" (Widdowson 1994: 385). What is assumed, nonetheless, is that default "owners" are usually connected to space as in the nation-state ideology; English merely suggests an exception without challenging the default framework.

Focusing on power relations, Braj Kachru (1992: 356–357) categorizes Inner Circle ("traditional cultural, and linguistic bases of English"), Outer Circle ("institutionalized non-native varieties in the regions that have passed through extended periods of colonization") and Expanding Circle (regions where English is a "foreign language") of English-speaking countries. Here, the Inner Circle English remains privileged as "native speaker" English, especially the "Standard English" used in Great Britain (Quirk 1988) or the United States. Kachru argues for, instead, considering all English varieties on equal terms, naming them "Indian English," "Korean English," etc. and suggests a pluralized understanding of English—"World Englishes." However, this approach still assumes language as a bounded countable unit with internal homogeneity (i.e., within each World English) and its connection to the space of the nation (Pennycook 2007).

In contrast to the above framing, this volume avoids the notion of discrete bounded units of language as well as its connection to space—both tightly linked to the nation-state. Instead, it looks at the space that emerges through mobile individuals, globally or otherwise, who brought with them language politics of diverse space and created layers of meaning that were conducive to certain linguistic actions. Rather than constructing things or phenomena through global networks as in global assemblage (Collier and Ong 2005), we employ the notion of performative linguistic space to examine the specific temporal intersections of language politics that motivate/dissuade individuals to act contextually. That is, we focus on the dynamics of emerging utterances and signs that are rooted in various spatial and linguistic politics which intersect with each other in a specific space temporally.

4.3 Concept of language in academic disciplines

The framing of language as bounded and internally homogeneous units that this volume critiques can be traced back to earlier academic discussions of language, partly because the nation-state ideology shaped the field of linguistics. The structural linguistics of Ferdinand de Saussure, for example, views language as a fixed code shared by a homogeneous speech community, overlapping the nation-state boundary (Baumann and Briggs 2000). Though challenged by contemporaries who saw language as heteroglossic, fluid, and constantly emerging via social interaction (Voloshinov 1973), the Saussurean notion endures in concepts such as "language borrowing," "multilingualism," and "translanguaging," all presupposing bounded and countable languages which are then "borrowed" or are coexisting or "mixed" (Doerr 2018; 2022; Pennycook 2004; Urciuoli 1995).

Specifically, in relation to space, Li Wei (2018) puts forth the idea of Translanguaging Space: "a space that is created by and for translanguaging practices, and a space where language users even break down the ideologically laden dichotomies between the macro and the micro, the societal and the individual, and the social and the psychological through interaction" (2018: 23). Translanguaging is about "not simply going *between* different linguistic structures, cognitive and semiotic systems and modalities, but going *beyond* them" and "Translanguaging Space has its own transformative power because it is forever evolving and combines and generates new identities, values and practices" (Li Wei 2018: 23).

Before continuing with the critique of translanguaging, it is important to address the conflicting stances in this volume regarding this concept. While Doerr strongly rejects using the concept of translanguaging as discussed below, McGuire eschews translanguaging because of its failure to fully account for disparity in the language resources of deaf people (De Meulder et al. 2019). In contrast, Đỗ and Poole find this framing useful for their exploration of spatial codes and employ the concept throughout their chapter.

Doerr has argued elsewhere (2018; 2020; 2022; forthcoming) that, for something to gain value for transcending conventional practices, it necessarily reinforces the meaningfulness of conventional practices. Just like globalization paradoxically reinforces the meaningfulness of national borders by celebrating the crossing of them—if national borders are meaningless, crossing them would not be an important feat (Doerr 2018; 2020; 2022)—celebrating translanguaging as subversive relies on and reinforces the very thing it seeks to transcend: division between languages.

"Translanguaging" *does* make sense *if* used to indicate interlocutors' intentional strategies. A translanguaging approach, as it was originally developed, instead of measuring a student's linguistic proficiency based on the degree of match to a bounded notion of target language, allows one to see the student's proficiency in their own linguistic repertoire developed throughout their life (Garcia and Kleyn 2016; Garcia and Li Wei 2014).

In the research context, however, identifying translanguaging practices needs to be done carefully. For example, saying, "let's eat tacos mañana," would be considered a translanguaging practice if uttered in a space where the word "mañana" is marked as non-English and even prohibited (e.g., "immersion" English-as-a-Second-

Language classroom) because it would have been uttered in order to intentionally subvert the rule. Such an utterance sends a meta-message of that subversiveness, which is done against the backdrop where the boundary is made to matter institutionally (e.g., the ban on non-English in the classroom).

However, if this example sentence was uttered in a space that encourages individuals to speak freely without worrying about "sticking to one language" (e.g., at home where people share similar vocabulary and communicate by freely drawing on them), it would be strange to call it a translanguaging practice because, for the speakers, the boundary between languages is not meaningful (if not nonexistent) and thus transgressing that boundary is not meaningful. However, this is the very type of space Li Wei describes as Translanguaging Space. That results, then, in Li Wei (as a researcher) imposing language boundaries on a practice that is not built on these boundaries. In other words, what is being imposed here with the notion of Translanguaging Space is not only the belief that language is a bounded, discrete unit where the distinction of "mañana" as English or Spanish is clear (even though many English speakers in the US would understand what it means) but also that the difference between English and Spanish, rather than between "dialects" in English or in Spanish, matters. This is what Judith Butler (1993) described as *citational* practices—bringing up the category as something that is meaningful, which is *performative* practice precisely because it reinforces the meaningfulness of that category.

Rendering the difference between English and Spanish as more significant than that between "dialects" in English or in Spanish is a scale-making practice. Scale-making (or scaling) practice is a concept developed in the field of human geography in which scale is "a relational, power-laden and contested construction that actors strategically engage with, in order to legitimize or challenge existing power relations" (Leitner et al. 2008: 159). It is a representational trope or discursive frame, "an epistemological construct that presents specific sociospatial orderings" (Moore 2008: 204). While being epistemological, scalar representations and acts of making them—scale-making practices—can have material effects through their deployment, as in the notion of "nation." Thus, the focus of analysis is the reifying practices of everyday actors and organizations that solidify particular scalar configurations in consciousness and practice, thus enabling certain ways of seeing, thinking and acting (McKinnon 2010; Moore 2008).

Using translanguaging as an analytical concept in observing and describing linguistic interactions is such scale-making practice, *citing* (Butler 1993) that specific boundaries (e.g., between Spanish versus English as opposed to Colombian Spanish versus Spaniard Spanish) are positioned as more important than other boundaries, all the while keeping the notion of language as a bounded entity intact. The aforementioned discussions of ethnic movements as well as World Englishes are also scale-making practices, shifting the unit of homogeneity from the nation to ethnic group or from the language called English to what is commonly called "English with an accent," respectively. In all these cases, the scaling practices maintain the stance of language as an internally homogeneous, bounded unit.

This volume is critical of this framing of language and is more consistent with a framework that sees language not as a prior system/unit tied to ethnicity, nation, or territory even though they appear to be as a result of "a sedimentation of acts repeated over time" (Pennycook 2004: 7) but as being constantly constructed anew through interactions in a given context: "languaging" (Akmajian et al. 1995). We focus on space and linguistic practices that emerge or are hindered in that specific space in context, rather than with the understanding of language as a bounded unit associated with a linguistic community and space as is common in studies on space and language, as we discuss next.

5 Space and language in existing research

Austin's lectures on performative utterances (1955/1962) are premised on the existence of certain "felicity conditions." These conditions have been categorized as context in terms of "recognizable conventions" that establish "the infrastructure through which the utterance gains its force as a particular type of action (Duranti and Goodwin 1992: 17). In other words, it is because these utterances occur in a particular context that they are effective in carrying out the action. Duranti and Goodwin's volume (1992) demonstrates how context is shaped by and shapes "talk." They explore the setting and assumptions in which speech occurs. In this volume, we employ "space" (though some ideas may appear to resemble phenomena that may be called "context"), indexicality, norms, practices, and/or ideologies. In this section, by situating our volume within existing research on space and language, we outline our three key contributions to linguistic anthropology as well as applied linguistics and sociolinguistics. In contrast with many of the works below, our volume avoids looking at space as a stage and does away with notions of spatialized linguistic communities.

Since the uptick in research in "language in space" in the mid-1990s (see Levinson 1996), there has been consistent interest in spatiality and language across disciplines. Our interdisciplinary volume engages specifically in the proactive and productive aspects of space—this is our first contribution to the literature. There is a tendency for some works in linguistic anthropology and applied linguistics to treat space as a stage where linguistic practices occur. For instance, Auer and Li's volume (2009) explores how people become, stay, act, and live as "multilinguals," touching upon issues of space (e.g., geographical spaces, monolingual classroom space, community language education as a "hidden" space). However, this and other similar works, stop short of centering space or theorizing its effects on linguistic acts. Carl and Stevenson (2009), for example, consider Central Europe a "multilingual space" in their analysis of the role of the German language in identification practices; however, theories of space are secondary to analyses of linguistic ideologies and practices. Conversely, our investigation into how certain spaces encourage, discourage, or even silence linguistic acts—utterances or signs—in ways informed by the individuals' movement between diverse spaces contributes a more active engagement with space and the resulting linguistic practices.

This volume's second contribution is our exploration of how movement of individuals between spaces creates contours of specific performative linguistic space, adding a dynamic analysis. Existing works on space and language often focus on one space and examine the intersection of space and language acquisition (e.g., Mix et al. 2010) or how the linguistic signs in space (i.e., linguistic landscape) both reflect and shape worldviews, ideologies, policies, and practices of the community as well as passers-by (Bakhaus 2007; Malinowski and Tufi 2020). In contrast, chapters in this volume show how the traces of individuals' past movements between multiple spaces create layered meanings of a specific linguistic space. Chapters show how individuals' subject positions activate certain ideologies in each space. When individuals carry these ideologies into a new space, traces of spatial practices are dragged along. In this dynamic process, layered meaning of the space in question is created as the interlocutors interact with other individuals and "activate" ideologies. The result is a specific performative linguistic space that encourages or discourages certain linguistic practices, temporally and contextually.

This essential movement is explored variously across the chapters. Doerr's chapter, as mentioned, investigates the narratives of language practices in Spain by US study abroad students with Latin American backgrounds moving between the space of their "homeland" where Spanish prevails as a former colonial language, the space of US immigration politics where English monolingualism prevails, the study abroad space of Spain where immersion is encouraged and Spanish-English bilingual ability became an asset, and the colonial space in Spain where Latin American varieties of Spanish carries negative connotations. Đỗ and Poole's chapter analyzes the effects of students' and faculty members' moving between perceived and lived spaces, specifically between the spaces prior to their arrival in Japan, the larger campus space in Japan, and the space of the English-Medium-Instruction program. Kumagai's chapter depicts students bringing different understandings of language learning into the virtual remote learning space, highlighting diverse effects of the move between in-person and virtual learning space. McGuire's chapter explores the dynamics of deaf youth in Japan who move between perceived "hearing" and "deaf" spaces shaped by contrasting ideologies and linguistic practices, bringing corresponding habitus into divergent spaces. Jakubiak's chapter illustrates the space of White Savior syndrome and space of critical anti-colonialism as volunteer tourist students move back and forth between their home, university, and volunteer tourist sites. In short, our investigations into the effects of the movements between spaces add new insights to the study of language in space, highlighting not only the layeredness that constructs the performative nature of the space but also its temporariness and contextuality, as specific individuals meet and interact linguistically in space.

Third, this volume does not ascribe linguistic communities to space. Our exploration of temporal and contextual aspects of utterances and signs in space differ from existing works which concentrate on linguistic communities associated with the space, with their borders being either unquestioned and assumed or investigated as being constructed. For example, some research examines individuals' relationship to the assumed linguistic community, albeit no unequivocal boundary, using Lave and Wenger's (1991) concept of "community of practice." Anya (2017), for instance, offers insight into how the space of a Brazilian city provides African American study abroad students with a new environment to learn not only language (i.e., Portuguese) but also the racialized identities they occupy as black individuals. However, the idea of a community of practice associated with the space underpins this analysis. Other works investigate dynamics around the boundary of linguistic communities. For example, Bagga-Gupta et al.'s (2019) volume explores "communicative practices in the making" in digital learning spaces by examining learning processes with a complementary focus on languaging and meaning-making across blurred boundaries. Hadi-Tabassum's (2006) research in a dual-immersion (Spanish-English) classroom unpacks the students' use of metalanguage as a way to resist Spanish/English borders and power differentials. It does so while building upon bhabha's concept of the "third space" (1994), a type of liminal, in-between space of hybridity that moves discussions and discourses beyond binary cultural categories. Engaging in questions of proficiency and language acquisition to explore the power relations among teachers and students, Hadi-Tabassum questions boundaries between linguistic communities. Although focusing on the blurring of the boundary and hybridity, its very focus not only creates the meaningfulness of such a boundary (as discussed earlier in our critique of "translanguaging" approaches) but also assumes that there are "non-hybrid" spaces with clear-cut boundaries of linguistic communities, which is not usually the case.

Chapters in this volume do not ascribe individuals to linguistic communities because the researcher's choice as to which linguistic communities to analyze can be arbitrary, drawing attention to communities that may not be the main concern of the individuals in the study, similar to what occurs with the aforementioned "methodological nationalism" (Wimmer and Glick Schiller 2002). Further, we posit that this framing is problematic because it assumes stable and discernible links not only between individuals and particular language(s) but also between individuals and the space they occupy. This framing relies on the problematic assumption of monolingualism, or more importantly "unit thinking" which, even when authors acknowledge "bilingualism" or "multilingualism," seeks to isolate, identify, and name the "languages" one uses as bounded units, instead of recognizing individuals' heteroglossia that renders such categorization meaningless (see Doerr 2022).

Suggesting a linguistic community on a certain scale in this way is a scaling practice which draws attention to that specific scale, as described earlier. Also, identifying and connecting linguistic communities to certain spaces assumes clear and stable connection between individuals and language (seeing language as bounded units) as well as space, which is not often the case. Rather, we approach linguistic practices without assuming or identifying the linguistic or speech community to which the individuals may feel they belong, similar to Voloshinov's approach to the meaning of words (1973) mentioned earlier: they emerge contextually and temporally only at the very moment of linguistic interaction. By moving away from an attention to linguistic communities and, instead, investigating speech and sign acts that (do not) occur in performative linguistic space at particular moments, we seek to capture the "messier" realities revealed through ethnographic research.

It is useful here to identify what this volume *does not* attempt to do in terms of theorization. These "nots" may be considered limitations or delineations, depending on the reader. This volume does *not* engage in the rich body of literature on spatial cognition in language (e.g., Levinson 2003) nor does it focus on experiential bases for language in space. Although contributors agree with the notion that "embodiment is quite literally how language works" (Bucholtz and Hall 2016: 174) and aim to move away from a deterministic view of linguistic practices to a more agentic embodied one, chapters do not concentrate on embodiment.

In sum, this volume focuses on contextual linguistic practices ushered in space and the relationships between them, without assigning linguistic communities to interlocutors, allowing us to avoid scaling practice on the part of researchers and contribute more nuanced, data-driven analyses of linguistic practices in performative linguistic space. In the final section, we will introduce how each chapter in this volume explores this central concept.

6 Structure of the volume

Each chapter examines diverse settings with various theoretical frameworks and approaches. In the second chapter, Doerr illustrates how performative linguistic spaces are experienced with historical, political, and educational layers in the context of studying abroad, by examining students' narratives from a US college about their study-abroad stay in Spain. The students with Latin American (Guatemalan and Colombian) background experienced the shifting meanings of their Spanish-English "bilingual" ability, from the historical legacy of Spanish colonialism in their ancestral homeland, to a liability in the monolingualist US political setting around immigrants, and then to an asset in the study abroad space in Spain where using local language is considered educational as well as practical in study abroad discourses. The historical legacy, however, re-emerged in Spain where their "colonial accents" received negative reactions. Doerr's chapter shows the performative linguistic space that emerged in Spain through the spatial movements of students.

The third chapter by Đỗ and Poole investigates the interplay of monolingual language codes and "translingual" practices within a space for English-medium instruction (EMI) at a Japanese university. Their ethnographic and autoethnographic data illuminate how the English monolingual language code shapes the institutional space of the College of Interdisciplinary Studies (CIS) within the broader university. In the physical space of the CIS where English monolingualism acts as a "spatial code," various inhabitants of the space including EMI policymakers, the university faculty and administrators as well as the students consider monolingual English ideology as the standard practice to be enforced. The interweaving relationship of physical, mental, and social spaces—and the movement between them—results in individuals carrying diverse linguistic ideologies, which are then negotiated by CIS students and faculty. For example, the social space of the CIS constructed through "translanguaging" practices challenges the hegemony of monolingualism. Đỗ and Poole's ethnography of the lived space in the CIS, where members subvert language codes, demonstrates how the various axes of differences among students are blurred in the interstice of monolingual and heteroglossic spaces. This chapter highlights the effects of movement between different types of linguistic spaces on speech.

In the fourth chapter, Kumagai shows how divergent meanings and practices of foreign language learning in one space—an in-person teaching space—can be carried into the virtual online space of remote teaching, creating a new divergent kind of performative linguistic space. Globally, the pandemic has pushed face-to-face learning to virtual spaces, shifting class interactions and learning experiences. Through qualitative interviews and surveys along with ethnographic observations of students in a Japanese language course at an American university, Kumagai finds that students' perceptions of this "unfamiliar, uncertain learning space" of the Zoom classroom is significantly affected by their understanding of classroom communication norms that they previously developed in the space of more conventional in-person learning. Kumagai reports two interpretations among students regarding the Zoom learning space: as a silencing one which restricts speech, and as a safe one that facilitates communication. The research further revealed that emotions (including anxiety and discomfort) generated when participating in a virtual space—due to technical aspects—prohibits simultaneous and impromptu speech, suggesting that physical spatial modality can have either productive or limiting effects. By analyzing the varied ways professors and students compensate semiotic modes that are un-available in virtual space, this chapter offers new insights into how virtual space af-fects speech practices in classroom contexts, and how movements between two physical spaces of learning—in-person and virtual—usher new learning experiences depending on the perception of and meaning attributed to spaces.

The fifth chapter by McGuire unpacks the assimilative linguistic practices that emerge from the uneasy navigation of both "hearing" and "deaf" performative lin-guistic spaces. It explores how space and languages shape—and are shaped by—interactional sense-making processes among deaf Japanese youth, by drawing on long-term ethnographic research of their linguistic practices. McGuire frames the discussion as socialization in habitus—"hearing habitus" and "deaf habitus"—de-veloped in relation to hearing and deaf spaces. While deaf spaces are neither static nor homogenous, the local Sign language is generally the lingua franca (in Japan, Japanese Sign Language) and often demarcates and shapes these spaces. In hearing dominant spaces, hegemonic audist and phonocentric views coax deaf youth into spoken language practices and speech acts. Students who were raised and educated in these hearing spaces internalize linguistic ideologies (and related stigmas), which can result in *dysconscious audism*, and carry these discordant views into deaf spaces. Whereas in deaf spaces, signing skills are highly prized, speech acts have little linguistic capital. These youth drag the spatial practices and meanings from the hearing spaces of the home and school into deaf spaces, only to discover new spatial meanings.

In the final chapter, the utility of investigating the movement between two spaces is highlighted by Jakubiak as she traces the physical and metaphoric spaces of speech when individuals move through their experience of volunteer tourism. Using data from multi-sited ethnography, Jakubiak investigates how for-mer volunteer tourists become critical of volunteer tourism (short-term, alterna-tive travel that combines volunteering with holidaying) while developing new subjectivities. This chapter draws upon literature on "coming out migrations" to examine the dislocating and disorienting liminal space of international voluntary service trips. Her analysis centers on the experiences of two alumni of voluntourism programs and the new ideological spaces that they inhabit over time. As participants traverse physical and temporal spaces—volunteer tourism sites, home, and univer-sity classrooms—they gain a new perspective of voluntourism which contrasts with the regime of truth about ideal civic action and global citizenship. Metaphorical "safe" and "brave" spaces emerge through which former volunteers are empowered to reject Orientalist narratives and White Savior tropes. In doing so, this chapter offers an ethnographic exploration of how post-voluntourism safe and brave spaces are productive of speech acts that critique dominant norms and practices.

The Afterword by Miller shows how the volume's concept of performative linguistic space can be useful in various contexts, even apparently "over the top" claims such as the use of a Japanese word, *kawaii*, in English as constituting cultural appropriation. By specifically applying the volume's approach that language politics travel with individuals to various spaces, Miller demonstrates how this debate can be better understood if we consider the racial politics that individuals are bringing into the space of discussion: infantilization and sexualization of Asian Americans in the US. Miller suggests possible expansion of this volume's main theme, even into unlikely spaces.

Overall, this volume shows the temporality and individualized effects—at the intersection of one's subject positions and past experiences—of the ways an individual's mobility affects linguistic space, which then ushers or hinders utterances or signs. It does so by portraying what space does linguistically to and with mobile individuals. This volume offers new lenses for understanding the relationships between space and linguistic practices that are shaped by individuals moving between spaces, with the aim of germinating ideas for further research—like the cross-disciplinary conversation between the two editors at a small café in Kyoto.

References

Aalbers, Manuel B. 2014. Do maps make geography? Part 1: Redlining, planned shrinkage, and the places of decline. *ACME: International Journal for Critical Geographies* 13(4). 525–556.

Agnew, John. 2005. Space: Place. In Paul Cloke & Ron Johnston (eds.), *Spaces of geographical thought*, 81–96. London: SAGE Publications.

Akmajian, Adrian, Richard A. Demers, Ann K. Farmer & Robert M. Harnish. 1995. *Linguistics: An introduction to language and communication*. Cambridge: MIT Press.

American Anthropological Association. 2020. "Anthropology of policing: The persistence of racialized police brutality and community responses." Webinar on YouTube. https://www.youtube.com/watch?v=9-LtlPp4Ih0 (accessed 26 July 2021)

Anderson, Benedict. 1991. *Imagined communities*. London: Verso.

Anya, Uju. 2017. *Racialized identities in second language learning: Speaking blackness in Brazil*. New York and London: Routledge.

Appadurai, Arjun. 1990. Disjuncture and difference in the global cultural economy. *Public Culture* 2(2). 1–24.

Auer, Peter & Li Wei (eds.). 2009. *Handbook of multilingualism and multilingual communication*. New York: Mouton De Gruyter.

Austin, John Langshaw. 1955/1962. *How to do things with words*. Oxford: The Clarendon Press.

Austin, John Langshaw. 1961/1979. *Philosophical papers*. Oxford: Oxford University Press.

Bagga-Gupta, Sangeeta, Ylva Lindberg & Giulia Messina Dahlberg (eds.). 2019. *Virtual sites as learning spaces: Critical issues on languaging research in changing eduscapes*. London: Palgrave Macmillan.
Backhaus, Peter. 2007. *Linguistic landscapes*. Bristol: Multilingual Matters.
Balibar, Etienne. 1988. The nation norm: History and ideology. In Etienne Balibar & Immanuel Wallerstein (eds.), *Race, nation, class: Ambiguous identities*, 86–106. London: Verso.
Balibar, Etienne. 1994. *Masses, classes, ideas: Studies on politics and philosophy before and after Marx*. New York: Routledge.
Bauman, Richard & Charles L. Briggs. 2000. Language philosophy as language ideology: John Locke and Johann Gottfried Herder. In Paul Kroskrity (ed.), *Regimes of language: Ideologies, polities, and identities*, 139–204. Santa Fe: School of American Research Press.
Bayart, Jean-Francois. 2007. *Global subjects: A political critique of globalization*. Cambridge, UK: Polity Press.
bhabha, homi. 1994. *The location of culture*. London: Routledge.
Blommaert, Jan. 2007. Sociolinguistic scales. *Intercultural Pragmatics* 4(1). 1–19.
Blommaert, Jan. 2021. Sociolinguistic scales in retrospect. *Applied Linguistics Review* 12(3). 375–380.
Bourdieu, Pierre. 1989. Social space and symbolic power. *Sociological Theory* 7(1). 14–25.
Bourdieu, Pierre. 1991/1982. *Language and symbolic power*. Cambridge: Harvard University Press.
Braun, Bruce. 2003. "On the raggedy edge of risk": Articulations of race and nature after biology. In Donald S. Moore, Jake Kosek, & Anand Pandian (eds.), *Race, nature, and the politics of difference*, 175–203. Durham: Duke University Press.
Broad, Kennith & Ben Orlove. 2007. Channeling globality: The 1997–1998 El Niño climate event in Peru. *American Ethnologist* 34(2). 285–302.
Bucholtz, Mary & Kira Hall. 2016. Embodied sociolinguistics. In Nikolas Coupland (ed.), *Sociolinguistics: Theoretical debates*, 173–197. Cambridge: Cambridge University Press.
Butler, Judith. 1993. *Bodies that matter*. New York: Routledge.
Cabantous, Laure, Jean-Pascal Gond, Nancy Harding & Mark Learmonth. 2016. Critical essay: Reconsidering critical performativity. *Human Relations* 69(2). 197–213.
Carl, Jenny & Patrick Stevenson. (eds.). 2009. *Language, discourse and identity in central Europe: The German language in a multilingual space*. New York: Palgrave Macmillan.
Castañeda, Paola. 2020. From the right to mobility to the right to the mobile city: Playfulness and mobilities in Bogotá`s cycling activism. *Antipode* 52(1). 58–77.
Centner, Ryan & Manoel Pereira Neto. 2021. Peril, privilege, and queer comforts: The nocturnal performative geographies of expatriate gay men in Dubai. *Geoforum* 127: 92–103.
de Certeau, Michel. 1984. *The practice of everyday life*. Berkeley: University of California Press.
Collier, Stephen J. & Aihwa Ong. 2005. Global assemblages, anthropological problems. In Aihwa Ong & Stephen J. Collier (eds.), *Global assemblages: Technology, politics, and ethics as anthropological problems*, 3–21. Malden, MA: Blackwell Publishing.
Coetes, Ta-nehisi. 2014. "The Case for Reparations." The Atlantic. June. http://www.theatlantic.com/magazine/archive/2014/06/the-case-for-reparations/361631/ (accessed 13 January 2017)
Comaroff, John. 1987. Of totemism and ethnicity: Consciousness, practice and the signs of inequality. *Ethnos* 52(3–4). 301–323.
Cresswell, Tim. 2006. *On the move: Mobility in the modern western world*. New York: Routledge.
Cresswell, Tim & Peter Merriman. 2011. Introduction: Geographies of mobilities—Practices, spaces, subjects. In Tim Cresswell & Peter Merriman (eds.), *Geographies of mobilities: Practices, spaces, subjects*, 1–32. Farnham, UK: Ashgate.
Doerr, Neriko Musha. 2015. Standardization and paradoxical highlighting of linguistic diversity in Japan. *Japanese Language and Literature* 49(2). 389–403.

Doerr, Neriko Musha. 2018. *Transforming study abroad: A handbook*. London: Berghahn Books.

Doerr, Neriko Musha. 2019. The politics of intersecting landscapes: Chronotopes and modes of governmentality of Pokémon GO and the real world. In Neriko Musha Doerr & Debra Occhi (eds.), *The augmented reality of Pokémon Go: Chronotopes, moral panic, and other complexities*, 41–64. Lenham, MD: Lexington Books.

Doerr, Neriko Musha (ed.). 2020. *The global education effect and Japan: Constructing new borders and identification practices*. New York: Routledge.

Doerr, Neriko Musha. 2022. *Fairies, ghosts, and Santa Claus: Tinted glasses, fetishes, and the politics of seeing*. New York: Berghahn Books.

Doerr, Neriko Musha. forthcoming. "Puke" in English and Māori: Post-translanguaging, post-unit-thinking, and not "losing Te Reo Māori" in Aotearoa/New Zealand. *Journal of Language, Identity, and Education*.

Dowling, Robyn & Catherine Simpson. 2013. "Shift–the way you move": Reconstituting automobility. *Continuum* 27(3): 421–433.

Duranti, Alessandro & Charles Goodwin (eds.). 1992. *Rethinking context: Language as an interactive phenomenon*. Cambridge: Cambridge University Press.

Egan, Robert. 2021. "Provoking responsibility': The struggle for recognition as an everyday cyclist in Dublin City. *Geoforum* 127: 23–32.

Eisenhauer, David C. 2021. The battle for the boardwalk: Racial formations in a segregated coastal resort. *Geoforum* 126(10). 403–411.

Fairclough, Norman. 2014. Semiotic aspects of social transformation and learning. In Johannes Angermuller, Dominique Maingueneau & Ruth Wodak (eds.), *The discourse studies reader: Main currents in theory and analysis*, 378–387. Amsterdam: John Benjamins.

Fichte, Johann Gottlieb. 1968 [1808]. *Addresses to the German nation*. New York: Harper Torch Books.

Finney, Carolyn. 2014. *Black faces, white spaces: Reimagining the relationship of African Americans to the great outdoors*. Chapel Hill, NC: University of North Carolina Press.

Floyd, Myron & Monika Stodolska. 2014. Theoretical frameworks in leisure research on race and ethnicity. In Monika Stodolska, Kimberly J. Shinew, Myron F. Floyd & Gordon J. Walker (eds.), *Race, ethnicity, and leisure*, 9–19. Champaign, IL: Human Kinetics.

Foucault, Michel. 1977. *Discipline and punish: The birth of the prison*. New York: Vintage Books.

Friedman, Jonathan. 2003. Globalizing languages: Ideologies and realities of the contemporary global system. *American Anthropologist* 105(4). 744–752.

García, Ofelia & Li Wei. 2014. *Translanguaging: Language, bilingualism and education*. London: Palgrave MacMillan.

García, Ofelia & Tatyana Kleyn. 2016. Introduction. In Ofelia Garcia & Tatyana Kleyn (eds.), *Translanguaging with multilingual students: learning from classroom moments*, 1–6. New York: Routledge.

Gellner, Ernest. 1983. *Nations and nationalism*. Ithaca: Cornell University Press.

Glick Schiller, Nina & Noel B. Salazar. 2013. Regimes of mobility across the globe. *Journal of Ethnic and Migration Studies* 39(2). 183–200.

Goodwin, Charles & Marjorie Harness Goodwin. 1992. Assessments and the construction of context. In Alessandro Duranti & Charles Goodwin (eds.), *Rethinking context: Language as an interactive phenomenon*, 147–189. Cambridge: Cambridge University Press.

Gorman-Murray, Andrew. 2007. Rethinking queer migration through the body. Social & Cultural Geography 8(1): 105–121.

Gregson, Nicky & Gillian Rose. 2000. Taking Butler elsewhere: Performativities, spatialities and subjectivities. Environment and Planning D: Society and Space 18: 433–452.

Gulson, Kalervo N. & Colin Symes. 2007. Knowing one's place: Space, theory, education. *Critical Studies in Education* 48(1). 97–110.

Hadi-Tabassum, Samini. 2006. *Language, space and power: A Critical Look at Bilingual Education.* Clevedon: Multilingual Matters.

Harvey, David. 1990. *The condition of postmodernity.* Cambridge: Blackwell.

Hedman, Christina & Ulrika Magnusson. 2022. Performative functions of multilingual policy in second language education in Sweden. *International Journal of Bilingual Education and Bilingualism* 25(2). 452–466.

Henderson, Jason. 2006. Secessionist automobility: Racism, anti-urbanism, and the politics of automobility in Atlanta, Georgia. *International Journal of Urban and Regional Research* 30(2). 293–307.

Johnson, David Cassels. 2010. Implementational and ideological spaces in bilingual education language policy. *International Journal of Bilingual Education and Bilingualism* 13(1). 61–79.

Kachru, Braj. 1992 [1982]. Models for non-native Englishes. In Braj B. Kachru (ed.), *The other tongue: English across cultures*, 48–74. Urbana: University of Illinois Press.

Kawai, Tomoyuki. 2016. "Anxiety Grows over 'Pokemon Go' Mishaps." Nikkei Asian Review, July 22. http://asia.nikkei.com/Business/Companies/Anxiety-grows-over-Pokemon-Go-mishaps. (accessed 11 June 2018)

Kymlicka, Will. 1995. *Multicultural citizenship: A liberal theory of minority rights.* Oxford: Clarendon.

Lave, Jean & Etienne Wenger. 1991. *Situated learning: Legitimate, peripheral, participation.* Cambridge: Cambridge University Press.

Leitner, Helga, Eric Sheppard & Kristin M. Sziarto. 2008. The spatialities of contentious politics. *Transactions of the Institute of British Geographers* 33. 157–172.

Levinson, Stephen C. 1996. Language and space. *Annual Review of Anthropology* 25. 353–382.

Levinson, Stephen C. 2003. *Space in language and cognition: Explorations in cognitive diversity.* Cambridge: Cambridge University Press.

Lewis, Nathaniel M. 2012. Remapping disclosure: gay men's segmented journeys of moving out and coming out. *Social & Cultural Geography* 13(3). 211–231.

Li Wei. 2018. Translanguaging as a practical theory of language, *Applied Linguistics* 39(1). 9–30.

Low, Setha M. 2003. *Behind the gates: Life, security, and the pursuit of happiness in fortress America.* New York and London: Routledge.

Low, Setha M. 2009. Toward an anthropological theory of space and place. *Semiotica* 175. 21–37.

Malinowski, David & Stefania Tufi (eds). 2020. *Reterritorializing linguisticlandscapes: Questioning boundaries and opening spaces.* London: Bloomsbury Academic.

Martin, Derek Christopher. 2004. Apartheid in the great outdoors. *Journal of Leisure Research* 36. 513–535.

May, Stephen. 2001. *Language and minority rights: Ethnicity, nationalism and the politics of language.* Harlow: Pearson Education.

MacKinnon, Danny. 2010. Reconstructing scale: Toward a new scalar politics. *Progress in Human Geography* 35(1). 21–36.

de Meulder, Maartje, Annelies Kusters, Erin Moriarty & Joseph J. Murray. 2019. Describe, don't prescribe. The practice and politics of translanguaging in the context of deaf signers, *Journal of Multilingual and Multicultural Development*, 40(10). 892–906.

Milroy, James & Lesley Milroy. 1991 [1985]. *Authority in language: Investigating language prescription and standardisation.* London: Routledge.

Mix, Kelly S., Linda B. Smith & Michael Gasser (eds.). 2010. *The spatial foundations of cognition and language: Thinking through space.* Oxford: Oxford University Press.

Moore, Adam. 2008. Rethinking scale as a geographical category: From analysis to practice. *Progress in Human Geography* 32 (2).203–225.

Nelson, Lisa. 1999. Bodies (and spaces) do matter: The limits of performativity. *Gender, Place & Culture* 6(4). 331–353.

Pennycook, Alastair. 1994. *The cultural politics of English as an international language*. London: Longman.

Pennycook, Alastair. 2004. Performativity and language studies. *Critical Inquiry in Language Studies: An International Journal* 1(1). 1–19.

Pennycook, Alastair. 2007. The myth of English as an international language. In Sinfree Makoni & Alastair Pennycook (eds.), *Disinventing and reconstituting languages*, 90–115. Clevedon: Multilingual Matters.

Phillipson, Robert. 1992. *Linguistic imperialism*. Oxford: Oxford University Press.

Picard, David & Michael DiGiovine. 2014. Introduction: Through other worlds. In David Picard & Michael Di Giovine (eds.), *Tourism and the power of otherness: Seductions of difference*, 1–28. Bristol: Channel View Publications.

Qin, Kongji. 2020. Curriculum as a discursive and performative space for subjectivity and learning: Understanding immigrant adolescents' language use in classroom discourse. *Modern Language Journal* 104(4). 842–859.

Quirk, Randolph. 1988. The question of standards in the international use of English. In Peter H. Lowenberg (ed.), *Language spread and language policy: Issues, implications, and case studies*, 229–241. Washington, DC: Georgetown University Press.

de Saussure, Ferdinand. 1965. *Course in general linguistics*. New York: McGraw-Hill.

Smitheram, Jan. 2011. Spatial performativity/spatial performance. *Architectural Theory Review* 16(1). 55–69.

Soja, Edward W. 2010. *Seeking spatial justice*. Minneapolis: University of Minnesota Press.

Spicer, André, Mats Alvesson & Dan Kärreman. 2009. Critical performativity: The unfinished business of critical management studies. *Human Relations* 62. 537–560.

de Swaan, Abram. 2001. *Words of the world: The global language system*. Cambridge: Polity.

Tomlinson, John. 1999. *Globalization and culture*. Chicago: University of Chicago Press.

Trinidad, Alma M. O. 2011. Sociopolitical development through critical indigenous pedagogy of place: Preparing Native Hawaiian young adults to become change agents. *Hulili: Multidisciplinary Research on Hawaiian Well-Being* 7: 185–221.

Tsing, Anna. 2000. The global situation. *Cultural Anthropology* 15(3). 327–360.

Tsing, Anna. 2005. *Friction: An ethnography of global connection*. Princeton: Princeton University Press.

Tyler, Melissa & Laurie Cohen. 2010. Spaces that matter: Gender performativity and organizational space. *Organization Studies* 31(2). 175–198.

Urciuoli, Bonnie. 1995. Language and borders. *Annual Review of Anthropology* 24. 525–546.

Voloshinov, Valentin. 1973. *Marxism and the philosophy of language*. New York: Seminar Press.

Wickert, Christopher & Stephan M. Schaefer. 2015. Towards a progressive understanding of performativity in critical management studies. *Human Relations* 68. 107–130.

Widdowson, Henry. 1994. The ownership of English. *TESOL Quarterly* 28(2). 377–389.

Wilk, Richard. 1995. Learning to be local in Belize: Global systems of common difference. In Daniel Miller (ed.), *Worlds apart: Modernity through prism of the local*, 110–133. London: Routledge.

Wimmer, Andreas & Nina Glick Schiller. 2002. Methodological nationalism and beyond: Nation-state building, migration and the social sciences. *Global Networks* 2(4). 301–334.

Winichakul, Thongchai. 1994. *Siam mapped: A history of the geo-body of a nation*. Honolulu: University of Hawaii Press

Neriko Musha Doerr

Performative linguistic space of study abroad: Immersion discourse, short-term programs, colonial legacies, and US immigrant space

1 Introduction

Study abroad is a spatial learning experience. Staying in a "new" environment away from home—"abroad"—students are expected to "study," to learn things that they cannot learn anywhere else, especially if they stay home. However, the space of the study abroad destination is not static but constructed contextually. It is constructed not only by its institutional setting but also by the presence of students with diverse backgrounds, who bring with them language politics from various spaces. Using the notion of performative linguistic space that emerges contextually and encourages or discourages certain utterances (see Doerr and McGuire, this volume), this chapter teases out two kinds of performative linguistic space which emerged in Spain when three students from a US college studied abroad there in 2011 and 2013.

The first kind of performative linguistic space emerged at the intersection of the notion of "immersion" and study abroad's need to attract more students. The discourse of immersion is one of the most prevalent discourses in study abroad, encouraging students to leave their comfort zone and engage themselves in the life of the study-abroad destination. This notion of immersion is often expressed as "live like locals," sometimes suggesting that any experience—even disorientation—in the study-abroad destination is a learning experience. Spending time with fellow compatriot students is strongly discouraged by the immersion discourse in the zero-sum game of limited study-abroad time (Brockington and Wiedenhoeft 2009; Cushner 2009).

Nonetheless, the students I interviewed reported that spending time with fellow American students was not only enjoyable but also meaningful and informative as they could learn about diverse practices within the US. They did use the notion of immersion but not as a way to pressure themselves to engage with the "locals" but to talk about how much they liked their experience there or to explain, if not justify, their choices (e.g., dropping a class, which did not affect learning experience because they could learn through immersion outside classes), or

https://doi.org/10.1515/9783110744781-002

to make commentary on the activity (e.g., as new, enjoyable, or not "packaged") or on the people (e.g., as different from them or as legitimate "locals").

This discourse of immersion intersected with the study abroad's need to attract more students, which manifested itself in the institutional setup. Study-abroad programs designed to attract American students tended to be short-term (one week to one month) and used English as the medium of instruction, which goes against the immersion discourse that encourages students to speak the local language of the destination. In this chapter, I will argue that the institutional design overrode the discourse of immersion and created a performative linguistic space that encouraged English utterances. Moreover, I will argue for revisiting the notion of immersion and suggest acknowledging the positive aspects of interacting with students from the same country, while also noting its pitfalls.

The second kind of performative linguistic space emerged in the experience of two of the students above who had migrated from Latin American countries to the US. They found themselves acting as translators for other American students, while feeling discouraged from speaking Spanish outside this context due to Spaniards' negative attitudes toward them. I discuss how a performative linguistic space emerged around them in Spain as an effect of their geographic mobility—between their original Latin American ("Guatemalan" and "Colombian") homeland, English monolingualist US, and Spain as a study abroad destination and as a former colonial mother country.

Although some researchers discuss space as stages on which the linguistic actions occur or of linguistic communities that are associated with the space in somewhat static ways, as discussed in the introductory chapter of this volume (Doerr and McGuire), I show in this chapter the complex dynamics of space at the intersection of students' past and present experience of various linguistic spaces gained through their geographic mobility. This chapter offers a new analytical angle to the body of study-abroad research, in which few works have discussed the effects of spacing on students' linguistic practices,

This chapter presents part of my research on experiential learning, particularly in the context of studying abroad (2015; 2016; 2017; 2020c). In what follows, I will review the literature on study abroad, especially in regard to space and to the notion of immersion, introduce my fieldwork and its methods, followed by the narratives of three students, and then analyze these narratives in terms of the emergence of performative linguistic spaces in relation to the discourse of immersion, institutional settings, and students' geographic mobility that connects diverse linguistic politics.

2 Spacing processes in study-abroad research

"Spacing" shapes the world (Cresswell and Merriman 2011: 15) as discussed in the Introduction of this volume (Doerr and McGuire). Space ushers, hinders, and directs mobility while being marked by it (Cresswell 2006; Cresswell and Merriman 2011; de Certeau 1984). This volume focuses on such processes specifically due to the geographic mobility of individuals who carry with them specific language politics of spaces they move between, turning the space temporarily into that specific performative linguistic space. This chapter focuses on such performative linguistic spaces that emerged in the context of studying abroad in Spain based on the analysis of the institutional setup and students' narratives about their experience.

Study abroad is a particular type of global movement of people, usually educated and often privileged young adults (Barnick 2010). Although global education takes various forms, including that which can be done at "home," study abroad has been seen as the prominent mode of delivery. In most European contexts, Beelen and Jones (2015) argue, as the office in charge of global education shifted from academic departments to administrative offices, the focus became the students' physical mobility rather than the content of their learning, although "Internationalization at Home" initiatives focus on the incorporation of topics from various parts of the world in the curriculum. In the US context where short-term study-abroad programs are becoming prominent due to the pressure to increase the number of students studying abroad (Chieffo and Griffiths 2009), students' physical mobility, rather than the subject content, continues to be seen as important.

Study-abroad researchers' discussions have centered on strategies to nurture "global competence" and turn students into "global citizens." In addressing the effectiveness of learning through immersion, well-planned pre-departure experiences (Bennett 1998; Brustein 2009); ethnographic projects (Roberts 1994; Roberts et al. 2001; Ogden 2006); reflective writing (Chen 2002); and volunteer work and co-op programs that would allow students to engage directly in the host community (Bringle and Hatcher 2011; Lewin and van Kirk 2009; Plater et al. 2009) have been suggested. Research discussions also focus on methods of measuring the students' global competence and related skills (Carlson et al. 1990; Laubscher 1994; Deardorff 2009; Jackson 2005; Lewin and van Kirk 2009; Plater et al. 2009; Porfilio and Hickman 2011).

An increasing number of studies critique study abroad as (re)creating power relations between study-abroad students and host societies, such as through advertising that celebrates consumerism and portrays the host society as an open "laboratory" to satisfy American students' desire for adventure (Zemach-Bersin 2009; also see Gillespie et al. 2009) or as full of immobile and parochial individuals, in contrast to mobile and cosmopolitan study abroad students (Doerr 2013).

There has been little research that sheds light on the dynamics of space in study abroad. The exception is research done by geographers, which can be categorized into two types. The first examines transient study-abroad students' place-making practices in the destination as they relate to larger-scale urban transformation—educational businesses, property developers, and local and national governments seeking to cater to study-abroad students—as well as the students' own negotiation of urban space (Collins 2010; 2012; Fincher and Shaw 2009).

The second type has focused on geography field courses that happen to occur abroad, leading to examining particular academic goals (Houser et al. 2011), such as learning ways to "read the landscape" by focusing on the cultural context, developing a sensitivity to history's footprints in everyday life (Moline 2009; also see Glass 2014; Lemmons et al. 2014; Rink 2017), rather than the common study-abroad focus on the attitudinal change (e.g., "cross-cultural sensitivity"), or language acquisition (Alred and Byram 2006; Carlson et al. 1990). Few geographers researching study abroad, however, discuss the ways in which particular space ushers certain actions, especially linguistic actions, or how they are affected by the students' geographic mobility—what we term performative linguistic space in this volume.

I have discussed elsewhere ways in which the project of study abroad constructs spaces through its discourses, such as that of immersion (2013) or adventure (2012), constructing the study-abroad destination and the students' home country as internally homogeneous and fundamentally different from each other. I have also discussed how study-abroad students themselves construct space at various scales—regional and national—in their act of narrating their experiences (2015) and contradictory dual perceptions of study-abroad destination space as homogeneously filled with "local" people, on the one hand, and as heterogeneously filled with "local" people as well as visitors such as themselves and tourists, on the other (2016), as I will describe further later.

This chapter approaches the issues from different angles and illustrates, first, the ways in which the notion of immersion did not result in creating the performative linguistic space it aims to establish (i.e., space that encourages students to speak the "local language") due to the institutional setup derived from the recent push to increase the number of students studying abroad. Second, this chapter focuses on how students' geographic mobility activates intersections of various language politics from spaces they have occupied and were shaped by, resulting in the emergence of various performative linguistic spaces.

3 Study-abroad destinations as "spaces of cultural difference": The discourse of immersion

The discourse of immersion operates with what I have called "unit thinking"—seeing the world as constituted by discrete and bounded units that are internally homogeneous (Doerr 2022a). One prominent example of unit thinking is the nation-state ideology that implies a problematic homology among "one nation, one people, one culture, one language, and one territory," each perceived as static and internally homogeneous (Doerr 2018).

The discourse of immersion constructs the study-abroad destination as the space of culturalist difference in four ways (Doerr 2013). First, the premise that students learn through immersion constructs the host society as culturally different from students' home society. If locals are similar "culturally" (or otherwise) to people in their home country, students learn little from merely immersing themselves in the host society.

Second, with no clear learning objectives, curricula, assessment, or teachers, learning through immersion—i.e., by just "living like a local"—is talked about by students first by identifying difference and then by describing how they emulated it. For instance, as I introduced elsewhere (Doerr 2017), an American student studying abroad in France explained her learning experience to me by first constructing French-vs-American differences (e.g., French wear flats while Americans wear sneakers) and then describing how she "acted French" by wearing what she deemed "French" (Doerr 2017).

Third, as cognitive dissonance and disorientation in the study-abroad destination is considered to provide a learning experience unique to study abroad, the host society is necessarily constructed as the space of difference; otherwise, cognitive dissonance and disorientation cannot occur. Researchers argue such experience gives students opportunities to develop the ability to fail, navigate unknown environments (Brockington and Wiedenhoeft 2009), and confront their own anxieties and limitations, resulting in self-awareness, confidence, adaptability, persistence, risk-taking, empathy, knowledge of another "culture" as well as one's own, and ability to shift perspectives (Cushner 2009).

Fourth, "global competence," "global citizenship," "intercultural competence," and other related learning outcomes of study abroad that are supposedly achieved through immersion hinge on constructing the host society as the space of difference (emphasis added in the list of items introduced below). Hunter, White, and Godbey (2006) have listed common threads in notions of global competence: (1) international knowledge (e.g., world history and events), (2) global skills (e.g., adaptability to *diverse cultures*), (3) global attitudes (e.g., openness toward *difference*) and (4) discipline-specific competence in collaborating *across cultures* (also, see Brockington and Wiedenhoeft 2009; Currier, Lucas, and Saint Arnault 2009; Cushner 2009). Richard Lambert's oft-quoted definition of global competence identifies five interrelated questions concerning (1) knowledge of globally cross-cutting issues (e.g., environment) or deep *area-specific knowledge*; (2) empathy for people with *different* backgrounds; (3) approval or favoring of *things abroad*; (4) *foreign language* competency; and (5) task performance in international arenas. Darla Deardorff (2009: 348) identifies common threads in the notion of global citizenship: "(1) global knowledge; (2) understanding the interconnectedness of the world; (3) intercultural competence, or the ability to relate successfully with those from *other cultures*; and (4) engagement on the local and global level around issues that impact humanity."

As mentioned, the discourse of immersion also operates by perceiving the study-abroad destination as internally homogeneous by discouraging study-abroad students from spending time with fellow compatriot students while studying abroad, implying there is nothing to be learned from such experience—i.e., because they are not "different" enough to learn something new, in contrast to the way students are said to learn from people in the study abroad destination whose "difference" is the source of learning. Students' interviews in this chapter, however, show they learned from other compatriot students, suggesting that people in their home country are diverse and offer new points for learning.

The language spoken in the host society is also seen as homogeneous and static in the discourse of immersion. Any conversation one can have in the space of the study abroad destination is seen as meaningful "immersion" to learn the language (Brockington and Wiedenhoeft 2009). This perception of a host society's language overlooks not only the changes and diversity of the linguistic practices—regional, class, and generational that are often hierarchically positioned, sometimes as a colonial legacy, as will be discussed—but also the standardization processes that forced some to emulate the standard language, as an effect of relations of power (Bourdieu 1991).

In sum, the discourse of immersion is premised on and further constructs the host society as the space of difference which is internally homogeneous: unit thinking of nation-states. As such, it assumes that life in the study-abroad destination was shaped independently from any global connections. To overcome this perception, I have argued elsewhere (2018; 2022c) for "structural competence"—the ability to see how aspects of daily life have been shaped by continuously shifting global arrangements of production, circulation, and marketing guided by global regulations and trade agreements—to highlight relational processes in constructing and even noticing "difference." I suggested replacing the notion of "global competence" based on the static view of difference (i.e., seeing certain practice or item as representing certain "culture" to be learned and negotiated) with that of "structural competence," the ability to comprehend and engage with the wider shifting structural forces—themselves shaped by the changing contours of global connections such as trading regulations, price fluctuations, fashion and consumer trends—that construct perceived difference.

In this chapter, I shift the focus from the ways the immersion discourse creates and perpetuates spatial difference at the level of concept to the discourse's effects, or lack thereof, on students' linguistic practices, or more precisely, students' language choices as narrated by students. I argue that it was the institutional setup that had a great effect on creating performative linguistic spaces by drawing certain kinds of students. As another kind of performative linguistic space, this chapter shows the effects of the students' past and present movements between various spaces and their language politics.

4 Fieldwork on study abroad

Most research on study abroad is done from the viewpoint of the sending side and it tends to "be accepted as a common-sensical truth . . . that study abroad is a good, in and of itself," with little supporting evidence, Amit argues (2010: 13; also see Barnick 2010; Schroeder et al. 2009). While ethnographic work on study-abroad students' experiences would partially fill this gap, given the prevalence of short-term programs (Chieffo and Griffiths 2009), such work falls outside of the older notion of ethnographic fieldwork as based on "intensive dwelling" in a single place and "extended co-residence" with the people one is studying (Clifford 1997: 71). However, this notion of what constitutes "legitimate" ethnographic work has been critiqued as grounded less in the quality of analysis than in, first, the history of anthropology— the discipline that spawned ethnography—as a legitimate academic discipline as opposed to travel/journalistic writing (Clifford 1997) and, second, the legacy of the colonialist assumption that non-Western people/research objects are immobile "natives" rooted in a particular space, as opposed to mobile and cosmopolitan Western anthropologists (Appadurai 1988).

Study abroad requires an ethnography of its own (see Murphy-Lejeune 2002), differing from conventional fieldwork in two ways. First, because living with study-abroad students in their host home or dorm would interfere excessively with their "immersion," participant observation often needs to be limited and interviews become more prominent. This can be solved in short-term (one to two-weeks) "island-style" study abroad trips, which are when a group of students led by a professor from the home university spend the entire time together, in which the researcher can go on the trip as a participant and carry out participant observation throughout, which I have done in ones to Sierra Leone (2012), Ghana (2014) and Peru (2016). The study abroad experiences discussed in this chapter, however, are from a longer (one-month) program and the data is mainly from the student interviews.

Second, because study abroad necessarily involves a trip, fieldwork needs to be "multi-sited" (Marcus 1995), in the student's home country and the destination. Interviews often need to be conducted before, during, and after their stay abroad in order to gain insights into their shifting perspectives. Accordingly, this chapter is based on multiple interviews conducted at several stages.

This chapter also uses a case study method focusing on students' specific subject positions and the contexts in which they are situated, supplemented by interviews with the study-abroad providers and other studies I have conducted. Talburt and Stewart (1999) critique study-abroad research as often generalizing students' experiences abroad mainly based on monocultural white middle-class students' experiences. They instead illustrate how the students' race and gender affect their experience. The case study method responds to this critique, seeking instead in-depth qualitative analyses that capture connections between various factors and nuanced and situated multi-front processes (i.e., vis-à-vis people in the destination, fellow American students, program providers, etc.) of learning that quantitative studies can overlook, thus providing a holistic understanding of particular students' study-abroad experiences. While this method has limitations in terms of lacking generalizability, the case study method of in-depth understanding of specific situated study-abroad experiences offers an important angle.

Regarding the research on the choice of "language" being used, it is important to use the interview method along with observation of such utterances, rather than relying only on the actual utterances. It is because such "language choice" can only be determined with the notion of language seen as discrete units—"English" or "Spanish," for example—on the part of the observer, an arbitrary process (e.g., the term "tacos" can be arbitrarily considered English or Spanish depending on the observer). That is, the discussion of language choice can only make sense through the speaker's narrative about it—how they label their language choice themselves (see my discussion of the problem of "translanguaging" as an analytical concept in Doerr 2020a; 2022a; and the introductory chapter of this volume). That is, this chapter is not a study of actual utterances which then I analyze as a researcher; rather, this chapter discusses the choice of language, which was encouraged or hindered by specific space as felt by the individuals who reported their choices.

For these reasons, in this chapter, I focus on narratives of language choices by three students from a US college in a study-abroad program in Bilbao, Spain and analyze them by situating them in wider social and cultural arrangements. The students were from Cape College (all names are aliases except for Richard, with whom I have published together under his real name), a public liberal arts college in the northeastern US with an enrollment of approximately 6,000 students (in 2011, around the time they studied abroad). The student body's ethnic identifications were "White, non-Hispanic" (73%), "Hispanic or Latino of any race" (11%), Black or African American, non-Hispanic (5%), Asian, non-Hispanic (5%), and two or more races, non-Hispanic (1.2%).

Two of the students I focus on here (Tracy and Maria, pseudonyms) were among four students who responded in 2011 to a call for research participants to be interviewed before, during, and after their study abroad trips that the director of Cape College's International Education Center sent out via email on my behalf to twenty-five students who were to study abroad via external providers. This self-selective process implies that those who participated are the ones interested in helping others (i.e., researchers) and sharing their experiences with others, and possibly do not mind their experiences being scrutinized. Thus, the results presented here may show more conscientious and self-reflective narratives than those who did not participate in my research. The third student (Richard) originally participated in my fieldwork of an alternative break trip in 2012. Because of his unique perspective as a participant in service-related work while being of low-socioeconomic status himself (others tended to identify themselves as "middle class"), I have collaborated with him in writing papers (2013b; 2014). He happened to study abroad in the same program in Bilbao as the two students above in 2013, which resulted in my further interviewing him regarding his experience and co-writing a journal article (2018), which I will be discussing in this chapter with a new focus on space.

The program they attended in 2011 (Tracy and Maria) and 2013 (Richard) in Bilbao, Spain, was designed specifically for study-abroad students, mainly from the US, at a local university there. It aimed to offer "a wide selection of interesting courses, and . . . favor[s] an enriching cultural *immersion* experience" (program brochure, p. 9; emphasis added). The program organizer told me in my interview that the program's goals included improving students' knowledge of the Spanish language, subjects they study, and Spanish culture—which she said they would learn from their host family and local friends. She personally wanted students to learn another way of life and tolerance of people different from them. Students from Latin American countries, she added, would also learn a new culture in Spain because Latin American and Spanish cultures are different. The program ran for one month, from June 27 to July 29 in 2011 and from 24 June to 30 July in 2013. The program included a three-day excursion to Madrid and Segovia before everyone was bused to Bilbao. It also offered excursions to Guernica and Pamplona.

Tracy was a psychology and education major finishing up her sophomore year before studying abroad. Self-identifying as "Caucasian," she had studied Spanish for thirteen years at school prior to her visit. Her daily schedule while studying abroad was Spanish language class from 10:00 a.m. to 12:00 p.m., home for lunch with her host mother for about 2 hours, and hanging around with friends, sometimes in her friends' dorm rooms or walking around town, she said.

Maria had finished her junior year majoring in economics and international business before studying abroad. Maria told me that she is "Hispanic, Latin American." Born and raised in Guatemala, she came to the US when she was nine. She is fluent in both English and Spanish. In my pre-trip interview, she said that she was excited to experience the culture and city, become mature, add an edge to her resume, and make friends. Maria took two business classes during the day from 8:30 a.m. (Classes end at 11:00 a.m. or 3:00 p.m., depending on the day) and spent the rest of the day with her fellow American students at the mall, beach, movies, or a bar.

Richard, a double major in psychology and marketing, finished his junior year before traveling to Spain. He self-identified as "Colombian," having immigrated at the age of one and spoke Spanish at home growing up. He had visited Colombia on two three-week trips (in high school and college). Richard chose to study abroad in Bilbao partly for its focus on business studies, partly for its location in Spain, where his uncle from Colombia lived, and partly because he knew the language. He stayed with his uncle's family before (one month) and after (one month) studying abroad in Bilbao, though for the latter stay, he mainly traveled to Malaga and Morocco, keeping his uncle's family as the base.

I interviewed each of the three students before, during, and after their study-abroad stay, as mentioned, lasting from 30 minutes to four hours. For the during-trip interviews and brief participant observation, I visited Bilbao for four days, July 13–16, 2011. I spent the first day there interviewing two staff members. I interviewed Tracy and Maria on July 14, two and a half weeks after their arrival in Spain. I interviewed Tracy in a park. Then we walked downtown, had lunch together, and visited her host family. After spending time with Tracy, I met with Maria who took me to her dorm and then showed me around downtown. We did the interview at a city plaza, went to a bar for tapas, and took the metro back to the dorm. During this visit, I also did participant observation in two classes and interviewed two of their teachers as well as two staff members. Richard's during-trip interview lasting for over an hour in 2013 was done via Skype, partly because I had visited and thus knew the same study-abroad program in 2011 that gave me some ideas about the site, hence focusing on what he has to say over seeing what the program site is like. This during-trip interview was supplemented by a formal post-trip interview totaling over four hours and extensive informal discussions about his experience over several months because we were also collaborating on writing a journal article about it (Doerr and Suarez 2018).

Ethnographic data are always a result of unique interactions between researchers and the researched, situated in layers of relations of power that require acknowledgment (Clifford 1988). I had taught as adjunct faculty at Cape College, and Maria had taken my class. Despite these institutionally established power relations, our interaction was unlike professor-student relations in the classroom, because not only was I not giving them grades (Maria was no longer taking my class) but also because I positioned myself as learning from them.

This chapter focuses on the interviews more than participant observation partly because of the way research was carried out and partly because I focus on language choices that specific space ushers or hinders that need to be viewed from the interlocutors' rather than the researcher's viewpoint, as mentioned earlier. In analyzing interviews, narrative studies inform us that our narrations about our experience are shaped by others' stories that provide the vocabularies and sequences that not only assure us that our experience is not anomalous but also turn fragmented parts of our experience into a coherent story (Plummer 1995). Discourses in study abroad provide such existing narratives to frame one's experience. This chapter shows, however, an alternative to common narratives in study abroad regarding one's subject positions. That is, whereas study-abroad discourses assume students to be monolingual (in English in the US context) white middle-class (Salisbury et al. 2011; Sweeney 2013), narratives of Maria and Richard show Spanish-English bilingual students helping other students who are not bilingual.

On the other hand, our narratives are shaped by questions asked by the interviewer—the *coaxer*—that elicit certain responses: the courtroom interrogator, the therapist, and the ethnographer are such coaxers (Plummer 1995). In daily conversation, the dialogic nature of utterances can make any interlocutor a coaxer (Bakhtin 1981). Narratives about a study abroad trip are told in various ways with various coaxers—professors and other students as well as assignment questions (see Doerr 2022b). Because it is inevitable to have such a dialogic aspect in narrative, it is important to identify such possible items that influenced the outcome.

Therefore, interviews presented here are narratives shaped by myself, an ethnographer thus coaxer, who prepared semi-structured interviews with open-ended questions about their backgrounds, what they learned—in which the choice of language was often asked because we were discussing learning the language—and what they enjoyed, which were then expanded further following students' interest in elaborating. Also, in order to get some commentary on the effects of the context of the interview, I asked during the post-trip interview what they felt were the effects of participating in my research.

Tracy responded that she wouldn't have reflected as much if she did not participate in the research, as my questions were more specific than what her friends' questions would be when they ask about her study abroad experiences. Maria stated how, during her stay there, "a couple of days before [Doerr's arrival], I was thinking 'Okay, she's coming and these are the things I feel about' . . . I was really . . . looking forward to this [interview] because I was like 'I can talk to her about this. She'll understand where I am coming from' . . . I feel like it helped shape my experience." This points to her probably focusing more on things she thought I would be interested in hearing.

As for Richard, since he co-wrote papers with me, as mentioned, his interview process was part of what we called elsewhere (2013a) "anthropological co-investigation." It involved weekly discussion of relevant literature that I introduced (e.g., Freire 1970; Foucault 1983) and brainstorming paper ideas based on Richard's observations and literature we read together. His interviews about study abroad introduced in this chapter were part of this on-going co-investigation discussing common assumptions about education, development, humanitarian aid, and study abroad for publication (Doerr and Suarez 2013b; 2014; 2018).

5 Language space of study abroad: Institutional setups over the discourse of immersion

The first type of performative linguistic space this chapter discusses is the space students were encouraged to speak English, despite the prevalent discourse of immersion that encourages students to speak the local language, as this section describes.

5.1 Studying abroad in English: Creating English space in the study-abroad destination

Many study-abroad programs, often short-term ones, offer programs that use English as the medium of instruction. This is due to the recent push in the US—in which colleges often set up a certain percentage gain—to increase the number of students studying abroad by making the programs more attractive (Chieffo and Griffiths 2009), as mentioned. Short-term programs draw a larger number of students because of the lower cost and lower level of required commitment from students, especially regarding time. English-medium classes also require less from Anglophone students, making them more attractive to those who prefer classes taught in a language familiar to them.

That is, while immersion that encourages students to interact with local people and speak the local language remains the key discourse in study abroad, the industry's recent push to increase the number of study-abroad students tends to defy the encouragement of language immersion, increasingly creating an officially-sanctioned space of English language in the study-abroad destination. For example, in 2018/19, 64.9% of students studying abroad (total of 306,141 students; total students in US higher education were 16,043,597) did so in "short-term" (summer or eight weeks or less) programs as opposed to 56.3% in 2007/08 (total of 262,416 students studying abroad). The "mid-length" (one semester or one or two quarters) program was 32.9% in 2018/19 as opposed to 39.5% in 2007/08 and "long-term" (academic or calendar year) was 2.2% in 2018/19 as opposed to 4.2% in 2007/ 08 (Open Doors 2010; Open Doors 2020). These programs tend to be English-medium programs, which are themselves increasing overall (Collier 2021).

The effects of this institutional setting, however, are not just the officially-sanctioned space of English but also the kinds of students who study abroad—students who cannot speak the local language, often monolingual English speakers—who in turn create the space in which English prevails wherever they go as a group: beyond that official space of the classroom, the dorm where they stay together and wherever else they visit, linger, and dwell. Two students introduced in this chapter are "native speakers" in both Spanish and English, and they reported they were in the minority.

5.2 Enjoying the company of American students and the performative linguistic space of English

The three students in question, studying abroad in Bilbao attending the program designed for study-abroad students, talked about spending much time with fellow American students, usually using English. It was an experience often talked about positively not only as enjoyable but also as a good learning experience.

Tracy listed making friends with fellow American students as one of the things she enjoyed the most in her study-abroad experience: "I like that I could have friends in different states when I go home. I like how varied the group is and how they bring different stuff to the table." In my post-trip interview with her six weeks after her return (9/12/2011), she said the part of the trip she liked the best was "connecting with people [from the US]. Like the different areas they live in." The only Spaniard she had gotten to know well was her host mother, she said. In the interview during her stay there, she said what she wanted to do before going home was to "explore as much as I can . . . Get closer with the [American] people I met here so that you know if I wanna visit, . . . Chicago, or DC [I have someone to see]." When I asked whether she had expected to make friends from the US while studying abroad, she said: "I kind of hoped that I would, but I didn't know if I would. But I'm glad that I did." Her comment suggested that she knew before her departure to study abroad that the program is mainly for American students and that she wanted to become friends with them.

When I asked whether she had experienced any misunderstandings, although I was expecting to hear about misunderstandings with Spaniards, Tracy instead talked about misunderstandings with other American students, indicating her main group of interaction: "when I say I'm from New Jersey, they just think we are all like people from the Jersey Shore [a reality TV show]." She said it was one of the things she learned during the study abroad as well—regional stereotyping by American students. This also suggested, as she explained earlier, that most of the interactions she had in Spain were with her fellow American students.

For Maria also, spending time with fellow American students was what she enjoyed the most, she responded in my during-trip interview. Approximately thirty American students from the same program were living in the dorm where she stayed, and Maria hung out with about twenty of them, she said. She talked about how much she loved their company: "I love it. There's always something to do . . . Nobody excludes anybody. It's very, very cool." Although at first, she felt embarrassed about her fellow American students' loudness that stood out among mellower Spaniards, she came to accept it: "It grew on me," she said.

Maria also reported learning much from fellow American students:

> People from different states are so different . . . There are these kids who are from Mississippi . . . They wear cowboy boots to go out and they tuck their shirts in. And we just talk about how different the way of life is from state to state. So, I'm learning about my own country while I'm here . . . My best girlfriend here, she's from . . . Chicago but she's [originally] from Lithuania . . . [so I also learned about] Lithuanian culture.

Being with fellow American students also allowed Maria to, somewhat paradoxically in light of the immersion discourse, learn Spanish culture—"taking on Spanish culture as a group"—she reported: "When I'm with my friends . . . if they want to practice Spanish, they just [talk to strangers] . . . So I've done that [with them] a lot," mentioning talking to strangers is something that she would not do alone. The company of fellow American students gave her the courage to interact with strangers in the study-abroad destination. She also reported learning cultural behavior in Spain by asking Spaniards questions on behalf of her fellow American students who could speak little Spanish, highlighting an increased opportunity to interact with Spaniards due to being with fellow American students.

Maria also learned about cultural behavior in Spain through observing her American friends' reactions to situations: "I realize the cultural differences the most when I see how frustrated all my [American] friends get . . . 'Why aren't they taking my American dollars?' . . . 'Why don't they just give me what I want?' . . . and then I realize 'Wow, the way of life here is very different'." Having grown up in Guatemala and then in the US, Maria was familiar with all practices, unable to distinguish what is Guatemalan, what is American, and what is Spanish which resembled Guatemalan ways. Only upon observing the reactions of fellow American students did she realize which sensibilities were American and which were Latin American/Spanish, albeit this may not be generalizable beyond the people she spent time with.

Richard stayed in the dorm as well, which he enjoyed:

> I'm glad I stayed in the dorm 'cause I met these cool kids, you know. It's much easier staying in the dorm, you know, 'cause with the host family, you kinda go and eat dinner and leave [for home at night] and then come back [the next day to school]. (post-trip interview)

He mentioned going to fiestas and bars with fellow American students and ending up talking with Spaniards there. It was a similar situation to the one Maria mentioned—taking on Spain as a group. That is, being in a group of American students did not necessarily mean they were shut out from interacting with the local Spanish people in the study-abroad space. Oftentimes, it was the other way around: the company of American students pushed them to interact with the local Spaniard more.

Here, taking on Spain as a group suggests the group of compatriot students acting as a buffer zone to experience the unfamiliar. As mentioned earlier, Richard chose Spain as his study abroad destination because of his uncle living there and because he can speak Spanish. Although he did not specifically mention the program being designed for American students as an appeal to him, this implies his comfort in being surrounded by something familiar while venturing out to study abroad.

He compared his experience of visiting touristic places on his own or with his uncle's family and doing so with American study-abroad students in my post-trip interview, mentioning the latter immersion as enjoyable whereas the former was not (i.e., "felt too touristy"). He found hanging out with fellow American students who wanted to do the same thing as he does was one of the most enjoyable experiences during this stay in Spain.

Tracy, Maria, and Richard all said the language they used with fellow American students was English, indicating their company meant the use of English with them. That is, the congregation of American students who did not necessarily speak Spanish fluently—a result of the institutional setup where the program is made for American students with no requirement of Spanish proficiency—created a performative linguistic space that encouraged utterances in English in the midst of Spain, although Maria and Richard did communicate with Spaniards in Spanish, often on behalf of their fellow American students. Although the discourse of immersion constructs the space of study-abroad destination as the space of local language, the discourse itself did not quite create a performative linguistic space that urges students to speak the local language.

5.3 The immersion discourse as the demonization of the company of fellow American students

These three students' accounts show that they all enjoyed the company of fellow American students and learned from it. Spending time with compatriots, however, is a practice condemned by the discourse of immersion with the fear that it prevents effective immersion. By doing so, the discourse of immersion hierarchizes study-abroad experiences, privileging particular types of programs and experiences over others. The use of English is often treated as an example of "not immersing"—not speaking the local language—in the host society.

For example, regarding programs for American study-abroad students, Hovey and Weinberg (2009: 37) characterize "high road" study-abroad programs as the ones that offer good immersion experience where "students become part of the culture by staying with local families and giving back to local communities . . . students attend classes and participate in activities with local students and are taught by local staff." In contrast, in "low road" programs, "students make *minimal effort to learn local languages* or customs, travel in large groups, and are taught in American-only classrooms. They live and go to bars with other Americans" (emphasis added: Hovey and Weinberg 2009: 36). Others support this general hierarchy of learning experience, privileging out-of-class experience over classroom learning (Chen 2002; Laubscher 1994; Peterson 2002), homestay over staying in a dormitory with American students (Chieffo and Griffiths 2009), semester-long stays over short visits of several weeks, and the companionship of locals over fellow American students (Deardorff 2009). At Cape College, the term "immersion" is often used and its implied hierarchy of learning was mentioned when students consulted with the staff at Cape College's International Education Center when deciding on the accommodation (e.g., "a host family provides more immersion than a dorm") and during orientation meetings.

That is, the experiences Tracy, Maria, and Richard raised as enjoyable and memorable for them are the kinds of experiences these researchers and the resulting discourse discourage, though not specifically by the staff in the program they attended. Tracy stayed with a host family, but she spent much time with fellow American students; Maria and Richard stayed in the dorm, which they liked, spending time with compatriots. This group of compatriots served somewhat as a safety bubble to venture out to Spain together, though both Maria and Richard had international travel experience before—Maria migrating to the US from Guatemala at a young age and Richard, traveling to Colombia to visit his family—though both with family.

5.4 The students' uses of the immersion discourse: Appreciating, justifying, and commenting on experiences

Focusing on the construction of space at the discourse level, I have argued elsewhere (2016) that the discourse of immersion constitutes study-abroad space as a space held in tension between homogeneous space-time and heterogeneous space-time, as mentioned. The homogeneous space-time views the host society as composed only of people of one nation, with every moment of their stay a meaningful learning experience. The heterogeneous space-time is constituted of "local space" inhabited by local people and "outsider space" comprised of study-abroad students or tourists, the space the students need to avoid. This duality allowed the students to highlight their proactive involvement in the local space by denouncing others who linger in the outsider space, such as spending time with other study abroad students or in touristic areas with other tourists. There is a productive tension between the two spaces where the former evokes an ideal state of the "nothing-but-local" and the latter provides students something to avoid as well as differentiate themselves from to demonstrate they are immersing themselves in local life (Doerr 2016).

In this chapter, I focus on different aspects of the ways students used the notion of immersion. The students I interviewed were aware of the notion of immersion and talked about learning from immersion, supporting the construction of the destination as the space of difference as well as the hierarchy of learning. Nonetheless, my interviews show that students also used the notion of immersion in different ways: to appreciate certain experiences (Tracy), justify certain choices (Tracy), or to comment on their activities and the people they interacted with (Richard).

Tracy used the term "immersed" to show how she is learning a lot, appreciating her experience in Spain in the during-the-stay interview. As a general comment on her study abroad experience, she said:

> I love it . . . Learning a lot . . . I'm always kind of like experiencing things, learning things . . . If we go for a walk, like you are surrounded by the language and you're *immersed* in it. And you know everything is experience. You get lost in the metro, you get off at the wrong stop . . . It's kind of like all learning experiences (emphasis added).

Tracy also used the notion of immersion to explain how her decision was the correct one. When she told me that she had to drop one of her two classes because of the workload, she used the notion of immersion to explain how it is okay and is working out: "I'm still learning plenty . . . and I feel like it's worth more than a class just to be . . . living with a host mom and speaking Spanish all the time. It's total *immersion* as opposed to, you know, whatever you'd do in an hour of class, so" (emphasis added). Her host mother, who lived alone, made Tracy speak Spanish a lot, which Tracy liked because it improved her Spanish. "That's the biggest impact in this stay," she said.

Maria also discussed learning cultural differences through daily interaction and observation—"the sellers here are just very pushy"; "Everybody's always presentable." However, she did not use the term "immersion" to describe her experience.

Richard's perception shows that the notion of immersion can be used as a commentary on activity and the people he interacted with. I discuss his use of immersion here more extensively than other students' because he had other experiences in Spain—living with his Colombian uncle's family and traveling around on his own—to compare his study-abroad experiences in terms of the notion of immersion (Doerr and Suarez 2018). Richard described staying with his uncle near Madrid in an area with "a lot of Hispanics" as "not immersion" and "not an authentic" Spanish experience. It was because he spent time looking around in Madrid on his own (i.e., "touristic things") or watching TV with his young cousin (i.e., "It had the feeling of babysitting"), he said. His experience while "studying abroad" in Bilbao and staying in the dorm with other American students, however, was immersion, along with his solitary travel afterward. My analysis of his perception suggests immersion was not actually about the act of "living like locals" as outlined below in four ways (for more details, see Doerr and Suarez 2018).

First, immersion was about being enjoyable. For him, "studying abroad" was more of an immersion experience because it was more enjoyable: "Just 'cause I had a lot of kids my age in Bilbao. . . . People that wanted to do stuff I wanted to do and so I mean I think I enjoyed my time a lot more." He even called the "touristic things" he did with fellow students "immersion" because it was enjoyable.

Second, immersion had to be a new experience for Richard. His uncle's lifestyle—Colombian and immigrant—was too similar to how he grew up to make him feel the experience was an immersion. Also, that newness included the sense of being "strangers"—staying with an extended family did not count as immersion for Richard. This resonates with how immersion is often considered as an experience of "cognitive dissonance" (Che et al. 2009).

Third, immersion was about activities he had control over. Traveling on his own was Richard's biggest "immersion experience," he explained: "I couch-surfed [i.e., found places to stay via web sites where people offering inexpensive lodging to travelers] and Airbnb-ed which . . . made my experience a lot better." In that sense, he felt the study-abroad program was too packaged—with accommodation and recreational activities being arranged for the students—to make it feel a sense of immersion.

Fourth, for an activity to be immersion, the person he was interacting with had to be "local"—the issue of belonging—which his uncle was not. His uncle identified himself as well as his son (against his will) as Colombian, not Spanish, Richard said. His uncle saw Spain as just another country to work in rather than his new homeland. Also, he felt his uncle was not accepted as a Spaniard by other Spaniards, being subjugated to racism: "they [Spaniards] make it known that whoever is not Spanish [i.e., an immigrant] is not Spanish."

The discourse of immersion was used by students like Tracy and Richard not so much to pressure themselves to interact with the local people but rather to show their appreciation of certain experiences (Tracy), to justify their choices (Tracy), or to make commentary on some activities as enjoyable, new, controllable, or to emphasize that the people interacting with were legitimate members of the local society (Richard).

5.5 Institutional setting vs discourse of immersion: Spacing and students' linguistic practices

These cases show that language choice in the study-abroad context was shaped mainly by the institutional settings of giving students a choice of staying with a host family (i.e., being forced to speak the local language as in Tracy's case) or of having English-medium classes that then recruits certain kind of students (i.e., those who do not speak the local language) to participate, although Spanish speaking students such as Maria and Richard did participate.

The immersion discourse shapes such an institutional setting as it encourages including the host family system that compels students to speak the local language, as seen in Tracy's example. However, other concerns, such as attracting more short-term study-abroad students, shape the institutional setting (e.g., having English-medium classes), which has a bigger impact on what language students end up predominantly speaking because they shape the student body of the program, creating specific performative linguistic spaces that urges utterance in a specific language.

The discourse of immersion itself had little effect on pressuring students to speak the local language. That is, although it constructed the space of the study abroad destination as that of the associated nation (i.e., Spaniard, also with condemned outsider space occupied by non-Spaniards) that is fundamentally different from the students' homeland (i.e., U.S.), it did not create performative linguistic space that urged utterance in the local language (i.e., Spanish).

Students practiced and enjoyed the one activity that the discourse of immersion especially discouraged—spending time with compatriot students—ironically learning much from this. This is also supported by some researchers who argue cultural comparisons are better done with someone from the same cultural background experiencing a different culture together because local people would not know what is different from the students' home society (Woolf 2010). In a different context of cultural adaptation, being with compatriots is accepted or encouraged for smooth learning experience. One example is a family volunteer tourism experience—called worldschooling or roadschooling—for the purpose of letting the children learn to "feel global" through traveling abroad and "doing good" without much anxiety because the "abroad" experience is done as a family, compatriots (Molz 2017). Another example, though often not compared to study abroad despite its relevance (for an effort to connect them, see Doerr 2020a; Doerr, Puentes, and Kamiyoshi 2020), is the cases of immigrants' successful cultural adaptation to the new society due to their ties to their own compatriot community (Portes and Rambaut 2001). In terms of language acquisition, researchers argue that immersion is not necessarily the most effective way to learn a language for college-age students (Doerr and Lee 2013); their racial appearance may affect interlocutors' approaches to them (Zheng and Samuel 2017); or they may learn better from instructions about grammar in their first language (Medgyes 1999).

The above discussions indicate that it is more productive to acknowledge the importance of spending time with fellow compatriot students with positive effects: it allows students to learn about diversity in the US (Tracy and Maria), reduces anxiety among students in interacting with the "locals" (Maria; Richard), and helps students realize things that are considered local or not (Maria; Woolf 2010). Instead of blanketly discouraging the company of compatriot students, I suggest acknowledging these positive aspects and engaging students in discussing the possible negative outcome (e.g., lack of interaction with the "locals").

That is, my analyses above on the institutional setting overriding immersion discourse in creating a performative linguistic space that encourages English utterances can be used to revisit the immersion discourse. In practice, for example, class activities can include discussion of diversity among American students, which can then be used to understand diversity in the host society. Students can do group work to go out and engage with the people in the destination together, alleviating some anxiety of doing activities on their own. Talburt and Stewart (1999) suggested the usefulness of discussing among students' diverse study-abroad experiences of students depending on their race and gender. Following that lead, students can also analyze their study-abroad experience in terms of their subject positions and share their experience in understanding the diverse perceptions and experiences. For study abroad researchers, this discussion points to the benefit of not only acknowledging the importance of institutional setting in creating a performative linguistic space that pushes students to choose certain language(s) but also to revisit the notion of immersion in terms of what it encourages (e.g., interact with the "locals") because its effects are limited or what it discourages (e.g., interact with compatriot students) because it can create a meaningful learning experience.

In sum, because of the institutional setup, students who were willing to study abroad and take classes in the language they are comfortable with gathered and created the performative linguistic space of English in Spain. They brought with them the language politics at "home" in the US that caters to the dominant group: to use the language that you are comfortable with, instead of learning other languages to cater to others such as immigrants. Even those who spoke languages other than English, such as Maria and Richard who needed to learn English in the US, reported that they were more comfortable using English in the classroom than Spanish because their academic career in the US was done in English. Nonetheless, as will be discussed in the next section, their situation as immigrants added complexity to the above effect.

6 Mobility and intersections of language politics: Latin America, the US, and Latin American Spanish-English bilingual speech in Spain

The first type of performative linguistic space this chapter discussed emerged in Spain as a study abroad destination, which encouraged utterances in English at the intersection of seeking to attract more students to move geographically to study abroad by offering English-medium programs and the discourse of immersion that encourages utterances in Spanish, the "local" language. There, the demographic that the institutional setting drew—(often monolingual) Anglophone students—had a bigger impact than the discourse of immersion in creating a kind of performative linguistic space that predominantly encouraged English utterances as Tracy, Maria, and Richard suggested, though the notion of immersion was used for other purposes.

Spain also drew students who spoke Spanish as well, as the cases of Maria and Richard show. In these cases, the performative linguistic space that emerged was a little more complex, occurring at the intersection of students' geographic mobility that shows traces of four different kinds of language politics connected to space and carried over by students themselves. I will tease out these four spaces in this section.

6.1 Performative linguistic space of ancestral homeland: Latin America and Spanish language

The first is the space of Latin American countries, the ancestral homelands of Maria and Richard, where Spain imposed its language (except for Brazil) to its colonial subjects. Immigrating from Guatemala and Colombia, respectively, Maria and Richard embodied the legacy of Spanish colonialism in their ability to speak Spanish. Although they migrated to the US at a young age—Maria at nine and Richard at one—it was their family background and upbringing that perpetuated this colonial legacy, turning the space of family and at times immigrant neighborhoods into a performative linguistic space of Latin American homeland that urges utterances in Spanish.

This legacy of Spanish colonialism manifested itself in Latin American migrant communities in Spain also, like where Richard's uncle lived. Former colonial subjects tend to migrate to their former colonial mother countries because they share language and often education as well as other social systems, the latter imposing them on the former as part of colonial processes. Ironically, such immigrant communities in Spain from former colonies provided a comfort zone for students like Richard who was the first member in his family to study abroad. Here, Spanish colonial legacy in language politics provided Maria and Richard with both Spanish proficiency and a comfort zone in Spain, encouraging them to choose Spain as their study abroad destination. Maria and Richard thus embodied and brought with them colonial language politics to Spain.

6.2 Performative linguistic space of a new homeland: Spanish language and immigrant space of the US

The second space is the US as their new home as immigrants, the trace of this US immigrant language politics Maria and Richard also embodied. In the US, Spanish utterances by immigrants are often silenced in mainstream settings, especially in schools. In part, the linguistic ideology of monolingualism as the "natural state," even though multilingualism is the norm in most parts of the world, shaped the understanding that Spanish-speaking migrants' use of Spanish is an obstacle to learning English, despite the reported benefits of using the learner's first language in learning their second language. Therefore, many schools adopted the practice of discouraging migrant students from using their first language up until recently (Baker 2009; Cummins 2001).

In part, the racist sentiments also discourage non-white minority immigrant students' speech in their first language. In a school setting, while white students' experience in Europe is often considered enrichment and something to be shared in class, non-white migrant students' experience of visiting their homeland (often non-European countries) is ignored and not considered enrichment (Moll et al. 2005). Reflecting this racist double standard, "bilingualism" of non-white migrant students is often not appreciated, if not silenced.

This double standard is also reflected in the notion of "global competence." White monolingual students learning to speak Spanish along with gaining other cultural knowledge through studying abroad is often praised as gaining "global competence," whereas minority immigrant students with similar knowledge and skills gained through their upbringing as immigrants are rarely celebrated in the college context (see Doerr 2018; 2020a; Doerr, Puentes, and Kamiyoshi 2020). That is, it is the context, the space (i.e., study-abroad), not the skills themselves, that makes certain proficiency into "global competence": when Spanish is useful in the study-abroad context in Spain, it becomes global competence whereas, in the mainstream US space, it can be considered an obstacle, if not a sign of a lack of patriotism to the US. Global competence is then situational and spatial, and thus necessarily *acknowledged* knowledge, attitudes, and skills (Doerr 2018).

In other words, the US mainstream institutional setting was a performative linguistic space that hindered their Spanish speech, whereas their family and community space—a transplanted Latin American performative linguistic space with Spanish colonial legacy—was a performative linguistic space that encouraged it. Therefore, in the US, the legacy of both US assimilationist policies and aforementioned Spanish colonialism shaped their daily linguistic acts, creating a layered linguistic performative space for Maria and Richard that differed from other study-abroad students. They then brought this language politics to Spain when they studied abroad there.

6.3 Performative linguistic space of study abroad: Bilingualism as an asset

The third space for them is that of study abroad space where the speech in the local language is encouraged, although students did not adhere to it, as mentioned. These language politics are shaped by both the institutional setting that encourages English utterance and the discourse of immersion that encouraged utterance of Spanish, the local language, as discussed earlier. Both Maria and Richard told me about helping other American students by translating Spanish for them. Maria reported, as the only one who "could get us out of any situation," she went to the hospital seven times during her one-month stay there: "Every time somebody gets sick, I had to be there translating." Richard reported helping others, along with five other Spanish-English bilingual students.

Helping other students with the language gave Maria and Richard a special place among other American students. Maria reported how her bilingual ability gave her a niche among fellow American students who always needed her, pushing her to be more outgoing than she usually is, which she enjoyed very much. Richard positioned himself as one of several students who could help other students by translating. In both 2011 and 2013, there were a handful of students with Latin American backgrounds among the students studying abroad from the US. This suggests that this may be a common occurrence in study abroad destinations, at least in Spain.

Here, the space of Spain as a study-abroad destination turned Maria's and Richard's Spanish proficiency into an asset that, with their inclination to help others, pushed them to speak Spanish. That is, the space of Spain as a study abroad destination became a performative linguistic space for them. The knowledge of the Spanish language itself does not automatically make it an asset as seen in the second space of the US mentioned above; rather, it becomes an asset in Spain when its speech is valued.

Moreover, Spain as experienced by Maria and Richard became a performative linguistic space that encouraged bilingual utterance in Spanish and English, as it encouraged them to be active translators for their fellow American students. It is a result of the intersection of two spaces: the US space of immigrants Maria and Richard brought with them where Spanish proficiency was not celebrated and hence they needed to be proficient in English, and the space of Spain as the study abroad destination where the local language is valued via the notion of immersion. It is this intersection that created a new niche as translators for Maria and Richard within the American study-abroad student group. Turning the liability of Spanish into an asset, the space of study abroad in Spain as a performative linguistic space ushered Spanish speech, accompanied by English speech.

To be more precise, it was not just the knowledge of Spanish but the knowledge of both Spanish and English—their bilingualism—that made them an asset to the group of American study-abroad students staying in Spain: as translators. That is, it was not just the space and what language is used there but also for whom—English-speaking American study-abroad students—their bilingual knowledge was used that made their linguistic skill an asset. It is worth noting here that children of immigrant parents tend to act as translators—often called "language brokers"—for their parents who may be less proficient in English than the children who grew up in the US. This language-broker role often becomes an important part of who they are (Weisskirch 2017). Richard (though not Maria) had reported this experience growing up in the US. So, translating for others may have come easy to Richard, if not Maria, who is used to that role growing up, transferring language politics in the US specific to his own subject position to his new position in Spain while studying abroad, illustrating trajectories of various performative linguistic spaces intersecting to further create a different performative linguistic space.

In contrast, two Anglo-American students with proficiency in the language of their destinations (Tracy in Bilbao and another student in Paris) gained through schooling did not report helping others in this way. This contrast may be due to the level of proficiency in the language, or the confidence, or the effect of "native speaker myth" that rendered "native speakers" as more proficient in that language. But this also points to an effect of the aforementioned intersections of the language politics—i.e., their proficiency that had been neglected had become valued—that encouraged Maria and Richard to be more proactive in becoming translators for their fellow student in a way Tracy did not. This is a result of intersections of performative linguistic spaces.

6.4 Performative linguistic space of former colonial mother country: Spain as colonial space

The fourth space with its specific language politics that contributed to turning Spain into a performative linguistic space for Maria and Richard is that of Spanish as the former colonial mother country. As such, it hindered the Spanish speech of students who spoke Latin American varieties. It came with the general prejudice against Latin American individuals, which was then recognized by their Spanish utterances. Spaniards asked Maria and Richard where they are from because of their Spanish fluency, recognizing them as not being Anglophone American. Maria reported that she started to hide her Latin American background in that context, preferring to identify herself as just "American":

> I say I'm American. I don't say I'm from Guatemala . . . People [Spaniards] . . . are very not nice when you say you are from Latin America. Their tone changes a little bit . . . So . . . [now] I just say I'm American. And they say 'Wow your accent's great' . . . I don't ever say I'm from Guatemala.

Here, her argument points to the subtlety of language politics ignored in the immersion discourse that merely encourages students to "speak the local language":

language is diverse and linguistic variations are often marked and positioned hierarchically, which can involve various types of power play when speaking.

Richard reported his experiences with Spaniards: "They think [of] Latin America as below [them] . . . Like we don't even speak Spanish to them . . . that's what somebody said to me." He also recounted an incident in which a Spanish driver hit his uncle's car. She was at fault, but the police blamed his uncle, blatantly exhibiting their bias. As she drove off, the woman hit his uncle's car again, right in front of the police officer—who ignored it.

In this general atmosphere of prejudice against Latin Americans, Maria and Richard preferred not to speak Spanish with Spaniards: their Spanish utterance was discouraged. Maria explained their negative attitude as stemming from the colonial legacy: "Spain was the home, the old [mother] country." This differs from the negative treatment of heritage language speakers who lack linguistic proficiency (Moreno 2009) or academic literacy (Riegelhaupt and Carrasco 2000), which can be connected rather to the proficiency rather than the hierarchy among linguistic varieties.

Maria and Richard, however, turned their experience of this prejudice into a learning opportunity of grasping the subtle social features of Spain that other American students had little access to. I have argued elsewhere (2018; 2020a) that this allows minority immigrant students studying abroad, especially as heritage study abroad, to have an additional viewpoint to understand the complexity of social relationships shaped by their history. Yet, this colonial legacy manifested in daily acts of prejudice did discourage them from speaking Spanish—Spain as a performative linguistic space of colonialism—hindering their Spanish speech, unless necessary such as when translating for Anglophone students.

7 The discourse of immersion, institutional setups, and intersections of four language politics

The narratives of their experience given by Tracy, Maria, and Richard above illustrate Spain as performative linguistic spaces which emerged contextually as a study abroad destination that welcomed Anglophone and Spanish-English bilingual students. As such, Spain encouraged but also hindered various speech. In this section, I recapture the argument I made to clarify the processes by which performative linguistic spaces emerged in Spain due to students' geographic mobility.

The discourse of immersion is influential in shaping study-abroad programs, promoting homestays which encouraged students to use the local language of the destination. However, institutional setups are shaped by other forces, such as a need to attract more students, resulting in an increased number of English-medium classes. The result is that study-abroad students do not need to know the local language of the study-abroad destination. This institutional setting created a performative linguistic space that ushered English utterances, counter-practices of what immersion discourse encourages as students spent much time with other American students, speaking English most of the time. The discourse of immersion itself was merely used in their narratives to appreciate their experience, justify their decisions, and make a commentary on their activities and on people with whom they interacted.

For students with a Latin American background such as Maria and Richard, Spain emerged as performative linguistic spaces in a complex way, specifically through their Spanish-English bilingualism that reflected their geographic mobility between their ancestral homeland, the US as their new home as immigrants, and Spain as a study abroad destination as well as former colonial mother country. Their Spanish proficiency (i.e., a trace of language politics in their ancestral homeland as a former Spanish colony) that has been treated as liability in mainstream school space though nurtured in the family/immigrant neighborhood spaces in the US became an asset in Spain not only through the discourse of immersion but also through the presence of mainly Anglophone students. This contrast of language politics in the US and Spain—a reversal of US language hierarchy between English over Spanish that silenced Spanish speech into one that values Spanish proficiency as an asset—encouraged Spanish utterances, giving Maria and Richard a special niche as translators. Nonetheless, Spain also hindered this enthusiasm in Spanish speech by treating Latin American varieties of Spanish negatively. This is also an effect of student's geographic mobility that changed the same Spanish utterance from being "correct" (in their Latin American homeland) into being "with an accent" (in Spain).

In short, Maria and Richard's Spanish proficiency turned from imposed colonial language (in Guatemala and Colombia where they were expected to speak Spanish), to an obstacle in learning English (in the US where they were discouraged from speaking Spanish), to a useful skill to help non-Spanish speakers (in Spain as study abroad destination where they were encouraged to speak Spanish) but also a less "desirable" form of speech due to a colonial "accent" (in Spain as former mother country that discouraged their Spanish speech).

The traces of language politics in various spaces study abroad students embodied turned Spain—as they experienced as the space of study abroad destination—into performative linguistic spaces, ushering and discouraging Spanish and English speeches in complex ways. Specific space does not emerge as a performative linguistic space on its own connected to certain linguistic communities. Rather, the space becomes performative as a result of interactions among individuals who move between various spaces, bringing with them language politics (itself portable with the individuals involved) of the various spaces they have dwelled and traversed. These individuals' interactions activate diverse ideologies that shape their multiple subject positions and their link to specific space politics. That is why we need to see the contextual nature of the performative linguistic space and how those involved in their speech practices perceive their linguistic actions.

8 Conclusion

We are urged to choose a language to speak about certain things in a certain space. Study abroad offers a specific kind of space to which students with differing backgrounds react variously at the intersection of dominant discourses that guide them and the institutional setups that affect demography. This chapter examined the students' narratives about their experience and traced ways in which the students' geographic mobility ushered performative linguistic spaces to emerge in Spain as both a study-abroad destination and as a former colonial mother country. This intersection shaped the space and the speech that occurred there.

Studying abroad is a spatial practice, which turned out to be shaped by various concerns other than merely going "abroad." Students themselves bring traces of other language politics from other spaces, which intersected with that of study abroad—the need to increase participants by offering English spaces and the discourse of immersion that encourages utterance of local language. Study abroad space is not a separate "abroad" space students jump into but space co-constructed by those present—those who had lived, dwell, and pass through there. Study abroad destination is a temporal and contextual performative linguistic space activated by geographically mobile individuals, including study abroad students who interact with diverse others including those in the study abroad destination as well as fellow compatriot students in various combinations.

References

Alred, Geof. & Michael Byram. 2006. British students in France: 10 years on. In Michael Byram & Anwei Feng (eds.), *Living and studying abroad: Research and practice*, 210–231. Clevedon: Multilingual Matters.
Amit, Vered. 2010. Student mobility and internationalisation. *Anthropology in Action* 17 (1). 6–18.

Appadurai, Arjun. 1988. Putting hierarchy in its place. *Cultural Anthropology* 3 (1). 36–49.

Baker, Victoria. 2009. Being "multilingual" in a South African township: Functioning well with a patchwork of standardized and hybrid languages. In Neriko Musha Doerr (ed.), *The native speaker concept*, 139–160. Berlin: Mouton de Gruyter.

Bakhtin, Mikhail. 1981. *The Dialogic imagination: Four essays*. Austin: University of Texas Press.

Barnick, Heather. 2010. Managing time and making space: Canadian students' motivations for study in Australia. *Anthropology in Action* 17 (1). 19–29.

Beelen, Jos. & Elspeth Jones. 2015. Redefining internatinalization at home. In Adrian Curaj, Liviu Matei, Remus Pricopie, Jamil Salmi & Peter Scott (eds.), *The European higher education area: Between critical reflections and future policies*, 59–72. London: Springer.

Bennett, Neville. 1998. *Asian students in New Zealand*. Wellington: Institute of Policy Studies.

Bourdieu, Pierre. 1991/1982. *Language and symbolic power*. Cambridge: Harvard University Press.

Bringle, Robert G., Julie A. Hatcher & Steven G. Jones (eds.). 2011. *International service learning: Conceptual frameworks and research*. Sterling: Stylus Publishing.

Brockington, Joseph L. & Margaret D. Wiedenhoeft. 2009. The liberal arts and global citizenship: Fostering intercultural engagement through integrative experiences and structured reflection. In Ross Lewin (ed.), *The handbook of practice and research in study abroad: Higher education and the quest for global citizenship*, 117–132. New York: Routledge.

Brustein, William. 2009. It takes an entire institution: A blueprint for the global university. In Ross Lewin (ed.), *The handbook of practice and research in study abroad: Higher education and the quest for global citizenship*, 249–265. New York: Routledge.

Carlson, Jerry S., Barbara B. Burn, John Useem & David Yachimowicz. 1990. *Study abroad: The experience of American undergraduates*. New York: Greenwood Press.

Che, S. Megan, Mindy Spearman & Agida Manizade. 2009. Constructive disequilibrium: cognitive and emotional development through dissonant experiences in less familiar destinations. In Ross Lewin (ed.), *The handbook of practice and research in study abroad: Higher education and the quest for global citizenship*, 99–116. New York: Routledge.

Chen, Leeann. 2002. Writing to host nationals as cross-cultural collaborative learning in study abroad. *Frontiers: The Interdisciplinary Journal of Study Abroad* 8. 143–164.

Chieffo, Lisa & Lesa Griffiths. 2004. Large-scale assessment of student attitudes after a short-term study abroad program. *Frontiers: The Interdisciplinary Journal of Study Abroad* 10. 165–177.

Chieffo, Lisa & Lesa Griffiths. 2009. Here to stay: Increasing acceptance of short-term study abroad programs. In Ross Lewin (ed.), *The handbook of practice and research in study abroad: Higher education and the quest for global citizenship*, 365–380. New York, NY: Routledge.

Clifford, James. 1988. *The predicament of culture: Twentieth-century ethnography, literature,and art*. Cambridge: Harvard University Press.

Clifford, James. 1997. *Routes: Travel and translation in the late twentieth century*. Cambridge: Harvard University Press.

Collier, Sabrina. 2021. Where can you study abroad in English? https://www.topuniversities.com/student-info/studying-abroad/where-can-you-study-abroad-english (accessed May 15, 2021)

Collins, Francis Leo. 2010. International students as urban agents: International education and urban transformation in Auckland, New Zealand. *Geoforum* 41. 940–950. doi:10.1016/j.geoforum.2010.06.009

Collins, Francis Leo. 2012. Researching mobility and emplacement: Examining transience and transnationality in international student lives. *Area* 44(3). 296–304. doi:10.1111/j.1475-4762.2012.01112.x

Cresswell, Tim. 2006. *On the move: Mobility in the modern Western world*. New York: Routledge.

Cresswell, Tim & Peter Merriman. 2011. Introduction: Geographies of mobilities – Practices, spaces, subjects. In Tim Cresswell & Peter Merriman (eds.), *Geographies of mobilities: Practices, spaces, subjects*, 1–32. Farnham, UK: Ashgate.

Cummins, James. 2001. *Negotiating identities*. Los Angeles: California Association for Bilingual Education.

Currier, Connie, James Lucas & Denise Saint Arnault. 2009. Study abroad and nursing: From cultural to global competence. In Ross Lewin (ed.), *The handbook of practice and research in study abroad: Higher education and the quest for global citizenship*, 133–150. New York: Routledge.

Cushner, Kenneth. 2009. The role of study abroad in preparing globally responsible teachers. In Ross Lewin (ed.), *The handbook of practice and research in study abroad: Higher education and the quest for global citizenship*, 151–169. New York: Routledge.

de Certeau, Michel. 1984. *The practice of everyday life*. Berkeley: University of California Press.

Deardorff, Darla. 2009. Understanding the challenges of assessing global citizenship. In Ross Lewin (ed.), *The handbook of practice and research in study abroad: Higher education and the quest for global citizenship*, 346–364. New York: Routledge.

Doerr, Neriko Musha. 2012. Study abroad as "adventure": Construction of imaginings of social space and subjectivities. *Critical Discourse Studies* 9 (3). 257–268.

Doerr, Neriko Musha. 2013. Do "global citizens" need the parochial cultural other?: Discourses of study abroad and learning by doing. *Compare* 43 (2). 224–243.

Doerr, Neriko Musha. 2015. Learner subjects in study abroad: Discourse of immersion, hierarchy of experience, and their subversion through situated learning. *Discourse: Studies in the Cultural Politics of Education* 36 (3). 369–382.

Doerr, Neriko Musha. 2016. Chronotopes of study abroad: The cultural other, immersion, and compartmentalized space-time. *Journal of Cultural Geography* 33 (1). 80–99.

Doerr, Neriko Musha. 2017. Learning as othering: Narratives of learning, construction of difference, and the discourse of immersion in study abroad. *Intercultural Education* 28 (1). 90–103.

Doerr, Neriko Musha. 2018. *Transforming study abroad: A handbook*. London: Berghahn Books.

Doerr, Neriko Musha. 2020a. "Global competence" of minority immigrant students: Hierarchy of experience and ideology of global competence in study abroad. *Discourse: Studies in the Cultural Politics of Education* 41(1). 83–97.

Doerr, Neriko Musha. 2020b. Introduction: Borders, Japan, and global education effect. In Neriko Musha Doerr (ed.), The Global Education Effect and Japan: Constructing New Borders and Identification Practices, 3–32. New York: Routledge.

Doerr, Neriko Musha. 2020c. Safe-guarding, social-pricing, and labeling: Technologies of border construction and discourses of border crossing in study abroad/away. In John Bodinger de Uriarte and Michael DiGiovine (eds.), *Study abroad and the quest for an anti-tourism experience*, 89–118. Lenham, MD: Lexington Books.

Doerr, Neriko Musha. 2022a. *Fairies, ghosts, and Santa Claus: Tinted glasses, fetishes, and the politics of seeing*. New York: Berghahn Books.

Doerr, Neriko Musha. 2022b. Modes of study abroad learning: Toward short-term study abroad program designs beyond the study abroad effect. *Frontiers: The Interdisciplinary Journal of Study Abroad*.

Doerr, Neriko Musha. 2022c. Structural competence beyond global competence: Overcoming the culturalist difference framework in study abroad. *Compare: A Journal of Comparative and International Education*.

Doerr, Neriko Musha & Kiri Lee. 2013. *Constructing the heritage language learner: Knowledge, power, and new subjectivities*. Berlin: Mouton de Gruyter.

Doerr, Neriko Musha & Richard Jose Suarez. 2013a. *Anthropological co-investigation as enhancing "learning the unintended": Subversion of "legitimate knowledge" in alternative break experiential learning.* Seminar on the future of anthropology in Schools of Education. Teachers College, Columbia University, New York City, October 18–19.

Doerr, Neriko Musha & Richard Jose Suarez. 2013b. *The allegory of cold showers and the politics of empathy: Production of diverse humanitarian subjects.* American Ethnological Society, Chicago, April 11–13.

Doerr, Neriko Musha & Richard Jose Suarez. 2014. *Allegedly vs unwittingly coming out: Class, subject positions, and the politics of tuning in to difference.* American Anthropological Association, Washington DC, December 3–7.

Doerr, Neriko Musha & Richard Jose Suarez. 2018. Immersion, immigration, immutability: Regimes of learning and politics of labeling in study abroad. *Educational Studies* 54 (2). 183–197.

Fincher, Ruth & Kate Shaw. 2009. The unintended segregation of transnational students in central Melbourne. *Environment and Planning A: Economy and Space* 41. 1884–1902. doi:10.1068/a41126

Foucault, Michel. 1983. Afterword: The subject and power. In Hubert L. Dreyful and Paul Rabinow (eds.), *Michel Foucault: Beyond structuralism and hermeneutics*, 208–226. Chicago: University of Chicago Press.

Freire, Paulo. 1970. *Pedagogy of the oppressed.* New York: Continuum.

Gillespie, Joan, Laarry Braskamp & Mary Dwyer. 2009. Holistic student learning and development abroad: The IES 3-D program model. In Ross Lewin (ed.), *The handbook of practice and research in study abroad: Higher education and the quest for global citizenship*, 445–465. New York: Routledge.

Glass, Michael R., 2014. Encouraging reflexivity in urban geography fieldwork: Study abroad experiences in Singapore and Malaysia. *Journal of Geography in Higher Education* 38 (1). 69–85. doi:10.1080/03098265.2013.836625

Houser, Chris, Christian Brannstrom, Steven M. Quiring & Kelly Lemmons. 2011. Study abroad field trip improves test performance through engagement and new social networks. *Journal of Geography in Higher Education* 35 (4). 513–528. doi:10.1080/03098265.2010.551655

Hovey, Rebecca & Adam Weinberg. 2009. Global learning and the making of citizen diplomats. In Ross Lewin (ed.), *The handbook of practice and research in study abroad: Higher education and the quest for global citizenship*, 33–48. New York: Routledge.

Hunter, Bill, George P. White & Galen C. Godbey. 2006. What does it mean to be globally competent? *Journal of Studies in International Education* 10 (3). 267–285.

Jackson, Jane. 2005. Assessing intercultural learning through introspective accounts. *Frontiers: The Interdisciplinary Journal of Study Abroad* 11. 165–186. http://www.frontiersjournal.com/Frontiersbackissaug05.htm (accessed 16 June 2014)

Laubscher, Michael R. 1994. *Encounters with difference: Student perceptions of the role of out-of-class experiences in education abroad.* Westport: Greenwood Press.

Lemmons, Kelly K, Christian Brannstrom & Danielle Hurd. 2014. Exposing students to repeat photography: Increasing cultural understanding on a short-term study abroad. *Journal of Geography in Higher Education* 38 (1). 86–105. doi:10.1080/03098265.2013.836745

Lewin, Ross & Greg Van Kirk. 2009. It's not about you: The UConn social entrepreneur corps global commonwealth study abroad model. In Ross Lewin (ed.), *The handbook of practice and research in study abroad: Higher education and the quest for global citizenship*, 543–564. New York: Routledge.

Loflin, Stephen E. 2007. *Adventures abroad: The student's guide to studying overseas.* New York: Kaplan Publishing.

Marcus, George. E. 1995. Ethnography in/of the world system: The emergence of multi-sited ethnography. *Annual Review of Anthropology* 24. 95–117.

Medgyes, Péter. 1999. Language training: A neglected area in teacher education. In George Braine (ed.), *Non-native educators in English language teaching*, 177–195. Mahwah: Lawrence Erlbaum.

Moline, Norm. 2009. International studies become pilgrimages: Geography in a multidiscipline overseas program. *Journal of Geography* 108. 94–104. doi:10.1080/00221340903102971

Moll, Luis, Cathy Amanti, Debrah Neff & Norma Gonzalez. 2005. Funds of knowledge for teaching: Using a qualitative approach to connect homes and classrooms. In Norma Gonzalez, Luis C. Moll & Cathy Amanti (eds.) *Funds of knowledge: Theorizing practices in households, communities, and classrooms*, 71–87. New York: Routledge.

Molz, Jennie Germann. 2017. Giving back, doing good, feeling global: The affective flows of family voluntourism. *Journal of Contemporary Ethnography* 46 (3). 334–360.

Moreno, Kristin Heather. 2009. *The study abroad experiences of heritage language learners*. PhD diss., University of Texas, Austin.

Murphy-Lejeune, Elizabeth. 2002. *Student mobility and narrative in Europe: The new strangers*. London: Routledge.

Ogden, Anthony C. 2006. Ethnographic inquiry: Reframing the learning core of education abroad. *Frontiers: The Interdisciplinary Journal of Study Abroad* 8. 87–112.

Open Doors. 2010. *Opendoors 2010 fast facts*. https://opendoorsdata.org/wp-content/uploads/2020/11/Open-Doors-Fast-Facts-2010-2019.pdf (accessed May 16, 2021)

Open Doors. 2020. *Fast facts 2020*. https://opendoorsdata.org/fast_facts/fast-facts-2020/ (accessed May 16, 2021)

Peterson, Chip. 2002. Preparing Engaged citizens: Three models of experiential education for social justice. *Frontiers: The Interdisciplinary Journal of Study Abroad* 8. 41–82.

Plater, William M., Steven G. Jones, Robert G. Bringle & Patti H. Clayton. 2009. Educating globally competent citizens through international service learning. In Ross Lewin (ed.), *The handbook of practice and research in study abroad: Higher education and the quest for global citizenship*, 485–505. New York: Routledge.

Plummer, Ken. 1995. *Telling sexual stories: Power, change and social worlds*. London: Routledge.

Porfilio, Brad J. & Heather Hickman. eds., 2011. *Critical service-learning as revolutionary pedagogy: A project of student agency in action*. Charlotte: Information Age.

Portes, Alejandro & Ruben G. Rumbaut. 2001. *Legacies: The story of the immigrant second generation*. Berkeley: University of California Press.

Riegelhaupt, Florencia. & Roberto Luis Carrasco. 2000. Mexico host family reactions to a bilingual Chicana teacher in Mexico: A case study of language and culture clash. *Bilingual Research Journal* 24 (4). 405–421.

Rink, Bradley. 2017. Sojourn to the dark continent: Landscape and affect in an African mobility experience. In Neriko Musha Doerr & Hannah Davis Taïeb (eds.), *The romance of crossing borders: Studying and volunteering abroad*, 93–113. London: Berghahn Books.

Roberts, Celia. 1994. Cultural studies and student exchange: Living the ethnographic life. In Michael Byram (ed.), *Culture and language learning in higher education*, 11–17. Clevedon, UK: Multilingual Matters.

Roberts, Celia, Michael Byram, Ano Barro, Shirley Jordan & Brian Street. 2001. *Language learners as ethnographers*. Clevedon: Multilingual Matters.

Salisbury, Mark H., Michael B. Paulsen & Ernest T. Pascarella. 2011. Why do all the study abroad students look alike? *Research in Higher Education* 52 (2). 123–150.

Schroeder, Kathleen, Cynthia Wood, Shari Galiardi & Jenny Koehn. 2009. First, do no harm: Ideas for mitigating negative community impacts of short-term study abroad. *Journal of Geography* 108. 141–147.

Streitwieser, Bernhard T. 2009. Undergraduate research during study abroad: Scope, meaning, and potential. In Ross Lewin (ed.), *The handbook of practice and research in study abroad: Higher education and the quest for global citizenship*, 399–419. New York: Routledge.

Sweeney, K. 2013. Inclusive excellence and underrepresentation of students of color in study abroad. *Frontiers* 23. 1–21.

Talburt, Susan & Melissa A. Stewart. 1999. What's the subject of study abroad? Race, gender and living culture. *Modern Language Journal* 82 (2). 163–175.

Weisskirch, Robert S.A. 2017. Developmental perspective on language brokering. In Robert S. Weisskirch (ed.), *Language brokering in immigrant families: Theories and contexts*, 7–25. New York: Routledge.

Woolf, Michael. 2010. Another mishegas: Global citizenship. *Frontiers: The Interdisciplinary Journal of Study Abroad* 19. 47–60.

Zemach-Bersin, Talya. 2009. Selling the world: Study abroad marketing and the privatization of global citizenship. In Ross Lewin (ed.), *The handbook of practice and research in study abroad: Higher education and the quest for global citizenship*, 303–320. New York: Routledge.

Zheng, Yi & Samuel, Arthur. G. 2017. Does seeing an Asian face make speech sound more accented? *Attention, Perception, and Psychophysics* 79. 1841–1859.

Ngọc Anh Đỗ, Gregory S. Poole

Languaging at an English-taught undergraduate program in Japan: Reconceptualizing spatial codes

1 Introduction

Brian Street (1993: 23) famously proposed that anthropologists and linguists re-think the culture concept as a verb, "to signal . . . the importance of treating the term 'culture' as a signifying process—the active construction of meaning rather than the somewhat static and reified or nominalising senses in which culture used to be employed in the discipline of anthropology, is sometimes still used in some linguistic circles, and has come to be used in everyday 'commonsense' lan-guage."[1] More recently, Cresswell and Merriman (2011: 7) similarly proposed the virtue of reconceptualizing space as "spacing," arguing that it is more useful to think not in terms of contained spaces, but rather ". . . the ongoing processes . . . through which the world is shaped and formed. Space, place and landscape are best approached as 'verbs' rather than as 'nouns'." Conceptualizing both culture and space in such a processual sense, as verbs, is a perspective that we adopt in this chapter as we investigate what Doerr and McGuire (this volume) have labeled "performative linguistic space." Through a consideration of how the spatial lan-guage codes employed by a small college community within a Japanese university trace the language ideology behind the observed linguistic practices, we contrib-ute another ethnographic example to the theme of this volume—how the pro-cesses of "spacing" and "languaging" perform power.

---

1 Street does not necessarily propose that we use "culturing" as an extrapolation or solution but rather argues along the lines of the following: ". . . the problem is that we tend then to believe the categories and definitions we construct in an essentialist way, as though we had thereby found out what culture is. In fact, 'there is not much point in trying to say what culture is . . . What can be done, however, is to say what culture does'. For what culture does is precisely the work of 'defining words, ideas, things and groups . . . We all live our lives in terms of definitions, names and categories that culture creates'. The job of studying culture is not of finding and then accepting its definitions but of 'discovering how and what definitions are made, under what cir-cumstances and for what reasons'. These definitions are used, change and sometimes fall into disuse'. Indeed, the very term 'culture' itself, like these other ideas and definitions, changes its meanings and serves different, often competing purposes at different times. Culture is an active process of meaning making and contest over definition, including its own definition. This, then, is what I mean by arguing that culture is a verb" (Street 1993: 25).

https://doi.org/10.1515/9783110744781-003

The ethnographic and autoethnographic data from our fieldsite, the College of Interdisciplinary Studies (pseudonym),[2] an English-taught program (ETP) at a comprehensive Japanese university, shows us that two competing language ideologies are constructed through the performance of linguistic space—the "languaging" practices of the actors. The students and faculty at the College of Interdisciplinary Studies (CIS), while explicitly endorsing a hegemony of monolingualism, simultaneously challenge this language ideology through engaging in linguistic practices we describe as "translanguaging" (Vogel and Garcia 2017). This is revealed by the actors as they perform "spacing." In the "practiced places" (de Certeau 1984: 117)—the social space constructed and negotiated by students and faculty—the "verbal repertoires" (Gumperz 1964: 137), or idiolects, of these informants show how a mental space of language ideologies are employed within and across the physical space of the classrooms, hallways, and lounges in a way that blurs the levels between this 'spatial triad' (Lefebvre 1991) of the physical, mental, and social (Soja 1989)."

In this chapter, first, we aim to lay out the theoretical positions that underpin our argument, namely the social process of performing space, or "spacing," the construction and maintenance of spatial codes, and the language ideology that is sometimes referred to as "translingualism" or "translanguaging." After an overview of our research methods and fieldsite, we then detail how the salient data points support a reconceptualization of space and language as verbs—"spacing" and "languaging" processes with which the authors in this volume are mostly concerned.

2 Space, "spacing," and "trans-spacing"

The importance of understanding space vis-à-vis social worlds, and in particular in relation to the social construction of language, has been recognized by scholars across the social science and humanities disciplines, including the field of linguistic anthropology (e.g., Low 2017; Agha 2006). Numerous studies have explored the relationship between various concepts of space and aspects of language (Auer et al. 2014), including language varieties in relation to geography (Johnstone 2013; Auer and Schmidt 2010), space and language education (Hadi-Tabassum 2006), and space and spatial representations (van der Zee and Slack 2003; Evans and Chilton 2010). Other work focuses, as we intend to do in this chapter, on spatiality and its relation to language ideology, language practice, and language use (Hadi-Tabassum 2006). Before exploring the relationship between space and language

2 In this study all individuals have also been assigned a pseudonym.

practice, it is important to ask how scholars have conceptualized space as it relates more generally to social interactions. In particular, three approaches guide our study—Soja's concept of physical, mental, and social spaces (1989), de Certeau's "practiced place" (1984), and Lefebvre's "spatial triad" (1991).

Soja (1989: 120) mentions three spaces, the physical, the mental, and the social space, and how these three spaces "interrelate and overlap." The physical space can be understood as places, as in the distinction between "place" and "space" proposed by de Certeau (1984). Place, or the physical space, is stable (de Certeau 1984: 118), usually seen as a "'container' of human life" (Soja 1989: 79). In this chapter, we reference the physical space or "place" as the CIS campus, the classrooms, the offices, and so on in their material form. The mental space in Soja's (1989) argument is associated with human cognition and perception, which corresponds to the language ideology(ies) discussed throughout this chapter. Finally, the social space can be interpreted through de Certeau's (1984: 117) notion of "practiced place" which is produced by social practices, translated into language practices in the context of this chapter.

Space, then, is less about either the physical, the mental, or the social specifically, but rather it is the interweaving of these three spaces, with an emphasis on the construction and negotiation between them by the inhabitants, which we refer to as "trans-spacing." As Lefebvre (1991: 26) has argued, "(social) space is a (social) product."[3] While the physical space of the campus can be used as a way to pinpoint the place of negotiation referred to in this chapter, these places do not restrict but rather enable the construction of the social space. The social space, then, is constantly negotiated, shifting in meaning, and constructed from the interactions of the multiple mobile elements occupying the space—the students, the faculty, and their shaped, fluid, and contested ideologies and perceptions (De Certeau 1984: 117).

Connected to Soja's (1989) three spaces mentioned above is Lefebvre's (1991: 40) proposal of a "spatial triad" (Figure 1), consisting of "spatial practice," "representations of space," and "representational space" which together correspond to perceived, conceived, and lived space, respectively. The first element, the dimension of "spatial practice," or perceived space, is constituted by the outside world and daily life, including mundane observable things and practices. This dimension of space is synonymous with Soja's physical space. The second element, "representations of space," also referred to as "conceptualized space" by Lefebvre (1991: 38), is where knowledge and ideology are applied to conceive and organize a space, corresponding

---

3 The debates around gender-inclusive public restrooms or the construction of "natural" spaces like wildlife refuges might be considered as examples of how space is a product of the mental, physical, and the social (Jakubiak, personal communication).

to Soja's mental space. The third element of the spatial triad, "representational space," is defined as the space of the lived experience of the "inhabitants" or "users" (Lefebvre 1991: 39) who also attempt to negotiate and transform the space, leading to its less coherent characteristic than physical and mental forms. This "lived" space can then be understood to correspond with Soja's social space. In our analysis of the data presented in this chapter, we apply Lefebvre's spatial triad, in combination with Soja's notions of the three spaces, with certain modifications.[4]

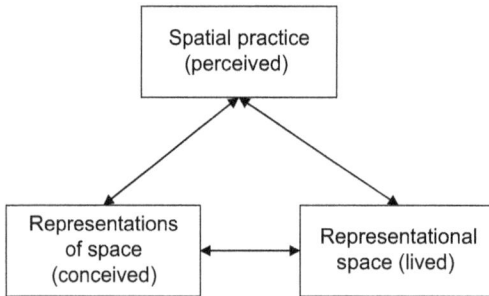

Figure 1: The relationship between the three spaces.

Spatial practice, or the physical space, in the context of this chapter refers to "place" in its material and allegedly stable sense. Since the focus of our research, CIS, is a college within a larger Japanese university, the physical/perceived space here includes the university and the faculty that deliver the college curriculum. Representations of space, the conceived or mental space, is manifested by the language ideologies that simultaneously serve as the spatial codes regulating, managing, and organizing the space of CIS. In order to navigate and operate within the CIS, the inhabitants or the users of the space are required to "read" or "decode" it. Lefebvre's (1991: 16) "spatial code" allows the inhabitants to decode or to "read" this space which, although rather fixed and generally accepted by those inhabiting the space, nonetheless, can also be negotiated and even challenged, especially in the representational space where lived experience is manifested. Torres-Olave's (2012) work on an ETP at a university in Mexico provides a fascinating example of how representational space is manifested through the negotiation of "geographies of difference" by students as they construct imaginations of "us" and "them" identities around the pronunciation of their own surname.

---

4 Namely, when discussing the spatial triad, Lefebvre (1991) refers to broader society; whereas in this chapter we wish to rescale the spatial triad to Japan's higher education generally and English-taught programs specifically.

To sum up then, *physical space* portrays the more stable characteristics of the CIS that lead to certain expectations of what language use is considered appropriate (usually monolingual English), although the fact that the college is situated within a larger Japanese university also elicits certain expectations of Japanese usage on the campus. *Mental space* is the supposedly dominant monolingual language ideology, specifically monolingual English use which is deemed the standard. However, as the actors move between spaces, what they observe in actuality (social space) can in turn change the mental space, as will be illustrated in the data analysis section. *Social space* is informed by the expectation tied to the physical space and partially shaped by the dominant monolingual ideology of mental space. However, there are diversions from the norm manifested in the form of translanguaging (intentional or not), which sparks constant negotiations between various actors occupying the space (both between students and between students and faculty members).

2.1 Spatial codes: Language ideologies

This section delves into the monolingual and translingual ideologies, the two spatial codes that fit with our ethnographic study. Translingual ideology is derived from the concept of translanguaging (discussed below) whereas the monolingual ideology is hegemonic and socio-politically constructed, and derived from monolingualism which is argued to be a modern invention in service to nationalism and the construction of nation-states (Li 2017: 19; Rothman 2008: 442). Monolingualism generates and institutionalizes the link between nation-state and language. In the context of this association, language is "named" (as in a politically and socially defined and labeled) primarily according to political boundaries or communities, and thus, the concept of named languages is also regarded as part of language policies arising with the advent of modern nation-states and nationalism (García 2017, cited in Turner and Lin 2017: 3). Naming a language implies an underlying prescriptive system, which encourages the perception of a "pure" form of language which all speakers, specifically L2 speakers, should strive towards.

Therefore, in this chapter, we consider "monolingual ideology" as the conceptualization that language is a separate entity that is bounded, with speakers expected to use only one "named language" at one time. As we discuss further below, the physical space of the larger Japanese university is primarily managed by the mental space of a Japanese monolingual ideology, whereas the English monolingual ideology is regarded as the hegemonic code and mental space of the ETP within the physical space of the campus where the program is located. On the other hand, as we will demonstrate later, a translingual ideology contests the dominant monolingual ideology and is reflected in the language practice and language use of both the students and faculty members inhabiting the space, which leads us to the third element of Lefevbre's (1991) spatial triad, representational space, or the lived/social space in Soja's (1989) typology.

In the context of this volume, we reiterate a point made in the introduction, namely that ". . . space is not performative on its own . . . it becomes performative as a result of the specific intersections of linguistic politics brought by individuals from the various spaces they have traversed . . ." (Introduction: 2). In the social space of language ideology, the individuality and diversity of actors challenges the established, dominant spatial code and allows the possibility for transformation to emerge, painting a fragmented and less coherent picture of this hegemony. The challenge against the dominant spatial code of a monolingual ideology arises through the performance of individuals' language use embedded in a translingual ideology and a myriad of corresponding translanguaging practices. Diversity is manifested in this social space since a translanguaging ideology embraces the concept of verbal (or linguistic) repertoire, or idiolect (discussed below), based on an interlocutor's individual language use. In this way, while lived/social space serves as the focus of our chapter, the interrelationship between the three dimensions of the spatial triad is also a critical point of analysis. The incorporation of these dimensions is reflected and manifested in how the hegemonic language ideology (the conceived/mental space) is used to regulate and organize the physical and social space, yet is also contested and transformed by the actual language practices of the inhabitants (the social practices that produce the social space). As Soja (1989: 120) points out: "not only are the spaces of nature and cognition incorporated into the social production of spatiality they are transformed in the process."

In this chapter, we attempt to illustrate the mobility of the actors (the students and faculty) between different spaces: between what often might have been a predominantly monolingual space of their previous linguistic environment (e.g., hometown) and the CIS, where translanguaging is encountered; between the three spaces of the physical, mental and social; and between the larger Japanese space and the English one situated within it; and then to address how the movement of such "trans-spacing" either reinforces monolingualism or provides the resources for practicing translanguaging, thus constructing a performative linguistic space for translanguaging. The movement between spaces—trans-spacing—allows the actors to reflect on their personal language ideology and language practices, which in turn helps guide their decision to either abide by the mainstream language ideology or to alternatively construct a performative linguistic space for translanguaging.

2.2 "Translanguaging"

Since social/lived space is at the heart of this analysis, the concept of translanguaging and the ideology of translingualism (being tied to the construction of social space in the context of this field site) are similarly crucial. An important element of the language practices of the actors at the physical space of our field site can be characterized as translanguaging which, as both a concept and a language ideology, is tied to the construction of social space at the CIS. A recently emerging concept, translanguaging can be linked to the proposal to shift the static and predefined characteristics associated with "language" as a noun, to an activity and continual process manifested in "languaging" as a verb (Maturana and Verela 1980, cited in Li 2017:16), much as Street (1993) proposed that "culture is a verb," as mentioned above. Recent interest in the concept has seen different aspects of translanguaging explored in numerous studies.

Some scholars emphasize that "translanguaging" is a theory that challenges the ideology of monolingualism. In both the theory and pedagogy of translanguaging, it is argued that the interlocutor's first language (L1) contributes to, rather than hinders (as purported in monolingualism), the process of learning a second language (L2) (Li 2017: 17). García and Li (2013) emphasize the "transformative" potential of translanguaging to challenge the pervasive language perspective of monolingualism. Nevertheless, there are still few studies that explicitly research specific examples of the relation between the mainstream language ideologies of monolingualism and translanguaging. Various studies consider translanguaging as a form of language use,[5] and others locate the focus on the pedagogical aspect of translanguaging by observing and analyzing language practices inside classrooms.[6]

---

5 Song (2016) refers to translanguaging in the description of language practices observed in "a bilingual home" between Korean and American English-speaking bilingual children and their parents. In another study, translanguaging is used to observe, describe and compare the language practice in two different settings, a multilingual and a monolingual classroom (Rosiers, Lancker and Delarue 2018). Translanguaging is also viewed as a potential pedagogy, consisting of such steps as providing translation of instructions in students' home language, allowing students to answer questions in whichever language they feel most at ease, or repeating phrases or words in language students are more familiar with as a means of clarification, assisting especially young children during their early phases of language development (Paulsrud, Rosén, Straszer and Wedin 2017; García and Kleyn 2016).

6 These researchers choose to approach translanguaging from an ethnographic perspective, emphasizing the practical aspect of translanguaging as a pedagogy with the potential to assist or benefit students in the process of knowledge acquirement (Paulsrud et al. 2017; García and Kleyn 2016; Rosiers et al. 2018). While the ethnographic accounts of translanguaging as a pedagogy provide valuable insights into how and why people translanguage and the values of this language practice, it is also noticeable that the fields and subjects of observation are frequently limited to

More importantly, most studies about translanguaging are about the visibility of translanguaging, not the absence of it. This tendency to focus on translanguaging itself is congruent with the perception of translanguaging as ubiquitous, even intrinsic to language use (Li 2011). However, other interpretations of translanguaging, such as strategic language use or pedagogy, seem to open the possibility that there is also a situational and observable absence of translanguaging. This absence of translanguaging is an intriguing topic of interest to us addressing why, how, and when it occurs in consideration with the sociopolitical framing and context in terms of "trans-spacing." In this way, we explore the relationship between monolingual ideology and translanguaging in the context of an ETP situated in Japan, through both autoethnographic and ethnographic approaches, expanding on Li Wei's concept of "translanguaging space" to include a Lefebvrian spatial triad that maps language ideology and practice.

In considering the mapping of this spatial triad, it is important to recognize that the various forms and aspects of translanguaging across different studies emphasize two sides to translanguaging: the projection or outward manifestation of translanguaging, for instance, a pedagogy in educational settings (Paulsrud et al. 2017) or Canagarajah's (2013) negotiation strategy, and the inward and inextricable manifestation of the interlocutors' language repertoire (García and Li 2013; Li 2011). Here we attempt to connect these two sides by exploring how the outward manifestation impacts the inward language ideology of the interlocutors and thus, reshapes their outward language practice (or what could be referred to as the movement between the physical, mental and social spaces), and what implications this shift has, in turn, on the construction and reconstruction of a performative linguistic space (see Introduction, this volume). The relationship between these two sides of translanguaging practices and the potentially transformative effect on space lies at the center of the interrelationship between the perceived/physical, the conceived/mental, and the lived/social space.

For our purposes, we consider translanguaging both as the "dynamic and functionally integrated use of different languages and language varieties" (Li 2017: 15) and as "a process of knowledge construction that goes beyond language(s)" (Otheguy, García, and Reid 2015: 283). These definitions allow for the possibility of a situational use, or absence, of translanguaging, within certain social spaces. In this

---

a specific classroom, particularly a language class, in a certain elementary school where the informants are young bilingual children at an early stage of language formation. It is equally crucial to expand the studies of translanguaging to include teenagers and especially adults whose language is at a more complete and complex stage. One of the few studies about translanguaging that selects university students as the informants for ethnographic accounts and interviews is by Li Wei (2011) in which the concept of "translanguaging space" is formed and applied.

chapter, we refer to translanguaging as an interlocutor's unified linguistic repertoire in which the linguistic components are not bound by the concepts of named languages (see Auer 2022). However, it is necessary to clarify that the interlocutors and their languaging are under the influence of, or informed by, such factors as the monolingual ideology (the mental space); thus, it is undeniable that the named languages have social reality. As will be seen later, in many instances, the interlocutors strategically emphasize and take advantage of the boundaries between named languages, and we refer to this as the interlocutors being informed by the social dynamics and ideologies in their application of linguistic repertoires.

Tightly linked to translanguaging is the important concept of verbal or "linguistic repertoire" or idiolect, defined as "a person's own unique, personal language, the person's mental grammar that emerges in interaction with other speakers and enables the person's use of language" (Otheguy, García, and Reid 2015: 289). Idiolect is constructed primarily through means of interaction, shaped and informed via one's unique "exposure and experiences of language use" (Bybee 2006, cited in Ellis 2011: 14) and directly contradicts the ideology of monolingualism and named languages. Linguistic repertoire reflects the interlocutor's actual language use and is not necessarily reflected by or congruent with the "external perspective of the society that categorizes and classifies named national languages" (Otheguy, García, and Reid 2015: 289). Interestingly, the South African linguist, Leketi Makalela (2016, 2019), has theorized "ubuntu translanguaging" ("no one language is complete without the other") as an expression of the linguistic repertoire of Bantu speakers, a notion that very much challenges the monolingual bias of European colonizers, as well as the rather static notions of idiolect that tend to ignore the dialogic importance of all utterances.

Although we do take Doerr and McGuire's point (Introduction: 18–19) that as researchers we need to be careful not to impose our own interpretations onto the interlocutors, especially when we are suggesting a way of looking at language practices, this does not necessarily extrapolate to limiting our work to the confines of an ethno-scientific or ethnomethodological approach (Garfinkel 1967). Our intention is to employ the concept of translanguaging as a way to describe and (formally) recognize the interlocutors' language (and spatial) practices as processual (and as such, unbounded), a description that is not possible within the dominant ideological sphere of monolingualism, where (uncountable) *language* use must, and can only, be described as "border crossings" between named, bounded (countable) *languages*.

In this sense, referring to an interlocutor's specific instances of language use as translanguaging is less about the actual intention of the interlocutors, and more about the recognition of the actual language practices (social space) which are not recognizable within the current paradigmatic mental space or ideological sphere of monolingualism and named languages. On the other hand, even while juxtaposing *language* use and *languages* use [sic], we are forced to capitulate to the latter, as a widely accepted worldview and embedded in an individual inter-locutor's language ideology. As researchers, we are also then bound to work within this established conceptual system, risking, of course, giving further cre-dence to and re-embedding the hegemony of monolingualism by using associated terms (such as "named languages," "L1/L2," etc.), in our discussion below. This is certainly a limitation that we recognize but have no way (yet) to effectively avoid, given the dominance of monolingual conceptions of language. Nonetheless, this limitation does necessarily limit our main aim which is to explore the relation-ship between monolingualism and translanguaging ideologies through ethno-graphic and autoethnographic approaches, as we discuss below.

3 Research methods and field site

In this chapter, we draw on data from several of our past projects (Doerr, Poole, and Hedrick 2020; Đỗ and Poole 2020; Đỗ 2018; Taguchi et al. 2017) analyzed within a framework of "spacing" and "translanguaging." These projects were all ethnographic in nature, with two of them being partly or wholly autoethno-graphic, and as such the data were collected using various qualitative methods: participant observation, interviews, textual analysis, self-observation, and reflec-tion. We hope that the combination of both insider and outsider lenses provides a fuller picture of how individual inhabitants of this specific ETP space navigate, interact and negotiate, when they conform to, take advantage of, or challenge the hegemonic spatial code.

The data were all collected during the 2017–2018 academic year, from the same field site, physical spaces, and contexts at the campus of a four-year, under-graduate ETP within a large Japanese university. We look at the data anew, ana-lyzing them from a perspective and framework that emphasizes social space using the spatial triad proposed by Lefebvre (1991). In particular, within the con-text of the fieldwork data, we examine three different types of space each of which is associated with an element of the spatial triad: spatial practice, represen-tation of space, and representational space have been examined, with the last one being the main focus. The data drawn from multiple projects, as mentioned above, will be used to depict and analyze how each Lefebvrian spatial category is constructed by the actors.

Our field site, the College of Interdisciplinary Studies was founded in 2011 and is a four-year undergraduate program at a large private university that targets both students from abroad (so-called *"ryuugakusei"*[7]) as well as local students in Japan who prefer English-medium instruction (EMI) to Japanese-medium instruction (JMI). Therefore, English as a named language is the prerequisite and required linguistic component of the applicants' linguistic repertoires as well as that of all the enrolled students and teaching faculty members who are part of the program. The CIS is not based in one faculty but spans six faculties and represents not only a degree program in the liberal arts but also a trend toward developing English-taught programs (see Bradford and Brown 2017) that highlights government and institutional initiatives in Japan identified as "the global education effect" (Doerr 2020a, 2020b; Doerr et al. 2020). Upon graduation, students are awarded a bachelor's degree in the liberal arts with a concentration in either Humanities and the Human Sciences, Business and Economics, or Politics and Policy Studies. Students are encouraged to study across the entire range of subjects offered in the curriculum, an approach that is supported by minimizing the number of required courses. While all classes are conducted in English, students have the option of and are encouraged to study the Japanese language alongside their major content courses.

As an English-taught program, and not a content-based language learning (CBLL) or content and language integrated learning (CLIL) program (Marsh 2002), world language learning is definitely not a purported goal of the CIS. The curriculum at the CIS is designed to provide students with content knowledge in the various disciplines of the liberal arts, ranging from the fields of economics and politics to humanities and sociology, through English-medium instruction (EMI). As such, the CIS is a content-focused program, with Japanese, English, or other additional language learning being an entirely unintended outcome.

The CIS has an enrollment of slightly more than 200 students for the 2020 school year,[8] and has had over 45 passports/nationalities (and even more named languages[9]) represented during the ten years since the program began. Class sizes

---

7 See Doerr et al. 2020 for a discussion of "study abroad students (*ryuugakusei*)" in the context of Japan.
8 It is worth noting here that students from other JMI undergraduate faculty not enrolled in the four-year CIS programs can also take CIS classes as well. Short-term study abroad students mostly from institutions outside Japan are sometimes based at the CIS as the host department and attend its classes for the duration of their stay. These additional groups of students add another layer of diversity and numbers, totalling around 300 students during any one semester.
9 As an example of linguistic diversity at the CIS, in the first class meeting of an introductory linguistic anthropology course we surveyed the 71 students in attendance and counted 35 distinct named languages and 4 major dialects spoken as L1.

are typically small, from five to thirty students for most courses. The CIS is a faculty with over 60 part-time and full-time instructors. Since students take many of their classes with the five full-time professors over the course of the degree program, they get to know these faculty and choose one whose specialization aligns with their interests as an advisor for their senior research project or honors thesis. The location of the CIS—a program taught in English situated within a larger Japanese university—and the diverse linguistic backgrounds from both the students and faculty members make it an interesting field site for studying language uses and the relationship with the space.

4 Ethnographic data: Two competing spatial codes

The fact that CIS is an ETP situated within Japan, where the first language is not English, creates an interesting division of space each with different spatial codes (languages). One space embraces monolingual English as its dominant spatial code, understandable since English is the language of instruction and fluency is a prerequisite for becoming a member of this space in the first place.[10] Although there are no explicit rules, the expectation amongst the inhabitants (namely the students and faculty) is that CIS is a rather monolingual English space in terms of teaching and learning, arguably the result of a language ideology carried over from the space of the actors' previous environment and clearly communicated to the applicants to the program through the admissions requirement of "native-level English" and hiring requirement of teaching entirely in English. In the other space of the greater university, monolingual Japanese is the hegemonic spatial code, and the expectation is for inhabitants to know and be able to use Japanese in order to efficiently and smoothly navigate, meaningfully interact, and effectively negotiate within the university campus space. The nature of each of these two social spaces, manifested in the default spatial codes, is both constructed and perceived by the respective inhabitants and outsiders of the two monolingual Japanese and English spaces. For example, in the space of the wider university, much of the public documentation, announcements, and communication is conducted entirely in Japanese. Conversely, CIS communications are rarely bilingual;

---

10 Most CIS students for whom English is not a dominant language at home score over 100 on the TOEFL iBT.

students, faculty, and staff visiting from other faculty assume that all interaction while at the CIS should be conducted in English.

These two spaces, while separated, can also merge and even collide, as elements from one space can be brought into another and vice versa. The inhabitants of the CIS space are also the inhabitants of the larger Japanese society and thus, have to navigate back and forth between these two social spaces. Furthermore, an individual inhabitant of the CIS space can be first and foremost, an inhabitant of another space that is neither of the two mentioned here. The international students (or faculty members who are not Japanese) are originally inhabitants of a different place (i.e. a different society or social community). As they move to the spaces of CIS and Japan, the elements (the acquired language knowledge, the language ideology and so on) from their previous space are also brought to the new spaces, as we illustrate below.

While the CIS space is the focus of this chapter, the other spaces can contribute to understanding the language space of the College and why it is operated the way it is. For the matter of comprehensibility, the physical space of the CIS can be divided into both formal and informal space, as pointed out by Taguchi et al. (2017). The formal space includes the classroom and the offices where the monolingual code is generally expected and prioritized since supervision is visible and surveillance is in effect.[11] On the other hand, though we observed a certain surveillance of self and the other in the informal spaces such as the hallway and lounges (see also Đỗ and Poole 2020) we also witnessed far more complex and flexible language practices probably due to differing expectations, norms, or implicit "rules" as compared to formal spaces. This division does not mean, as shown in later sections, that the formal space is strictly monolingual (surveillance is incomplete), or the monolingual code does not operate in the informal space (surveillance is sometimes present). The monolingual code is still believed to be the norm in both formal and informal spaces by both students and faculty members, but to various degrees.

---

[11] Students surveil their language use knowing that monolingualism is the expected norm, if not the "rule," per se, especially in the physical space of the classroom—a Panopticon of sorts. In this context we might compare this with Foucault's concept of panopticism in which the surveillance becomes self-regulated. "He who is subjected to a field of visibility, and who knows it, assumes responsibility for the constraints of power; he makes them play spontaneously upon himself; he inscribes in himself the power relation in which he simultaneously plays both roles; he becomes the principle of his own subjection" (Foucault 1995: 202–203).

4.1 "Spacing" and "languaging" practices

The monolingual ideology in the mental space acts as the dominant spatial code and operates in the physical space, influencing the social space of the CIS. Here we present data that shows how the students and faculty members are moving between various spaces (see also Doerr and McGuire, in this volume), notably the space of the previous environment before moving to the CIS, and the spatial triad, bringing along, incorporating and reflecting on various language practices and ideologies. We show how translanguaging practices possess a similar power to construct a distinct performative linguistic space within the larger CIS space primarily shaped by the hegemonic monolingual spatial code. Through translanguaging practices, the inhabitants find a way to express and establish their identities and thus, destabilize the perceived coherence of the CIS space.

A recorded interaction between two students who are fluent in both Japanese and English shows how a distinct social space is established through translingual practices within the physical space of the lounge in the CIS. One of the students is a bilingual Japanese speaker whereas the other has a multilingual family background and though strongly identifies as a Japanese speaker also attaches their identity to their other linguistic legacies. When talking about school, the first student was asked by the other when they should start a project to which they replied with "Plan stage *wo yari hajimeru*." [*We should start the* plan stage]. Although the two words, "plan" and "stage," are separately common *gairaigo* (loan words) and as such part of the Japanese lexicon, the combined phrasing, "plan stage," as one term and not two separate words, is not normally used in Japanese. This, in addition to the fact that the students used the English pronunciation of the term "plan stage" (not the Japanese, *puran suteeji*), demonstrates a case of translanguaging. Oppositely, Japanese pronunciations of loanwords occurred as well, as with this translanguaging utterance from a bilingual student in the same social space, "Did your *garakei* have *kamera*?" (Did your *flip phone* have *a camera*?), in which the loanword *kamera* was deliberately pronounced not with English but with Japanese phonemes since the topic of the conversation, a "*garakei*, or Galápagos 'flip' mobile phone,"[12] was unique to the Japanese context.

Other recorded exchanges in the CIS space suggest instances of translanguaging being used as "discourse markers" (Schiffrin 1987) in the informal space of the school lounge. Such instances include utterances such as: "*Nanka demo saa . . .* isn't

---

12 This is a portmanteau derived from "Galá" (Galápagos) and "*kei*" (*kei-tai*, or mobile phone) that represents one example of the "Galápagos syndrome" in business—an isolated design example of an otherwise global product (in this case, the "feature" or "flip" mobile phones that were still very popular in Japan until the late 2010s, even after smartphones became ubiquitous).

it . . ." (combining the particle of assertion *saa* with *demo,* "but," after the familiar, non-interrogative form of the interrogative *nanika, nanka,* to mean *"I don't know but like . . .* isn't it . . ."*) or "There's this *nanka anou . . ."* (again, using *nanka* as a discourse modality that functions as "a sign that signifies the situation in which one does not or cannot find an appropriate signifier" (Maynard 2000: 1217), along with the interjection *anou* to mean "There's this *like, err . . ."*). In another example, on the subject of "job hunting" activities (*shuushoku katsudou*) amongst students getting ready to graduate, translanguaging between interlocutors at CIS in an informal space produced such utterances of translanguaging as: "Some companies *nanka ii yo tte*" [*They said that* some companies *are kind of attractive*] and "*Zettai* they have the information on there [i.e., the company website]" [They *definitely* have the information on there].

These speech events establish a translanguaging space in which the translingual code is perceived as the norm, within the larger supposedly monolingual space of the CIS. This translanguaging space is easily and naturally established due to the fact that the students share a large part of their linguistic repertoires and because the environment is an informal setting that allows a certain flexibility and freedom regarding language use compared to the more formal space of a classroom (which tends to conform to the monolingual ideology of the mental space).

Another recorded interaction within the CIS space in Taguchi et al. (2017) illustrates the formation of multiple and simultaneous social spaces to serve different purposes through the uses of language that deviate from the monolingual norm of the mental space. The speech event took place after class but within the physical space of the classroom and involved three students, two whose dominant home language is Vietnamese (A and B) and one (C) for whom American English is dominant (and Vietnamese is not a part of their linguistic repertoire). Some of the overlapping in the three students' linguistic repertoires is composed of features from the two named languages—English and Japanese, with Vietnamese being the shared linguistic components between A and B.

A: Kỳ này chị có 2 lớp thầy A. [I have two of Prof. A's classes this semester]

B: Lớp nào vậy chị? Seminar với . . . ? [Which classes are those? Seminar and . . . ?]

A: Intermediate Seminar với Colonialism. Làm bài tập hết sạch thời gian luôn. [Intermediate Seminar and Colonialism. I have to spend all my time on these class assignments.]

B: Em cũng vậy, có một lớp mà làm hết 5, 6 tiếng luôn. [Same, I only take one class from them this semester, but it takes me at least 5 to 6 hours to finish the assignment.]

A: (Nods in response.)

B: Nhưng mà cũng tại vì em procrastinate nữa nên mới thế. [But also because of my procrastination, it took that much time to do the assignment.]

Immediately after, B invited C to have some snacks using English: "You want some?" B turned to invite A and immediately switched to Vietnamese: "Mời chị." [Please have some] to which A replied in English: "Thank you."

This interaction similarly establishes a translanguaging space within the larger monolingual space of the CIS, which also took place in the physical and symbolically formal space of a classroom. Technically speaking, the physical space is the classroom which is, on the mental space level, perceived to dominantly operate on the monolingual code. The fact that the class has ended, and the authority was no longer present, transforms the physical space of a classroom into that of something similar to a lounge where other spatial codes are allowed and different surveillance strategies are employed depending on the contexts of the mental space level, a similar observation of which is mentioned also by Torres-Olave (2012). This conversion, together with the background of the interlocutors, constructs the social space where flexible translingual code is the norm. The fact that this conversation occurs after the class has officially ended allows the translingual code to emerge naturally between the two Vietnamese-speaking students as a way of establishing a social space based on the bond over shared linguistic repertoire while excluding the non-Vietnamese speaking student from this community and bond. The interaction occurring afterward that includes the American English-speaking student establishes another social space that no longer excludes this student, then is converted back to the social space that *does* exclude them. In other words, in this interaction that took place within the physical space of a classroom, two different social spaces are in operation, one of which is signified by the translingual code while the other is signified by the mental space of monolingual ideology. The social space signified by the translingual code shows how interlocutors are employing the social reality of the boundaries between the named languages to their benefit, illustrated by the purpose of excluding C (and any indirect interlocutors of the conversation) when A and B translanguaged.

Another informal space that is a resourceful space for translanguaging worthy of discussing here is an online textual chat between four CIS students, two of whom are fluent in Arabic, English, and Japanese while the other two are fluent in both English and Japanese.

D: Is E at school? Lol

G: No hahaha

D: E *doko* [E, where are you?]

E: Yeah. *Demo* classes *yabai* [Yeah. *But the* classes *are so crazy*]

H: 「ｲ」の宿題わかる人?笑 [*Does anyone know what the homework is for I's [class]? (LOL!)*]

D: *Wakaranai* [*No idea*]

G: Finding an article from one of the topics *desho?* [Finding an article from one of the topics, *isn't it?*]

Although this SNS chat[13] is less bound by the physical space of the school campus (the connection remains however due to the topic of the exchange), it is bound by the physical space of a keyboard, which makes this example interesting. On a smartphone, the interlocutors can type in Japanese using either a keyboard with Latin script (*ro-maji*) or a Japanese keyboard with Japanese syllabaries and Chinese characters, and the above conversation illustrates both. H's initial use of a Japanese keyboard makes it inconvenient to switch the physical space to a Latin script keyboard and thereby employ other linguistic components available in their repertoire. This parallels the mental space of a monolingual ideology observed in the physical space of the school campus. The result is that H joined the chat with a Japanese sentence typed in Japanese characters, which stands out compared to the other interlocutors' mix of English and Japanese linguistic components typed in Latin script (*ro-maji*). Additionally, being a private group chat between several CIS students with rather similar linguistic repertoires, this space functions in the same way as informal spaces such as the school lounge discussed earlier, but with even less interference from authority. The interlocutors are constructing a social space with translingual code as the norm. In this performative linguistic space, kept separate also by the boundary between the physical world and the virtual world, the students are able to further downplay, even go so far as to ignore, the influence of the monolingual ideology (the mental space) expected by most inhabitants in the CIS campus (the physical space), allowing them to communicate using what they consider to be a more natural, comfortable, and fuller linguistic repertoire.

Indeed, as revealed through interviews, some students agree that translanguaging helps express themselves better and more accurately and facilitates the

---

13 The SNS chat used in this chapter was collected by utilizing the screenshot function available on the smartphone device by one of the authors from the students of the CIS in a separate project by Taguchi et al. (2017). The interlocutors in these chat instances are a group of CIS students in which the author who collected the data is one of the members.

flow of the conversation ("I mix when I just can't find the words," "I guess I can express myself better, yeah, cuz [with] some words you can't explain in other languages"). Interestingly, CIS students describe their language use as a way to avoid the "troublesome" (*mendoukusai*) mental shifts that boundaries around named languages would otherwise impose–in other words, by creating a performative linguistic space that encourages strategies of translanguaging through which they employ their entire linguistic repertoire, avoiding the awkward communication strategies that a monolingual ideology otherwise entails. Students mention that translanguaging just "comes out naturally" for them, especially when the situation does not require them to self-police their languaging. In other words, in the performative linguistic space created within the CIS campus (the physical space) that requires little conformity to a monolingual ideology (the mental space), we can observe a social space where the inhabitants make fuller use of their linguistic repertoires, as can be seen in the above examples from informal settings.

4.2 Monolingualism—A hegemonic code for supporting space coherence

Monolingual code, as is illustrated by the data below, is the hegemonic ideology at the mental space level that organizes and dictates the physical and social spaces of the CIS. As Lefebvre (1991: 38) proposed, "a spatial practice must have a certain cohesiveness" but not complete coherence, and the spatial code is perceived to be necessary to maintain this degree of cohesiveness. In the spatial practice of the CIS, student and faculty inhabitants create and maintain community cohesion through monolingual English as a common ground given the widely different socio-historical and linguistic backgrounds and identities. Monolingual English becomes the default and prioritized language practice in much of the CIS space. Contradictory as it may sound, the diversity of the CIS contributes to and justifies the reinforcement of the monolingual code, as illustrated by our data below.[14] While the translanguaging practices can challenge the alleged coherence and stability of the CIS space as discussed in the following section, the reverse is also true. The prevalence of the monolingual ideology is, to a certain extent, internalized, reproduced, and surveilled by the inhabitants thus influencing the language practices that construct the social space.

---

14 Others have pointed out that if and when the environment is rich in terms of linguistic diversity the interlocutors may perceive the need for a single linguistic code to effect communication (Jakubiak, personal communication; Cameron 2001) which could be another facet of monolingual ideology.

In research elsewhere (Đỗ and Poole 2020), Đỗ describes their early language experience as a student in the CIS. During the first two years of the program, Đỗ found it almost impossible to translanguage due to several factors. On the one hand, Đỗ mentioned that their friends and fellow students did not share a large part of their linguistic repertoire, hence the need to restrict their idiolect to a mono-lingual code. On the other hand, the avoidance of translanguaging was rooted in the power of the monolingual code that operated dominantly in their previous space, the Vietnamese education system and society, before moving to Japan to join the CIS. The common perception in their previous space reflecting this hegemonic monolingual code is that language mixing is "a poor attempt at showing off" (Đỗ and Poole 2020: 159). A side consequence of this dominant monolingual code deeply embedded in the space of Vietnam is that the author was insufficient in Japanese proficiency which meant they had no "right" to use Japanese linguistic components in their idiolect when conversing. The self-imposed surveillance of the author's own linguistic repertoire contradicts Canagarajah's (2013: 10) description of trans-languaging: ". . . one can adopt language resources from different communities without 'full' or 'perfect' competence in them." Languaging is personal and internal to the interlocutors (Otheguy, García, and Reid 2015); nonetheless, it is informed, shaped, and shifted by the influence of monolingual ideology that the interlocutors were exposed to, consumed, and internalized. The interweaving relationship be-tween one physical space (Vietnam) and mental space (Vietnamese monolingual ideology) shapes the actual language practices in the social space of a different physical space (the CIS) and mental space (English monolingual ideology). Đỗ expe-rience illustrates how elements and heterogeneous spatial politics from an inhabi-tant's previous space can be interwoven with certain adaptations into the new space, a performative linguistic space. Furthermore, it exemplifies the hegemonic characteristic of the monolingual code that reaches across various spaces.

In research by Đỗ (2018), a student at CIS, "M" self-reflected on their language practices and the other inhabitants' perception that in certain situations monolin-gual English is the ideal spatial code not only in the mental but also the social space of the CIS. Despite their rich linguistic repertoire composed of linguistic fea-tures from English, Japanese, Arabic, and Russian, M chooses to be selective of their idiolect, strategically molding the way they speak based on their assump-tions about the people they are speaking to, in order to "fit in" to the environ-ment. M mostly resorted to monolingual English at the beginning of their time at the CIS when they were still new to everyone. Furthermore, they adhered to the monolingual code when communicating in a larger group. Explaining the reason for this choice, M says that monolingual English is more inclusive in those situa-tions whereas translanguaging might risk excluding other interlocutors. M's choice of language use is reasonable considering their unfamiliarity with the interlocutors' language background and whether they share an overlapping linguistic repertoire. As a result, M naturally reverts to monolingual English, since this is considered the expected and shared linguistic "space" among the inhabitants of the CIS and thus, monolingual English is perceived as inclusive in this situation where an interlocutor (M) encounters "unfamiliar" diversity. Another reason for M's frequent suppression of their own linguistic repertoire when interacting with unfamiliar people in the CIS space is the fear of being negatively perceived by others. This sentiment was shared by one of the authors previously (Đỗ and Poole 2020), as well as several other students through interviews: ". . . while you try to talk and you use other words [languages] to express then it may seem that you sound uneducated," or "[m]ixing [languages] sounds like I can't use one language or the other because words are being replaced so vocabulary level in languages might seem low [to others]. That's why there is a need to keep switching to fill in [lexical] gaps."

The tendency to use monolingual English to avoid negative evaluation is often a result of the students' experience in their space prior to the CIS, which then auto-translates to the expectation tied to language use in the physical space of the CIS. This illustrates how the students' mobility between different spaces led to the incorporation of a (monolingual) language ideology and practice into the new space (the CIS). Policing and surveilling one's own linguistic repertoire to align with the hegemonic spatial code is considered a safe strategy to avoid offending anyone or being viewed negatively as not competent in a named language, especially in situations where an interlocutor is interacting with unfamiliar surroundings.

This line of thinking is shared by another CIS student's feelings of exclusion when Japanese is used in classes due to his "insufficient" Japanese. As can be seen from both students' accounts, the monolingual code, in certain cases, is not contested by the presence of the (language) diversity of the space. If anything, the monolingual code is reinforced and justified for the purpose of inclusivity, a "safe" intermediate medium of interaction. The monolingual ideology of the mental space that attaches to the CIS physical space is perceived and reproduced in the social space, just as Bourdieu (2018 [1991]: 108) has argued: "Social space is inscribed both in the objectivity of spatial structures and in the subjectivity of mental structures [. . .]," through the strategic selection or restriction of an interlocutor's own linguistic repertoire, despite their otherwise natural tendency toward engaging in translanguaging practices when communicating with other interlocutors who they know share many linguistic features.

4.3 Utility of translanguaging within a predominantly monolingual space

Despite showing in the previous section that the monolingual code is used by in-habitants to organize and maintain a certain coherence in the physical and social spaces, and that the interlocutors believe that in many circumstances a monolin-gual spatial code is crucial due to various reasons (e.g., fears of being negatively evaluated by others, not wanting to exclude others, etc.), there are also instances of interactions that demonstrate how the actual language practices of the social space contradict this hegemonic spatial code, and thus challenge the justification and domination of the monolingual ideology. In this section, we identify this ten-sion between the monolingual ideology and the translingual practices through ethnographic data from the CIS.

The clash, or the tension, between the monolingual spatial code and the lan-guage practices that shape the social space of the CIS can be best observed inside the physical space of a classroom, a formal space where the monolingual ideology is dominant owing both to the presence of an authority, the instructor, and the ensuing self-surveillance that such a space enforces. The classroom is where most inhabitants expect some form of "standard language" use, and such standards are usually established and supervised by the instructors in charge of the class, both explicitly and implicitly. The standard is expected to align with the monolingual spatial code since, as repeated throughout the chapter, it is the hegemonic code of the CIS. Nonetheless, the reality of the social space is not as straightforward. The monolingual code is constantly challenged whether consciously or unconsciously, by not only the students who are expected to adhere to the established code but also by the instructors who have access to the right and authority to establish the spatial code of the classroom space.

The tension related to language uses within the classroom space can be rep-resented in form of the power relationships between the teachers and students, as pointed out by Hadi-Tabassum (2006: 70): "power relationships are [. . .] con-stantly determining the strategic manipulation of space and those power relation-ships are often expressed through both the use of language and through the movement of the body within that space." The teachers' strategies in constructing and manipulating the classroom space can vary from one to another. Some might attempt to establish the spatial code upfront while others opt for a more flexible option or use their power to invite the students to reconstruct the generally ac-cepted power relationships, as well as the spatial code. The same thing can be said for the students.

Đỗ and Poole (2020) present a case of language use inside the classroom that diverts from the dominant monolingual code for communication purposes. A group of six CIS students with different language backgrounds was working on an exercise when a Korean-speaking student described what he saw: "Strong wind in the northwest." His message confused some other members as they mistook "wing" for "wind," thus seriously disrupting the group conversation since the exercise relied heavily on verbal communication. The members who heard the phrase correctly attempted to clarify the meaning using various methods, from using hand motion to imitate the wind to repeating the phrase slowly in clearer diction. None were successful in clearing up the confusion until one student translanguaged—"Wind, like, *kaze da* [wind, eh]." Everyone was finally able to understand the phrase correctly. Though it is a bit obvious, this observation seems to us to highlight how a conversation occurring in the social space can fail and attempting to adhere to the monolingual spatial code merely reinforced this communication breakdown. On the contrary, translanguaging cleared up the misunderstanding effectively with one phrase, which was deemed especially important in this case due to the time pressure of the group work. Contrary to the belief illustrated above showing how monolingual spatial code is reinforced and justified for its efficiency and inclusivity in certain situations, translanguaging is strategically effective, and inclusive, in other cases. That the student deviated from the dominant monolingual spatial code (proven by the whole group communicating in monolingual English until that breaking point, and even after the disruption most group members still relied more on monolingual code, i.e., repeating the word in a clearer tone), reflects how the accepted norm can be easily challenged, especially when the situation calls for it. The example provided here might be labeled less as "translanguaging" than as an act providing a direct translation of the word, which is technically correct. However, considering the context, we believe that semantics (the main function of translation) is not the problem. The misunderstanding initially was one of phonetics, both in the production and perception of the uttered word. Thus, the interesting observation for us was that the student was able to utilize their full linguistic repertoire to efficiently clear up the mishearing (misperception) by providing a replacement with a completely different phonetic sound sequence. This utilization of the interlocutors' full linguistic repertoire also stands out especially because of the entirely monolingual (English) nature of the conversation until that point, and the use of "*kaze* [wind]" was, more or less, a translingual "jostle," occurring as a result of both the realization of the intended meaning ("wind") and the break in the monolingual flow.

As dominant as the monolingual spatial code is perceived to be inside the CIS's classroom, this same space is where both the class instructors and students are aware of the diverse language practices of the social space. As mentioned previously, the instructors can establish the spatial code for the physical space, the classroom.

They perceive the English monolingual practices as the common and established practices in the formal space of the CIS (perceived space), conceive their class to be operated in accordance with the monolingual code (conceived space), but eventually encounter the lived experience when they themselves break the perceived and conceived code (lived space), or when the students divert from the established code directly by engaging with their full linguistic repertoire. This data again illustrates a theme throughout this volume by showing how the performative linguistic space of translanguaging is created within a supposedly monolingual English space of the classroom through the students' constant mobility between (and reconstruction of) the perceived, conceived, and lived spaces prompted by the actual conversational needs, incorporating the spatial codes of the English-dominant (CIS) and Japanese-dominant spaces (the Japanese university).

In one of the classes in the CIS, an instructor who considers English their dominant language but also incorporates Japanese components in their language repertoire established the standard spatial code for the class that complies with the institutional monolingual ideology by asking the students to "[u]se 100% English, please. I can speak some Japanese, but not perfectly; I don't want to make any mistakes." The instructor's direct request reflects, as already illustrated, how the monolingual code is generally perceived as the safe and efficient way of communication. However, despite being the person making the request, the instructor themself often deviated from the spatial code they established by translanguaging during the lecture: "He's one of the grandfathers, the *daisenpai* [senior], of the topic . . .," "I'm running from *Ritsudai* [Japanese abbreviation for Ritsumeikan University] to here so . . .," or "After he left *Doudai* [Japanese abbreviation for Doshisha University] he *amakudaried*[15] (. . .) down to Kyoto *daigaku* [University] [sic]." Based on this observation, the instructor's translanguaging practices seemed to have occurred subconsciously since they themself made the request to maintain a spatial code of monolingual English in the class.

The instructor was not the only one contesting the monolingual spatial code in that classroom. A student translanguaged using Japanese phrases when standing up to state their opinion, which was considered bold considering the instructor's establishment of the monolingual English spatial code previously and the nature of the action. Stating one's opinion in front of the class is subject to the pressure of being supervised by other inhabitants of the space (the instructor and other students), which is different from private talk with classmates inside a

---

15 *Amakudari*, literally "descent from heaven," usually refers to the "parachuting of a (former) government (or company) official to a (senior) position in a private (or subsidiary) company" (Poole 2010: 157).

class. The hegemony of the monolingual spatial code, as well as the supposed co-herence of the physical and mental space, was destabilized by this student's lan-guage use. This observation demonstrates that the monolingual ideology, despite its pervasiveness in the physical and mental spaces of the CIS, is constantly con-tested and negotiated by both sets of interlocutors, one (the instructors) with rela-tively more authority and the power to establish the code, and the other (the students) with relatively less authority who are expected to abide by the code by default.

On the other hand, an interesting case from Đỗ and Poole (2020) seems to be the complete opposite of the above observation but nonetheless portrays the ten-sion between the monolingual spatial code and the translingual practices of the inhabitants of the space. In another class, the instructor neither made any direct request regarding language use inside class nor in any way directly established a standard spatial code. On the contrary, the instructor was the initiator of trans-languaging inside the class. However, upon hearing a student's translanguaging when they were making a presentation in front of the class, the instructor inter-rupted to request that the student speak in English only, saying "this is an English course." Later in an interview, the same student explained that they were just fol-lowing the "mode of language" set by the instructor. Despite that, the students' freedom in language use is suppressed by the instructor's "delimitation of the stu-dent space" (Hadi-Tabassum 2006: 70), leading to the students having to restrict their linguistic repertoire in the classroom space.[16] In this case, the monolingual ideology was reestablished by the authority of the space. The social space situated in the physical space of the classroom is thus reshaped to match the mental space of the monolingual norm.

However, the interlocutor with ostensibly more authority can rely on the cues provided by those with supposedly less authority inside a class to construct the common spatial code. For example, in another class, the instructor displayed a high awareness of the monolingual English code in the classroom, which can be as-sumed to stem from their efforts to include all students (Japanese speakers and non-Japanese speakers). The instructor made sure to attach the English translations to any mentioned Japanese words or phrases, at least for the first time. Simulta-neously, they acknowledged that this course centered on Japanese religions, and furthermore, the CIS space is embedded in a larger space where monolingual Japa-nese is considered the hegemonic code, thus translanguaging could be strategically viable. This allowed the instructor to respond to the students' indirect invitation to

---

16 Unlike other contexts where restrictive institutional or national language policies may shape space (e.g.Wiley 2002), the CIS has no explicit policy statements on language use.

employ translingual code. During the self-introduction, a student answered in monolingual English for the most part but concluded with *"Ijou desu"* [That is all] to which the instructor answered in pleased humor, *"Ijou! Hai!"* [The end! Ok!] and motioned for the next self-introduction. While all other students used English, the instructor did not translanguage again. This observation illustrates the ongoing negotiation between the monolingual ideology and the translingual practices in the classroom space. The negotiation did not turn into an actual tension due to the flexibility and acceptance of both involved parties, and therefore, both monolingual and translingual codes are employed situationally. The inhabitants' language practices "[create] new linguistic landscapes (not only visible but audible) that have the potential to shift perceptions and challenge the monolingual habitus" (Lamb and Vodicka 2018: 18).

As mentioned earlier, the students are not the only ones challenging the monolingual code and the coherence of the space; the instructors carrying an expectation to preserve the coherence of the space through the maintenance of a monolingual spatial code can do the same. In one class in the CIS, the instructor frequently translanguaged and set no standard code for the classroom space. When a student entered the class late, the instructor asked: "Can you grab a course outline, please? *Hai, douzo* [Here you are (handing the student a handout)]." Or when they explained the questionnaire, '. . . *onegaishimasu* [Please do your best]. (Continues in English) . . . Can you write your *kokuseki* [nationality] . . .'" After finishing the explanation that the students were to choose any of the five questions, they continued, *"Hai! Tanoshinde kudasai* [Okay! Enjoy]. *Docchi demo* [whichever you like]." At the end of the class, when the class became too loud because the bell had gone off, the instructor said *"Chotto matte kudasai"* [Just a moment, please] as an attempt to manage the class.

Similarly, in Đỗ and Poole (2020), one of the authors, Poole, reflects on how they translanguage in many of their interactions with students inside the classroom for various reasons. For one, since Japanese studies is an important part of the curriculum at the CIS, Japan is often the central topic of discussion, and so it is natural to use Japanese when doing so. Another more overt reason is that translanguaging is used as a source of friendliness, helping to construct a community—we are "translanguagers." In this case, the instructor is aware of their power relationship with the students and therefore, taking advantage of this power to invite the students to the discourse of power and language use within the classroom space. By doing so, the instructors and students are working together to dismantle the hegemonic monolingual ideology of the mental and physical spaces and towards the acknowledgement of the social space—the translanguaging practices. The instructor acknowledges "the right to be different" and "the right for different groups or collective explorations of such differences and, as a consequence, the right to pursue development on some territorial and collective basis that departs from established norms" (Harvey 2000: 251).

The social space of the CIS constructed by translingual practices can help the students reflect and dismantle their internalized language ideology that shapes their mental space. In Đỗ (2018), a student of the CIS acknowledges that people in the CIS have rather different attitudes toward language use, particularly translanguaging, compared to what is commonly accepted in their home country. They have never been criticized for translanguaging in the CIS as they were in their home country, saying: "everyone does it [in the CIS]." As a result, they become more comfortable in conveying their thoughts in the CIS space due to their language repertoire not being as restricted as it was in their previous space. This case illustrates how the elements acquired in the CIS space can be carried back to the inhabitants' previous space, while also signifying the instability of a hegemonic monolingual spatial code, a type of performative linguistic space.

The students can assume their agency through the language practices that challenge the monolingual norm of the CIS space, thus tipping the perceived power relationships between the teachers and students, as well as the coherence maintained by the English monolingual code. On the other hand, the instructors can take advantage of their power in an attempt to reconstruct the classroom space, making it lean towards what Harvey (2000) has termed "spaces of hope," which is then recontextualized as a more linguistically inclusive space that benefits an environment like that of the content-based CIS program, through initiating translanguaging practices in opposition to the monolingual spatial code (Lamb and Vodicka 2018).

5 Conclusion

This chapter illustrates how an analysis of space, especially the dynamics between the spatial triad (trans-spacing), can have potential in providing another way to explore and analyze various instances of "languaging." The interlocutors at this college in Japan engaged in the active construction of meaning, an ongoing process that shaped their language ideologies. Rather than static and reified, these understandings were constructed through the performance of "spacing" and "languaging" practices. Although monolingualism was explicitly endorsed and implicitly surveilled by students and faculty, this hegemony was challenged by the competing "performative linguistic space" of translanguaging. The dynamic of these competing ideologies was revealed through a triad of interweaving spaces—the mental spaces within which individual linguistic repertoires are surveilled, the physical spaces where these idiolects are then performed (campus classrooms, hallways, and lounges), and finally the negotiation of a social space which revealed an implicit ideology of translingualism that not only contests but also competes with the ideology of monolingualism. As discussed in this chapter, the interlocutors are informed by other factors including the monolingual ideology and the social reality of named languages. The interlocutors are constantly moving between the space triad, using both monolingualism and translanguaging practices to their advantage through either emphasizing (e.g. establishing a translanguaging space with the purpose of exclusion) or ignoring the boundaries (e.g. establishing a translanguaging space as a means of inclusion) between the named languages, as could be seen from the data provided in the chapter. The interlocutors, through their languaging, are actively manipulating the borders of these ideologies, relying on a social strategy that Sugimoto (2010: 297) has described as the "manipulation of ambiguity," enabling social actors ". . . to interpret various situations at their discretion." Such a manipulation can take place either within or outside institutional settings such as the CIS but demonstrates the value of a performative linguistic space in the creation of ambiguity of ideology to allow for fluid interactions in material spaces that are otherwise designed for concretely-defined purposes.

It has been illustrated in the chapter that the students and faculty members not only physically move across national borders and between spaces within the CIS, but also conceptually move across a spatial triad consisting of perceived (physical), conceived (mental), and lived (social) spaces. This latter movement is manifested in the way the mentally conceived space may, to a certain extent, dictate the spatial code of the physical and social spaces, and the social space may simultaneously influence how the mental space is conceived. This then serves to activate diverse ideologies of actor positionality (see Introduction to this volume).

This dynamic indicates to us that the emergence of ETPs in Japan, such as the CIS, has enabled a new and different kind of space in which there exists a language practice that challenges the dominant monolingual ideology.[17] This can be observed through the fact that whereas some interviewees themselves hold the idea that translanguaging is a sign of being "incompetent" in a language (being informed by the dominant ideology of monolingualism of the mental space), the informal physical spaces such as the school lounge or the private group chat with other CIS students allow them to frequently lean on and engage with the comfortable performative

---

17 HE practitioners in Japan have long acknowledged a hegemony of academic English practices (e.g. Eades 2000) of which the normalization and surveillance can effectively become a form of "linguicism" (Skutnabb-Kangas 2000, 30), or linguistic discrimination.

linguistic space of translanguaging. Although we have framed translanguaging as a language ideology (cf. Canagarajah 2013), originally it was proposed as a pedagogic tool of planned use in dual literacy programs (Lewis, Jones, and Baker 2012)—as we alluded to above, our contribution here has been to explore an example of the relation between monolingualism and translanguaging as ideologies. In this sense, the arising challenge calls for a reconsideration of effective and inclusive language use within the pedagogy of the educational setting in particular and Japanese HE in general. In particular, in this HE setting, by recognizing the interplay between language ideology and language use, between representational space (lived), conceptualized space (conceived), and spatial practice (perceived), we might not only recognize translanguaging as either an ideology or language practice but also, and importantly, advocate for an ETP pedagogy in Japan that embraces rather than marginalizes or competes with both the ideology and practice of translanguaging, echoing similar calls in other HE systems worldwide (e.g., Mazak and Carroll 2017).

However, it should be reiterated that instead of a reduction of the discourse down to a zero-sum dichotomy between monolingual ideology and translingual practices and an argument for the replacement of monolingual code with translingual code (especially after the data has illustrated how interlocutors can use monolingual code to their benefit), it is more effective to regard student and teacher agency at the CIS as an example of "engaging with others to create dynamic places in which multilingualism and plurilingualism are seen as an everchanging but always present norm," which is also referred to as "spaces of hope" (Lamb and Vodicka 2018: 18), and in an equal position to monolingualism. As a performative linguistic space, in some ways, the CIS has been constructed by its inhabitants as a social space that embraces the flexible and diverse nature of a variety of language uses and idiolects, an active process not confined to an ideology of monolingualism. As shown from the above data, this social space has the capability to reconstruct the mental space previously occupied by the monolingual code to newly incorporate the code of translanguaging. In other words, to effectively construct "spaces of hope," translanguaging should not be limited to only the social space, but also be elevated and woven into the mental space at the ideological level.

References

Agha, Asif. 2006. *Language and social relations*. Cambridge: Cambridge University Press.

Auer, Peter. 2022. "Translanguaging" or "doing languages"? Multilingual practices and the notion of "codes". In Jeff MacSwan (ed.), *Multilingual perspectives on translanguaging*, 126–153. Bristol: Multilingual Matters.

Auer, Peter, Martin Hilpert, Anja Stuckenbrock & Benedikt Szmrecsanyi (eds.). 2014. *Space in language and linguistics: Geographical, interactional, and cognitive perspectives*. Berlin: De Gruyter Mouton.

Auer, Peter & Jürgen E. Schmidt (eds.). 2010. *Language and space: An international handbook of linguistic variation*. Vol. 1. Berlin: De Gruyter Mouton.

Bourdieu, Pierre. 2018 [1991]. Social space and the genesis of appropriated physical space. *International Journal of Urban and Regional Research* 42(1). 106–114. https://doi.org/10.1111/1468-2427.12534.

Bradford, Annette & Howard Brown (eds.). 2017. *English-medium instruction in Japanese higher education: Policy, challenges, and outcomes*. Bristol: Multilingual Matters.

Cameron, Deborah. 2001. Globalization and the teaching of "communication skills." In David Block & Deborah Cameron (eds.), *Globalization and language teaching*, 67–82. London: Routledge.

Canagarajah, Suresh. 2013. *Translingual practice: Global Englishes and cosmopolitan relations*. London: Routledge.

Cresswell, Tim & Peter Merriman. 2011. Introduction: Geography of mobilities—Practices, spaces, subjects. In Tim Cresswell & Peter Merriman (eds.), *Geography of mobilities: Practices, spaces, subjects*, 1–18. Surrey: Ashgate Publishing.

de Certeau, Michel. 1984. *The practice of everyday life*. Berkeley: University of California Press.

Đỗ, Anh N. 2018. *Translanguaging in monolingual reality: A study of the self and others*. Kyoto: Doshisha University. B.A. Honors Thesis.

Đỗ, Anh N. & Gregory S. Poole. 2020. Translanguaging practice within an ideology of monolingualism: Two autoethnographic perspectives. In Neriko M. Doerr (ed.), *The global education effect and Japan: Constructing new borders and identification practices*, 147–172. London: Routledge.

Doerr, Neriko M. (ed.). 2020a. *The global education effect and Japan: Constructing borders and identification practices*. London: Routledge.

Doerr, Neriko M. 2020b. Introduction: Borders, Japan, and global education effects. In Neriko M. Doerr (ed.), *The global education effect and Japan: Constructing new borders and identification practices*, 3–32. London: Routledge.

Doerr, Neriko M., Gregory S. Poole & Roy G. Hedrick III. 2020. "Post-study-abroad students," "never-study-abroad students," and the politics of belonging: The global education effect of Japan's English-medium instruction. In Neriko M. Doerr (ed.), *The global education effect and Japan: Constructing new borders and identification practices*, 119–146. London: Routledge.

Eades, Jeremy S. 2000. "Why don't they write in English?" Academic modes of production and academic discourses in Japan and the West. *Ritsumeikan Journal of Asian Pacific Studies* 6. 58–77.

Ellis, Nick. 2011. The emergence of language as a complex adaptive system. In James Simpson (ed.), *Handbook of applied linguistics*, 666–679. London: Routledge.

Evans, Vyvyan & Paul Chilton (eds.). 2010. *Language, cognition, and space: The state of the art and new directions*. Sheffield: Equinox Publishing.

Foucault, Michel. 1995. *Discipline and punish: The birth of the prison*. 2nd edn. New York: Vintage Books.

García, Ofelia & Tatyana Kleyn (eds.). 2016. *Translanguaging with multilingual students: Learning from classroom moments*. London: Routledge.

García, Ofelia & Wei Li. 2013. *Translanguaging: Language, bilingualism and education*. New York: Palgrave MacMillan.

Garfinkel, Harold. 1967. *Studies in ethnomethodology*. Englewood Cliffs: Prentice-Hall.

Gumperz, John. J. 1964. Linguistic and social interaction in two communities. *American Anthropologist* 66: 137–53.

Hadi-Tabassum, Samina. 2006. *Language, space and power: A critical look at bilingual education*. Bristol: Multilingual Matters.

Harvey, David. 2000. *Spaces of hope*. Edinburgh: Edinburgh University Press.

Johnston, Barbara. 2013. Ideology and discourse in the enregisterment of regional variation. In Peter Auer, Martin Hilpert, Anja Stukenbrock & Benedikt Szmrecsanyi (eds.), *Space in language and linguistics: Geographical, interactional, and cognitive perspectives*, 107–127. Berlin: De Gruyter Mouton.

Lamb, Terry & Goran Vodicka. 2018. Collective autonomy and multilingual spaces. In Garold Murray & Terry Lamb (eds.), *Space place and autonomy in language learning*, 9–28. New York: Routledge.

Lefebvre, Henri. 1991. *The production of space*. Oxford: Blackwell.

Lewis, Gwyn, Bryn Jones & Colin Baker. 2012. Translanguaging: Origins and development from school to street and beyond. *Educational Research and Evaluation* 18(7). 641–654. 10.1080/13803611.2012.718488.

Li, Wei. 2011. Moment analysis and translanguaging space: Discursive construction of identities by multilingual Chinese youth in Britain. *Journal of Pragmatics* 43(5). 1222–1235. https://doi.org/10.1016/j.pragma.2010.07.035.

Li, Wei. 2017. Translanguaging as a practical theory of language. *Applied Linguistics* 39(1). 9–30. https://doi.org/10.1093/applin/amx039.

Low, Setha. 2017. *Spatializing culture: The ethnography of space and place*. London: Routledge.

Makalela, Leketi. 2016. Ubuntu translanguaging: An alternative framework for complex multilingual encounters. *Southern African Linguistics and Applied Language Studies* 34(3). 187–196. 10.2989/16073614.2016.1250350.

Makalela, Leketi. 2019. Uncovering the universals of ubuntu translanguaging in classroom discourses. *Classroom Discourse* 10(3–4). 237–251. 10.1080/19463014.2019.1631198.

Marsh, David. 2002. *CLIL-EMILE The European dimension: Actions, trends and foresight potential*. Brussels: European Commission.

Maynard, Senko. 2000. Speaking for the unspeakable: Expressive functions of *nan(i)* in Japanese discourse. *Journal of Pragmatics* 32(8). 1209–1239. https://doi.org/10.1016/S0378-2166(99)00091-0.

Mazak, Catherine M. & Kevin S. Carroll (eds.). 2017. *Translanguaging in higher education: Beyond monolingual ideologies*. Bristol: Multilingual Matters.

Otheguy, Ricardo, Ofelia García & Wallis Reid. 2015. Clarifying translanguaging and deconstructing named languages: A perspective from linguistics. *Applied Linguistics Review* 6(3). 281–307. https://doi.org/10.1515/applirev-2015-0014.

Paulsrud, BethAnne, Jenny Rosén, Boglárka Straszer & Åsa Wedin (eds.). 2017. *New perspectives on translanguaging and education*. Bristol: Multilingual Matters.

Poole, Gregory S. 2010. *The Japanese professor: An ethnography of a university faculty*. Rotterdam: Sense Publishers.

Rosiers, Kristen, Inge V. Lancker & Steven Delarue. 2018. Beyond the traditional scope of translanguaging: Comparing translanguaging practices in Belgian multilingual and monolingual classroom contexts. *Language & Communication* 61. 15–28. 10.1016/ j.langcom.2017.11.003.

Rothman, Jason. 2008. Linguistic epistemology and the notion of monolingualism. *Sociolinguistic Studies* 2(3). 441–457. https://doi.org/10.1558/sols.v2i3.441.

Schiffrin, Deborah. 1987. *Discourse markers*. Cambridge: Cambridge University Press.

Skutnabb-Kangas, Tove. 2000. *Linguistic genocide in education- Or worldwide diversity and human rights?* Mahwah, NJ: Lawrence Erlbaum Associates.

Soja, Edward W. 1989. *Postmodern geographies: The reassertion of space in critical social theory*. London: Verso.

Song, Kwangok. 2016. "Okay, I will say in Korean and then in American": Translanguaging practices in bilingual homes. *Journal of Early Childhood Literacy* 16(1). 84–106. 10.1177/1468798414566705.

Street, Brian. 1993. Culture is a verb: Anthropological aspects of language and cultural process. In David Graddol, Linda Thompson & Michael Byram (eds.), *Language and culture: Papers from the annual meeting of the British association of applied linguistics held at Trevelyan College, University of Durham, September 1991*. 23–43. Bristol: Multilingual Matters.

Sugimoto, Yoshio. 2010. *An introduction to Japanese society: Third Edition*. Cambridge: Cambridge University Press.

Taguchi, Shinnosuke, Salem Young, Anh N. Đỗ & Gregory S. Poole. 2017. Translanguaging as community building: Linguistic identity and ideology at a college of liberal arts in Kyoto. The Japanese Society for Language Sciences. Kyoto Women's University.

Torres-Olave, Blanca M. 2012. Imaginative geographies: identity, difference, and English as the language of instruction in a Mexican university program. *Higher Education* 63. 317–335. DOI: 10.1007/s10734-011-9443-x.

Turner, Marianne & Angel Lin. 2017. Translanguaging and named languages: productive tension and desire. *International Journal of Bilingual Education and Bilingualism* 23(4). 423–433. 10.1080/ 13670050.2017.1360243.

Van der Zee, Emile v. & Jon Slack (eds.). 2003. *Representing direction in language and space*. Oxford: Oxford University Press.

Vogel, Sara & Ofelia García. 2017. Translanguaging. *Oxford research encyclopedia of education*. https://doi.org/10.1093/acrefore/9780190264093.013.181

Wiley, Terence G. 2002. Accessing language rights in education: A brief history of the U.S. context. In James W. Tollefson (ed.), *Language policies in education: Critical issues*, 39–64. Mahwah, NJ: Lawrence Erlbaum Associates.

Yuri Kumagai

Moving from physical to virtual learning spaces: Learning a foreign language during the COVID-19 pandemic in a Zoom classroom

I think we're just naturally more afraid to speak when we're in online environments. You feel more distant with your professor and your classmates . . . It just takes more courage to speak in online class. —Carrie, a 3rd year Japanese language student

1 Introduction

In Spring 2020, the world faced an unprecedented challenge due to a deadly pandemic caused by COVID-19. It has affected every aspect of our lives, and teaching and learning are no exceptions. Remote teaching became the only way we delivered lessons regardless of discipline, and videoconferencing tools such as Zoom became the essential means with which to create a virtual classroom. In mid-March 2020, the private women's college[1] in New England where I teach Japanese language quickly shifted to remote teaching. The college completely closed its campus, and all students were sent home except for a limited number of students—mainly international students—who could not return to their homes. As one of the important goals of language teaching in our program is to develop students' oral proficiency, we resorted to using Zoom as the main platform via which we conducted synchronous online teaching.

Zoom allows us to have a virtual classroom where all participants—a teacher and students—come together despite being in different locations and in different time zones (even in different countries). Sometimes referred to as a "cyber face-to-face" environment or a "live online classroom" (Wang, Chen, and Levy 2010), Zoom promises to provide an environment that is similar to the physical face-to-face classroom by allowing teachers and students to establish audio and video communication. Synchronous online teaching, as opposed to asynchronous teaching, is said to have "an immediate and beneficial application to language learning because it provides face-to-face communication at a distance" (White 2006: 256; see also

---

1 The "college" in this study is a postsecondary institute of higher education.

https://doi.org/10.1515/9783110744781-004

Wang 2004), thus allowing instructors to replicate in-person classroom instructional techniques (Hill et al. 2004).

Even prior to the pandemic, online education was not truly a new phenomenon, particularly in higher education. The first entirely online course was offered in 1981 in the US (Harasim 2000), and since the early 1990s, colleges and universities all over the world have begun to offer courses and even entire degrees online, thanks to advancements in technology (Wallace 2003: 242). "Distance education"[2] is an umbrella term often used for formal education in which the teacher and students are physically separated (both online and offline formats), while the term "online education" refers to classes that are offered entirely online. Various terms such as "e-learning," "digital learning," "electric distance learning," "virtual learning," and "computer-mediated learning" are also used to describe education that is based on electronic tools and media through the Internet and network technologies (Ghazal, Samsudin, and Aldowah 2015).

Before the pandemic, the use of videoconferencing tools such as Zoom or Skype in the context of formal language teaching and learning in higher education was mostly limited to curricular projects such as e-tandem and telecollaboration (also known as "online intercultural exchange"), which connect geographically distant partners (individuals or classrooms) to provide opportunities for virtual interaction and exchange (Helm and Guth 2016; O'Rourke 2007; Ware and O'Dowd 2008). In other words, these synchronous online exchanges and interactions are a part of a larger educational practice, not a sole means of instructional endeavor. In addition, what has been contextually unique and different about online instruction during the COVID-19 pandemic is the fact that various parts of the world were under lockdown and, in many cases, people were not even allowed to leave their homes. As a result, teaching and learning online was an emergency measure, and those of us who were not used to this form of education were "forced"—to use Moorehouse's (2020) word —to enter unfamiliar territory without being fully equipped with the requisite skills and knowledge.

With this as a background, in this chapter I seek to understand how, if at all, moving between in-person learning space and online space affects linguistic practices from the view of performative linguistic space—the theme of this volume as

---

2 Specifically for language education, White (2006: 248–9) introduces Wang and Sun's (2001) four generational model for the evolution of distance language learning: a first generation model is print-based (correspondence) courses; a second generation model is first broadcast technologies and then audio-and video-based multiple media language courses developed in the 1970s; a third generation model uses information and communication technology such as CD-ROMs and Web presentation of course materials and is asynchronous; and the current, fourth generation model is characterized by internet-based real time technology.

discussed by Doerr and McGuire (this volume). I will do this by examining students' experiences and perspectives of studying Japanese language amid the COVID-19 pandemic. Per Doerr and McGuire, the notion of performative linguistic space is that space shapes what types of linguistic interactions are ushered, coaxed, or silenced by temporal and contextual interactions between the space and individuals' subject positions as well as the ideologies they carry over from one place to the other.

In a Zoom classroom, we imagine that we are occupying the same virtual space, but are we really? How, if at all, are we compensating for various semiotic modes that are not available in virtual spaces? Do students feel the same or different as compared to in-person classroom learning? To investigate these initial questions, I conducted a post-course survey with the students in my first-year and third-year Japanese language courses at the end of the Spring 2020 semester. What drew my attention was that the students in my first-year course did not see much difference between the regular in-person classroom and the virtual Zoom classroom, while the students in my third-year course noted that they felt "totally different." What factors contributed to creating such differences in perceptions and feelings? Those who felt differently in the Zoom classroom described their emotions with expressions such as "didn't feel as personal" or "not as engaging." The preliminary analysis of the survey suggests that this discrepancy is due to the students' expectations regarding what communication means in a language classroom, whether they see it as controlled verbal use of words or as exchanges of ideas and relating to each other with the target language. Intrigued, I conducted individual interviews with the students in the Fall of 2020 to further examine how students see and experience a Zoom classroom as a learning space. These interviews constitute the date used for the current study.

By drawing upon this data set, I attempt to answer the following questions: What kinds of spaces do students perceive the Zoom classroom to be in comparison to those familiar learning (in-person) spaces? What emotions and feelings are evoked in the Zoom classroom? What features of Zoom and the students' preconceived understanding of learning space contribute to such perceptions and emotions? What types of routines and patterns of interactions are negotiated and (re) established in the Zoom classroom as performative linguistic space emerges? And, ultimately, how do all of these factors affect the learning of a foreign language in a Zoom classroom? In what follows, I first briefly introduce the literature pertaining to learning spaces and online classrooms, and then illustrate the social context of the COVID-19 pandemic in which the present Zoom classroom is situated. Next, I describe the study, findings and discussion, and conclude the chapter with implications for online classrooms.

2 Place vs. space, (virtual) learning space, and synchronous online classrooms

2.1 Place vs. space

In order to clarify how I am using the words, "space" and "place" in this study, I briefly discuss the way relevant literature define space versus place. Scholars in the field of human geography view places as social constructions (Cresswell 2004; Massey 2005). They argue that places are created through action by people doing things in a particular space (Cresswell 2004). By talking about the space as a setting in which actions are performed, it becomes identified and defined as a place where certain activities are carried out. Similarly, in the field of learning space—and specifically in online, e-learning contexts—Washlstedt et al. (2008: 1024) note that "a space becomes a place when meanings, constructed through social interaction, cultural identities and personal involvement are supported and embedded into the environment." In other words, "place" is what is real to people whereas "space" is a more abstract version of the place (Cresswell 2011).

However, the ways in which scholars use the terms "place" and "space" are not without disagreement. Doerr and McGuire note in the Introduction of this volume that scholars have often defined and used the terms "space" and "place" differently, and sometimes in contradictory ways. Thus, they refer to Bourdieu (1989) to further contend that the distinction between space and place is "nothing but a contestation of who gets to impose their vision (and division) of the world onto others" (Introduction: 3). Accordingly, they decided not to entertain the distinction between the two terms, and use "space" throughout the Introduction.

In reviewing literature on learning space research, Ellis and Goodyear (2016: 156) also concluded that much writing does not distinguish between "space" and "place" and often uses the terms interchangeably. Nevertheless, they observed that there is a tendency to prefer the term "place" when people's lived experience is involved. Given these discussions, since this chapter is trying to make sense of how the virtual online classroom—an abstract, conceptual space—is perceived and felt by students, I use the term "space" throughout, except for when referring to a physical location or an area with a concrete structure such as one's home or room.

2.2 (Virtual) learning space

Research concerning learning spaces seeks to understand the connections between the qualities and specific features of learning places, successful learning activities, enjoyable learning experiences, and—ultimately—good learning outcomes (Ellis and Goodyear 2016). To recognize such connections, Ellis and Goodyear (2016: 150) argue that it is necessary to understand "complex, shifting assemblages involving human beings and things: material, digital and hybrid" in a space. It is also necessary to explore students' and teachers' experiences and to foreground subjective meanings and sense-making.

Learning space research—though a relatively new field—has so far mostly been concerned with "physical" schools and universities, often referred to as a "brick and mortar" context. Ellis and Goodyear (2016: 159) illustrate a typical classroom:

> In physical learning spaces, there will normally be somewhere for students to sit, or stand, and often somewhere for a teacher to base themselves. Various tools and other artefacts will be part of the room design: projector screens, data projectors, white-boards, flipcharts, microphones and loudspeaker, spotlights, and so on. Moreover, users of the room bring tools and other artefacts with them: notepads and pens, audio-recorders, laptops, etc.

The arrangement and design of the space carry an unspoken message: the space shapes students' behaviors and actions and promotes certain types of learning as well as certain kinds of communication behaviors. In other words, the performative linguistic space of a classroom encourages and discourages certain linguistic practices.

Similar explorations and examinations need to be extended to the physical classroom's online, virtual counterpart. As Oblinger (2006: 1) argues, "space—whether physical or virtual—can have an impact on learning." Just as various tools and artifacts in a physical classroom mediate the way students learn, in the virtual spaces—such as the Zoom classroom discussed in this chapter—offer unique affordances as well as limitations. Similarly, various tools, objects, and even humans and pets in the participants' surrounding physical places interact with the students' behaviors and learning.

As online education gained prominence, research on learning spaces specific to a virtual context—"e-learning space"—began to emerge in the early 2000s. Virtual space and learning have been studied from viewpoints such as architecture, learning task design, affordances, usability, social dynamics, learner-teacher interactions, and aesthetics (White 2006). Washlstedt et al. (2018: 1025) draw upon Shepherd's (2003) discussions about four success factors for any learning space—accessibility, support for different activities, being comfortable, and being sociable—and state that the main differences between an online and traditional (in-person) learning space center around the issues of being comfortable and sociable. Thus, they call for designs that support various types of social interaction within e-learning environments. Drawing on the notion of Lave and Wenger's "community of practice," Barab, MaKinster, and Scheckler (2004) discuss the difficulty of promoting trust and a sense of community in a virtual environment (despite popular ideas and terms such as "virtual community" and "online community") because people often feel isolated and distanced, and thus cannot or are not willing to establish relationships with each other.

As shown, existing literature on virtual learning space attempts to examine its specificity and discusses various issues pertaining to the online space as a static, distinct unit that completes itself internally. In contrast, this chapter endeavors to unravel how online learning space is neither static nor internally coherent; rather, it is shaped by the spatial politics that participants bring with them as they move from in-person space to an online learning space.

2.3 Synchronous online classrooms

Research on synchronous online classrooms often highlights benefits in comparison to other modes of distance learning. White (2006) identified several advantages offered by virtual classrooms, including increased learner confidence and motivation, opportunities for immediate interaction and feedback from instructors, and new opportunities for collaborative learning activities. That is, previous research emphasizes the advantages that are derived from the online classroom's synchronicity of instruction. Furthermore, in comparison to the traditional, in-person classroom, the synchronous online classroom makes attending classes easier, from saving time (no need to commute to schools) to reducing education costs (Arbauth 2000; Manegre and Sabiri 2020). Scholars also note a better attendance rate in online classes due to the convenience of attending classes from the students' preferred locations (Nurieva and Garaeva 2020).

Oftentimes, synchronous online classrooms are viewed as simple replications of face-to-face classrooms (Hill et al. 2004). While there are features that indeed help to replicate aspects of the in-person classroom, researchers discuss "mindset" (Brad 2020)—which instructors and students alike bring to the event—as a major factor that influences and shapes the learning environment, causing differences between synchronous online classrooms and in-person classrooms. Drawing on Rehn et al. (2018), Moorhouse et al. (2021: 2) discuss specific skills that are necessary for teachers to conduct synchronous virtual classes: the ability to teach and communicate content across a screen, to engage learners using two-dimensional images, to facilitate interaction in a digital classroom, to attend to students' emotional needs across physical distances, to maintain a sense of presence despite not being physically together, and to troubleshoot technical difficulties. The importance of social presence is a well-discussed topic in online classroom research (e.g., Aragon 2003; Tu and McIsaac 2002; Yamada 2009), and Lomicka (2020) lists three principles that are necessary to harness a teacher's virtual presence and connect with students: being present, being authentic, and interacting with learners.

During the COVID-19 pandemic, Zoom, a collaborative, cloud-based videoconferencing service, became one of the dominant platforms used for online synchronous instructions (Guillen et al. 2020; Kim 2020). Zoom allows instructors to open a virtual classroom where all participants come together to communicate in real time, regardless of geographical location. Individuals connect to Zoom via a computer, tablet, or mobile device. The platform also allows live sessions to be recorded, thus enabling instructors to post the resulting video on a course management system (such as Moodle) for students to (re)view at a later date. Zoom has numerous other features, including allowing individuals to toggle their webcams on/off, to mute/unmute their microphones, to share their screens with other participants ("share screen"), and to send text messages through "chat" to the entire group or privately to a selected individual.

Now that a few years have passed since the declaration of a pandemic, researchers have analyzed various issues pertaining to language instruction in synchronous online teaching settings (almost all related to the Zoom platform)[3] during the COVID-19 pandemic. The topics investigated by these studies include students' experiences (Famularsih 2020), students' and teachers' attitudes toward the synchronous online classroom (Nurieva and Garaeva 2020), instructional designs (Chan and Wilson 2020), and teaching competencies (Moorhouse et al. 2021) that facilitate a successful synchronous online class.

The discussions presented by these recent studies can be categorized according to three aspects of the synchronous online classroom: technical, pedagogical or instructional design, and interpersonal. Studies that address the technical aspect discuss both the positive and negative features of Zoom as a tool. For example, simplicity of installation, high quality of audio and video, stable and reliable connections, and available tools (e.g., screen share, virtual background, active speaker

---

3 Kristóf (2020) lists Skype, Zoom, Google Hangouts, and Microsoft Teams as the most popular applications for videoconferencing (not necessarily in the educational context) and presents characteristics and parameters of each application. Similarly, Correia, Liu, and Xu (2020) highlight Zoom, Skype, Microsoft Teams, and WhatsApp as the most widely used videoconferencing systems in e-learning and evaluate their features regarding impact on the quality of the online educational experience. They conclude that Zoom has the highest number of learning-related features and is the most supportive system for experiential learning.

view, desktop and application sharing, private and group chat, "raise hand" function, breakout rooms) are mentioned by both students and teachers as positive features, whereas, depending on the geographical location where the study was conducted, elements such as slow Internet connections and difficulty in joining sessions are raised as problems (Famularsih 2020; Nurieva and Garaeva 2020).

Studies on the pedagogical or instructional design aspect have discussed teachers' perspectives concerning difficulties in adapting to and designing new online instruction (Chen and Wilson 2020). Specific concerns raised were the amount of work needed for preparing materials, what and how much homework to assign to students (Famularsih 2020), limited opportunities to influence students' classroom behaviors (e.g., discipline and holding attention), and the impossibility of identifying the authorship of homework submitted by students (Nurieva and Garaeva 2020).

Finally, studies that address the interpersonal aspect have raised concerns about the lack of interactivity and engagement among participants, as well as a lack of initiative and motivation by students (Famularsih 2020; Nurieva and Garaeva 2020; Moorhouse 2020; Moorhouse et al. 2021). Nrieva and Garaeva (2020) report that students remained silent, did not attempt to ask questions or offer additional information, and were indifferent and uninterested. The instructional pattern became more teacher-centered than in face-to-face sessions, and the amount of "teacher talking time" increased (Moorhouse et al. 2021: 9–10). Group and whole class discussions are characterized by longer silences and shorter student responses (Moorhouse 2020). Together, these studies highlight the difficulty in creating a learning space where students are willing to take risks to engage more with classroom activities.

While these studies present us with some insights regarding what the synchronous online classroom may look like and how it may differ from the regular face-to-face classroom, what is not discussed are reasons why students behave in the ways they do in the online space. Thus, this chapter investigates: what features or aspects of the videoconferencing tool as a performative linguistic space influence and shape the way students feel and behave, and thus influence linguistic practices? What kind of space is an online classroom as it is perceived and understood by students? How are such perceptions and understanding affected by the move away from in-person space? These are the questions I attempt to answer in order to fill the gap in the literature. Although my data and analysis are specifically about Zoom (as it was the tool I used for teaching), knowledge gained from this study is applicable to other similar platforms such as Microsoft Teams or Webex. The findings from this study not only inform technical aspects for facilitating language instruction in the field of computer-assisted learning, particularly that of synchronous online teaching, but also contribute ethnographic insights to the notion of performative linguistic space that this volume proposes.

3 Zoom classrooms as learning space during the pandemic

In March 2020, the pandemic forced most colleges and universities to close their campuses, sending students back (mostly) to their homes and to start remote online instruction. In order to have a synchronous, face-to-face learning environment, our program decided to offer all Japanese language courses via Zoom. I recorded all of my classroom sessions and posted them afterwards on Moodle (course management system) for those students who missed a class or who desired to review the lessons. There was some concern among the faculty in the department about requiring students to have their cameras on during class, as this may reveal their family's economic status or living conditions by displaying their physical surroundings. Thus, I stated in my syllabi that putting/keeping one's camera on was optional, yet recommended during the class. I made this recommendation because research shows that non-verbal cues such as facial expressions, lip movements, eye-gaze, postures, and gestures facilitate easier communication, especially in foreign language learning (Sueyoshi and Hardison 2005; Kellerman 1992; von Raffler-Engel 1980). As it happened, all of my students kept their cameras on throughout the lessons, except for when they had some technical issues such as unstable Internet connections or problems with their devices. A few students used the feature called "virtual background,"[4] possibly to block the view of their physical surroundings or else for fun.

In a whole class session ("Main room") in Zoom, I asked students to keep their audio muted when not speaking in order to minimize the background noise. When they wanted to voluntarily answer or ask questions, I encouraged them to raise their physical hands (as I told them that I could see everyone's face on my second computer screen) or simply unmute themselves and speak up. I regularly used the feature called "share screen" to show PowerPoints slides for grammar explanations, example sentences, various images to elicit students' responses, and discussion questions, as well as to watch online videos together. The students also took advantage of this function when they gave their class presentations.

---

4 The "virtual background" feature allows participants to display an image or video as your background during a Zoom Meeting.

I have also extensively used the "breakout rooms" feature. Breakout rooms allowed me to assign students to different "rooms" in which they can only interact with students in their own "room" during a designated period of time. In the breakout rooms, two to three students in each room practiced grammar exercises (in the lower-level courses) or engaged in discussions on the assigned readings (in the upper-level courses), which I thought would emulate paired or small group activities in physical classrooms. I visited each room to monitor the students' progress and to answer any questions they had. Whenever I visited the rooms, everyone's video and audio were both on, and the students confirmed during the interviews that they kept their audio and video on during the breakout-room-activities unless there was a technical problem.

To understand students' experiences and behaviors in a Zoom classroom, we need to situate the space created by Zoom within a wider social context. The COVID-19 restrictions—though they varied depending on where one lived—limited our physical movement, forcing us to stay at home as much as possible. At the beginning of March 2020, the Governor of the state where the college is located declared a state of emergency as cases of COVID-19 began to spike. Schools as well as non-essential businesses were ordered to close, and a stay-at-home advisory was issued. The college immediately responded to the mandate, closing the campus soon afterwards and resumed classes remotely after a two-week break as a time for students to relocate and for faculty members to prepare online classes. As the COVID-19 situation continued to worsen worldwide, international as well as national travel restrictions and bans were issued, people were required to wear a mask when outside of the home, social distancing of six feet apart was called for, and indoor activities and events were strictly regulated.

What COVID-19 brought about, in effect, was the emphasis of borders and boundaries between nations, regions, and households, as movements beyond the boundary were warned to be dangerous. For example, students who were studying abroad in Japan were brought back to their homes, while the students who remained on campus housing during the lockdown were not allowed to socialize with other students in the dormitory and were instructed to pick up each meal as "grab-and-go" from campus cafeterias and eat alone inside their rooms.

Ironically, in contrast to the social and physical boundaries that were reinforced as described above, within the confine of one's home or room, boundaries between various activities became blurred. For almost all students (and for other people as well), their home and room became the only place where anything was happening. Their computer screen became the portal through which they did everything from taking classes to doing homework, working, socializing, and enjoying pastimes. Situated within this unique social context—multiple layers of space, where the physical boundaries between activities are erased—is the Zoom classroom that this study is attempting to unpack.

4 The study

4.1 The college, the Japanese program, and curricula

The college I teach at is located in a small New England town in the US. It is a highly selective women's liberal arts college with about 2,800 students. The students come from 48 states and 68 countries. The college has an open curriculum and is known for its progressive, feminist-oriented education.

The Japanese program offers four years of language courses with literature/culture courses taught in English. Each year, a handful of students major or minor in Japanese language and culture. First and foremost, our language program focuses on developing oral proficiency from the very beginning of the students' language studies. The maximum number of students per course is set at 15; for upper-level courses (i.e., third- and fourth-year courses) the student numbers rarely go beyond 10. The courses for the first two years are intensive courses which meet five days a week for 50 minutes per class, whereas the third-year course meets three days a week for 75 minutes and the fourth-year course meets two days a week for 75 minutes.

Before the COVID-19 pandemic, for all in-person Japanese language courses,[5] students sit in a semi-circle facing the front of the classroom where the teacher stands in front of a whiteboard on which lesson slides will be projected. The first three semesters of the courses (i.e., first-year and the first half of the second-year courses) are based on a textbook that is grammar-focused and communicative-oriented. In these courses, the teacher briefly introduces new grammar items for the day (usually using PowerPoint), and students are instructed to practice them in small groups or in pairs. Most of the class time is spent on various types of oral activities. The teacher moves around among the groups to monitor the students' progress and to offer help if needed. During classes, students are instructed not to open the textbook or to take notes (as all materials can be found in the textbook). This is to encourage students to pay close attention to what is happening in the

---

5 Although each instructor is responsible for designing and planning their course and each individual lesson, general descriptions of Japanese courses provided here are formats and procedures agreed upon and carried out by all instructors in our program.

classroom. For similar reasons, students are not allowed to have a personal computer or digital devices (e.g., a cell phone, a tablet) out on their desks.

The fourth and fifth semester courses (i.e., the second half of the second-year and the first half of the third-year courses) use another textbook which is theme-based (rather than grammar-based), and reading and discussing themes introduced in the text are the focus of the classes. Sometimes grammar is practiced in these classes, but not to the same extent as in the lower-level courses. Classes offered in the sixth semester and beyond (i.e., second half of the third-year course and above) do not use textbooks; rather, the instructors choose authentic texts (e.g., newspaper articles, short stories, etc.) depending on the students' interests and course theme and develop their own lesson materials. For these "upper-level" courses in an in-person setting, students do have their own textbook or other reading materials out on the desk; they also take notes, as new vocabulary or expressions are incidentally introduced throughout the class. These classes, too, have pair or small group interactions as an integral part of the lessons. In a smaller, less threatening context, students first discuss the assigned reading by verifying their understanding of the texts and exchanging ideas pertaining to the reading questions. The class then reassembles as a whole, and the students verbally share their thoughts about the material.

In Zoom classrooms, the general format remained the same as the in-person classrooms. All teachers in the Japanese program tried to follow the same curriculum from the previous years, in order to maintain the consistency and integrity of the program's overarching four-year curriculum. For lower-level courses, everything that the students needed for each day's lesson was on the PowerPoint slides shared by the teacher. Since teachers cannot share their screens with students when the class is separated into breakout rooms (due to Zoom's limitations), we uploaded a PDF version of the PowerPoint to Moodle prior to the lesson. For upper-level courses, too, we shared the PDF before the class began; in these cases, the PDF also included a list of discussion questions for the breakout room activities.

Transitioning from an in-person setting to the online Zoom setting was not easy and was often frustrating for both teachers and students. There were many technical steps to follow simply to share one's screen, and if one did not do it correctly, one would lose the screen with students' faces or be unable to share the sound of audio or visual files with students. As Moorehouse (2020: 2) aptly wrote, "the VLC [videoconferencing] sessions are still more 'bumpy' . . . than face-to-face sessions."

4.2 Interview and participants

This study is based on interviews I conducted with twelve students from the second-year, third-year, and fourth-year Japanese language courses during the Fall 2020 semester. The interviews were intended to gain insights about the students' experience with Zoom classrooms, following up on the Spring 2020 survey. While the original survey was done with my first-year and third-year students (who became second-year and fourth-year, respectively), I also interviewed students from the third-year course, as I was teaching the third-year in Fall 2020 (but not Spring 2020). I did not interview the first-year students from the Fall 2020 semester, because for them the Zoom instruction was their only experience taking a Japanese course at the college level. That is, they did not have experience of moving between two spaces—i.e., in-person and online spaces—to make any comparisons.

In the Fall of 2020, I sent an email that invited all students in second-, third-, and fourth-year Japanese courses to participate in an interview. Amongst them, twelve students responded and agreed to be interviewed. All of the students had taken my courses previously or were currently enrolled at the time. I conducted interviews in English using Zoom. Each interview lasted between 30 minutes to one hour. I used the recording as well as Zoom's auto-transcription function; though the auto-transcriptions by Zoom are not very accurate, they nonetheless made it easier to transcribe the interview data.

Brief profiles of the interview participants are shown in Table 1 below. All are female, and the names are pseudonyms.

Table 1: Participants' profiles.

Name	Course level (at the time of the interview)	School year	First language	Residence (physical location when attending online classes)
Emily	2nd year	Sophomore	English	South, USA
Nikki	2nd year	Sophomore	Chinese	China
Rebecca	2nd year	Sophomore	Chinese	China
Tai-Shu	2nd year	Sophomore	Chinese	China
Amy	3rd year	Junior	English	Northeast, USA
Carrie	3rd year	Junior	Chinese	Northeast, USA
Chris	3rd year	Senior	English	Northeast, USA
Rou	3rd year	Junior	Chinese	Northeast, USA
Cathy	4th year	Senior	English/Chinese	Singapore
Eri	4th year	Sophomore	English	Northeast, USA
Josephine	4th year	Senior	English	Northeast, USA
Katy	4th year	Senior	English	Northeast, USA

5 The Zoom classrooms as performative linguistic learning space

As with in-person classrooms, the ways students feel and behave in Zoom class-rooms depend on numerous factors: class size may contribute to different degrees of intimacy among students; the length of class meetings may affect how much each student feels one can speak during the class; the degree of familiarity with one's teacher and classmates may impact how comfortable and connected one feel to others; the discussion-based class encourages students' oral participation (as opposed to lecture-based classes); whether teachers control the turn-taking or encourage free-floating interactions may affect how students engage in class discussions; and some students are naturally more talkative while others are more reserved. This chapter will show that these factors play a much stronger role in the Zoom classroom than they do in in-person classrooms.

Students described their feelings and emotions in a Zoom classroom with expressions such as "impersonal," "feel distant," "not as engaging," "less real," and "awkward." What factors evoke such feelings? Below, I compare the Zoom classroom with in-person classrooms by highlighting the ways in which student's feelings and actions—new linguistic practices—are shaped and activated by their moving from accustomed, familiar in-person spaces to a new, unfamiliar virtual space: effects of performative linguistic space.

5.1 A Zoom classroom situated in a space without boundaries

A Zoom classroom does not exist in a vacuum. As previously described, it is situated within layers of spaces. Each layer of space has its own social meaning, shaping a person to feel and behave in certain ways. Josephine described having a different mindset when attending Zoom classes as compared to physical ones:

> I think that you enter Zoom classes with a very different mindset than you do physical classes. Well, you can attend class in your pajamas in your house, and five minutes ago you just woke up, . . . versus, getting up, getting ready for school, getting in my car, driving, parking, and walking on campus in the freezing cold. So, not having that, I think definitely changes the mindset from, like 'okay, I'm here, I'm ready to learn', to 'okay I'm here, I'm going to get through this class, and then I'm going to go back to sleep'. . . . And, then also the fact that everything is online. Now what I do for leisure and what I do for school, all of them are online, and what I do for work. It's like those boundaries are gone. (Josephine, a 4th year Japanese language student)

Likewise, Katy said:

> It feels a lot different to, you know, like, go to a classroom and sit down at the desk and . . . Here it's like I roll out of my bed to my chair. And being in my room all day. I think it makes it hard for me to focus on one thing when I'm doing all that; I always do everything at the same place. (Katy, a 4th year Japanese language student)

Similar emotions were expressed by many other students. Within the confines of their own rooms, in which boundaries between activities were gone, students attended the Zoom classroom to learn and engage. For students such as Josephine and Katy, the lack of "traditional" physical movement from their own room to a classroom hindered them from directing their attention to learning—being surrounded by too many distractions did not constitute an ideal learning space for them. For others, lack of movement and being in their own familiar space affected them in the opposite way, ushering them to feel safe and be ready to participate in learning. In both cases, students were keenly aware that they were not simply "in" or "out" of a classroom space; they were simultaneously occupying multiple spaces, each with competing forces.

5.2 Emulating an in-person learning space

5.2.1 "Camera on" to mimic physical face-to-face interactions

As described earlier, because of the emphasis and importance placed on the development of oral communication skills in Japanese language courses, all of the interviewed students felt that it was important to see each others' faces by having their cameras on during the class. Keeping the camera on made the Zoom class feel "more like being in in-person class" (Amy, Tai-Shu). It allowed them to see each others' facial expressions and body language, which made it "easier, especially in a foreign language; if you don't have the right word, your expression kind of helps you [in] conveying your meaning" (Amy). It was a way to feel "a sense of interacting with a real person" (Tai-Shu), to make it "a little more conversational" (Eri), and to signal that they are "being respectful to others by expressing [that] I'm listening to you" (Tai-Shu), all of which "makes it more humane" (Rou). In other words, keeping a camera on helps a Zoom classroom to emulate the experience of everyone being in the same place.

While keeping a camera on and reading others' facial expressions and body language help to facilitate better communication, the two-dimensional aspect of the camera does not provide a full range of cues with which to convey one's intentions. One of the major concerns that all students raised was a fear of "overlapping" with other persons or "interrupt[ing] or speak[ing] at the wrong time" (Chris). To avoid such moments, students paid close attention to other students' facial expressions and body language displayed on a screen trying to read other's intentions, or "just stay silent." Nevertheless, as Katy explained, "It's kind of harder for me to tell because everyone's just kind of sitting there like straight-faced and it's really hard for me to tell if someone's right about to, you know, say something or not. And so I think I hesitate more to say something."

In the in-person classroom, it is not just facial expressions but other cues (such as the way one is sitting and carrying their body, the direction of gaze, etc.) that help us gauge other people's intentions. As Chris said, "physical cues sort of get lost when we are all heads, two-dimensional heads." While all Japanese courses at this college contained fewer than fifteen students—small enough for all of the participants' faces to fit on one page on the screen (in gallery view)—in larger classes, one student said that she did "click through all pages to check on before [she] speaks" (Josephine). Even though overlapping talk does occur in a regular in-person classroom and reading everyone's face is nearly impossible due to the semi-circle seating arrangement, lack of physical proximity to each other in the online space amplified the students' fears. As Moorhouse et al. (2021: 2) note, "multimodal actions (gesture, facial expression, etc.) that aid teaching and inter-action in [face-to-face] classrooms can operate in a very different way in [syn-chronous online lessons] depending on the access and position of cameras and participants' screen size ratio." Moorhouse et al. (2021) further state that it is not the lack of "faces" that differentiates the synchronous online classroom from the physical classroom, but rather the physical proximity and presence of the teach-ers and learners.

In the Zoom classroom, not only did students feel the need to read others' faces (and body movements) in the hope of having better interactions, but keep-ing one's video on also functioned as a mechanism to impose self-discipline by being seen by the instructor. As Katy explained, "if I have my video on, I feel like the professor is more likely to look at me and then I feel more pressure not to like, look at my phone or not to read on another page because I feel like it might be obvious."

On one hand, attending a regular in-person class forces students to physically leave their own room/house and to enter another space that has a specific pur-pose: to learn. The physical classroom—a learning space—is designed for learn-ing to occur by minimizing factors that lead to distractions and is intended to be used for that specific purpose only. On the other hand, when attending class on-line via Zoom from their own rooms, students are surrounded by many distrac-tions without surveillance by the instructor and their classmates. Having one's "camera on" is one way for students to keep themselves "accountable" (Amy) and "more focused" (Carrie, Eri, Tai-Shu) on the tasks at hand.

5.2.2 "Breakout rooms" to recreate physical small group activities

In my daily instructions via Zoom, I took maximum advantage of the "breakout rooms" function and had students spend the majority of class time in pairs or in small groups. I did so with the hopes of reproducing a learning context associated with physical, face-to-face classrooms, thus promoting student interactions. Indeed, previous scholars (e.g., Gonzalez-Lloret 2020; Payne 2020) have proposed the utilization of breakout rooms for this very purpose. During both physical and online small group activities, students in the lower-level courses were assigned grammar exercises to practice orally, and students in the upper-level courses helped each other to understand the reading assignments and discussed the assigned questions before returning to a whole class discussion.

Students felt and behaved differently depending on whether they were in the whole class space (main room) or in breakout rooms. The small size of the breakout rooms was more conducive for encouraging students to engage in interactions with their classmates. Students said that being in the breakout space made them "most comfortable" (Emily) and "easier to have communication" (Josephine) which "is similar" (Carrie) to a regular classroom, yet "not exactly the same . . . without someone's [physical] presence" (Cathy). The students further explained what made the small group activities in breakout rooms different from a regular classroom was that there was no way to seek immediate help or response from the teacher as well as the (deafening) silence in the background—characteristic of breakout rooms, as I will discuss later.

Both instructor and students together tried to create a similar performative linguistic space (a language classroom) that they are familiar with, yet, as shown, numerous spatial factors prevented a Zoom classroom from simply emulating an in-person classroom. Meaning, purposes and behaviors that people experientially associated with a particular place (i.e., one's own room) were in conflict with allowing the *intended* performative linguistic space to emerge; what resulted was a new, different kind of performative linguistic space.

5.3 Multi-tasking behind the screen

In a Zoom classroom, students are juggling multiple tasks mentally as well as physically. For example, for a simple task such as asking a question, students went through taxing thinking processes as Carrie's words illuminate:

> When I'm in an in-person environment, I just naturally jump in because it feels natural just to jump in. But in an online environment, I sometimes debate whether I should just jump

in, or if you're going to call on someone, or if I should raise my physical hand or raise my virtual hand . . . and now it's so much more complicated. (Carrie, a 3rd year Japanese language student)

Physically, students were also busy multitasking on screen: trying to read others' faces, looking at lesson materials (e.g., PowerPoints and online reading texts), checking the course management system (Moodle), consulting online-dictionaries or online-translators, etc.

Students also engaged in multiple layers of interaction during class. When physically present together in class, "nudging" (Emily) or "poking" (Chris) a nearby classmate to have a small chat or to ask for help is a natural behavior. But in a Zoom classroom, they could not do that "without having it broadcast to the entire class" (Emily).[6] Being in separate places but attending the same space forced many students to seek other means to connect to each other. "To alleviate ways when it gets very confusing" (Cathy), students established a support system to compensate for the lack of physical presence of classmates, using other communication tools for texting (e.g., WeChat, Messages):

> Once in a while I'll use my phone. If I'm really confused, I'll message my friend and be like, do you understand this, am I just lost, should I ask about it, kind of thing. (Eri, a 4th year Japanese language student)

> Sometimes if we didn't get what you say, or just lose some connection with the Internet or just we have a little confusion, we just ask what happened. (Rebecca, a 2nd year Japanese language student)

Activities undertaken by students in the Zoom classrooms were not necessarily all "on-task," but could also be "off-task," as Katy's previously introduced quote suggested ("look at my phone"; "read . . . another page [on the Internet]"). When attending a Zoom classroom, even though the students were facing the computer screen as though paying attention to what was officially happening in class, they could be looking at a completely different Internet site or doing something totally unrelated (e.g., browsing the Internet or chatting with friends).

Accordingly, the students were in multiple spaces simultaneously in addition to the learning space in which the teacher was trying to conduct the day's lesson. While similar multitasking phenomena may happen to a certain degree in regular face-to-face classes, the types of off-task activities—as well as the extent to which they are practiced—differ considerably in online spaces, due to the fact that

---

6 Although students can chat with each other privately using the Zoom's function of private "chat," according to the students I interviewed, they never used the function for fear of sending a message by mistake to the entire group (including the teacher).

students are not allowed to have any computer devices out (including phones) during the in-person Japanese classes.

5.4 Feeling awkward and being complicit in creating a silent space

"Awkward" is the word most frequently and repeatedly used to describe some of the moments in the Zoom classroom by the interviewed students. Examples of what made them feel awkward included when "no one says anything [and is] just sitting there straight-faced" (Katy), or in a breakout room where "[it's] just me and them, and it's completely silent until one of us starts to speak" (Emily), unlike regular in-person classrooms where there was always background noise and students could hear other people talking and engaging in activities. In a Zoom classroom, "silence" seems to be one of the defining features that constitute the space. Silence evoked the students' feeling of "awkwardness," yet they themselves often participated in creating the silent space due to their fear of overlapping—one of the reasons they remain silent.

5.4.1 Assessing the worth of one's own words for "unmuting" and when on "speaker view"

In the Zoom environment, muting oneself when one is not speaking is considered proper etiquette so as not to disturb others with unexpected background noise. Though it seems like a minute detail, the step of unmuting oneself in order to speak up caused some students to remain silent. As Tai-Shu noted, "you need to click the button, which has one more step. So, it will prevent me from asking questions."

Several students perceived this technical aspect of the mute/unmute process as also symbolizing the worthiness of their utterances, thus affecting their willingness to speak up.

> I have to have a profound question because I not only have to have a question, I need to then figure out how I'm going to ask the question in Japanese. I would have to be really, really, really confused and really, really have a question to actually unmute, pop up, and ask it. [You need] more confidence in asking questions. (Carrie, a 3rd year Japanese language student)

Similarly, Eri said:

In a regular class, I could just like jump in and say the smallest thing. But [in a Zoom class-room] if I unmute myself, I feel like I have to have a fully formed thought. I feel like I can't just say like, "Oh yeah, I agree". . . . I feel like I have to create a new idea or like really build on top of somebody else's point. I think I feel more nervous to purposely raise my hand or unmute myself, and I'm going to say something, instead of just saying it. It is very different. So, there's more tension within myself, I guess. (Eri, a 4th year Japanese language student)

Another technical aspect that affected the ways in which students participated in class was the feature called "speaker view" in which Zoom automatically displays a large view of the speaker who it believes is speaking. For some students, this feature caused anxiety and led to a fear of making mistakes. As Emily explained:

It projects you in front of all the people. It highlights you, especially if you're on speaker view . . . So, it feels like people's undivided attention is on you whereas when you're in a [regular] classroom, you can still be listening to them, but looking around the room or look-ing at someone else or looking at the professor instead of looking at the person who is actu-ally talking . . . It's a little bit scarier to make mistakes, because everyone can hear those mistakes and of course you're on the big screen when you do make those mistakes. And I know we shouldn't be afraid of making mistakes when we [are] learning language; that's a part of the process, but there's always a little bit of nervousness that comes with it. (Emily, a 2nd year Japanese language student)

Even though using the language—expressing ideas, asking questions, and making mistakes—is the most fundamental and necessary part of learning a language (and all of our students are aware of this), some features of Zoom simply work against the goal of language learning.

5.4.2 Hiding behind the screen

All of the students that I interviewed said that they became quieter and speak less in a Zoom classroom. They said that because they "can hide behind the computer" (Josephine), they generally feel less pressure to speak up. Katy tried to make sense of her own such behavior:

I'm not sure if I know exactly why, but I think somehow it doesn't seem as real, or not as high stakes when you're online. Whereas if you're in a classroom with the teacher, I feel like there's more pressure. You know, the teacher is like looking around at each student, you know, waiting for someone to say or answer the question. Yeah, so I guess maybe on-line, there's less physical or emotional pressure to speak up. It feels like, it's everyone's si-lent and it's easier to just stay silent than to break through and be the one to speak up. (Katy, a 4th year Japanese language student)

It was usually the teacher who took up the task of filling such silent moments—the "awkward" moments—by calling on each student one by one. Consequently, this routine reinforced the traditional foreign language classroom discourse of the initiation-response-feedback (IRF) and the initiation-response-evaluation (IRE) interaction patterns (Thoms 2012). These patterns are quite dominant in in-person classrooms, particularly in lower-level language courses; however, breaking away from such patterns, and having free-floating interactions, is often considered essential in upper-level language classrooms. The implications of re-establishing this classroom discourse pattern in Zoom classrooms—even in upper-level courses —will be addressed later in this chapter.

The students' subjectivities, experiences and beliefs about what is to be a "good student"—e.g., paying attention, being cooperative, willing to participate, etc.—in a language classroom as well as the politics of learning were carried into this online performative linguistic space where certain linguistic practices were hindered and even silenced due to students feeling awkward, trying not to overlap, and wondering whether their words had worth.

5.5 Feeling "safe" in a familiar place

For some students, the feeling of "less pressure" to speak up when hiding behind the computer seems to be derived from a sense of security. Amy, who "liked the online class better" than the in-person class, said:

> I'm still in my room so I feel like I'm kind of in a safe space. So, I feel less pressure, because in the back of my head, I know that if I have to, I can just like leave without intruding on anybody. So, there's that safety net. (Amy, a 3rd year Japanese language student)

Unlike a large lecture course in which a student can quietly sneak out of the room without anyone noticing, leaving a physical face-to-face Japanese language classroom with fewer than 10 students (and everyone sitting in a semi-circle) would certainly draw attention to oneself, requiring one to provide an excuse for leaving. However, in a Zoom classroom, students do not have as many physical and psychological restrictions and feel less pressure to be in front of the camera all of the time.

Similarly, being behind the computer and thus being in a physically separate place from others gave some students, particularly those with social anxiety, a sense of comfort. Rebecca explained:

> I think Zoom is basically supportive for those who have social anxiety. Because we are not really like meeting others, face-to-face, so it reduces kind of anxiety by using Zoom than [if]

we are in normal class. Because we are not really face-to-face to see others, it's kind of safe behind this computer. (Rebecca, a 2nd year Japanese language student)

All of these students' comments highlight the situatedness of the Zoom classroom. It does not exist separately or independently from its social context; it exists at the intersection of a familiar, safe place and a virtual space with some uncertainty. For some students, their physical location—a familiar place—becomes a distraction that interferes with their focus on participating in learning activities in the virtual space; for others, a sense of security and control gained from knowing that they are in their own safe place (that is, physically distanced from a potentially unnerving, stressful place) allows them to be more confident and engaging. On the whole, students were keenly aware that they are simultaneously "in" and "not in" a classroom space. This is to show the way in which individual students interpret the emerging performative linguistic space—and subsequently feel, act and carry out communicative practice—differs significantly, which creates a complex, unique learning space.

5.6 Being in the same plane of space

One interesting observation that students made was the ease of feeling connected with the instructor afforded by the aforementioned "gallery view"[7] feature. In a physical classroom space, the arrangement of a room communicates the power relationships between the teacher and the students, as well as the rules and expectations that students need to follow (Blum 2020; Oblinger 2006). As described earlier, students sit in a semi-circle facing the teacher during in-person Japanese language courses at my institution. The teacher stands in front of a whiteboard when conducting the lesson, and the students are expected to face both the teacher and the whiteboard. Alternatively, if the room has a seminar table, the teacher sits at the head of the table and students sit a certain distance from the teacher around the table. In either case, there exists a separation and boundary between the teacher and the students.

In contrast, in a Zoom classroom, because everyone is in the "same plane of space" on screen (at least in gallery view), it communicated to some students a sense of equal footing or egalitarianism. Katy said:

---

7 The "gallery view" feature lets users see thumbnail-sized faces in a grid pattern. Participants have to manually select this mode.

> If you're [in an] in-person class, I always feel there's a little bit of a separation between the teacher and the students, because, you know, you come to the classroom and the students are all sitting at desks kind of together, and when the teacher comes and the teacher is kind of at the head of the class in a separate space. But on Zoom, you know, if the teacher opens the Zoom call and then students start to trickle in, you're all in this same plane of space. And I think it's easier to kind of see the teacher as just one of you, in the same group. (Katy, a 4th year Japanese language student)

Ironically, the sense of equal footing that some students felt with the teacher seems to have contributed to the most troubling characteristic of a Zoom classroom voiced by the upper-level students: the sense of "disconnect" amongst the students. According to them, students were focusing almost exclusively on the instructor, and not on their classmates.

> I think it's quite sad because we haven't been reacting to each other. I think we are talking to a teacher, but we don't really talk with the other students. When we're doing discussion right now, it is like "what do you think, Cathy?" or "what do you think, Josephine?," but I don't think many of us react to each other. (Cathy, a 4th year Japanese language student)

> If you know that the teacher is gonna just call on different people all in a row, then you learn to expect that. And then you start preparing yourself for the teacher's question . . . I think I am less likely to try to build off of someone else's thing; I'm more focused on the question posed by the teacher. And maybe that is [because of] the expectation that I'm going to be called on. Or like the teacher is going to ask me to answer makes [me] kind of focus on the question and not as much on what's being said about the question by other students. (Katy, a 4th year Japanese language student)

The sense of disconnect amongst students may be an (unfortunate) outcome resulting from various factors, all co-constructed by both the teacher and students. In a Zoom classroom, students become quieter due to a multitude of reasons as discussed above. In response, the teacher tends to resort to calling on each student, resulting in teacher-dominant, or teacher-centered interactional patterns (Moorhouse 2020), which then becomes a routine or an unspoken norm. This leads to a resurgence of the traditional IRE/IRF classroom discourse pattern discussed earlier. While this pattern, in general, is more dominant in the lower-level language classes, as the lessons tend to focus on having students practice new grammar patterns orally, it becomes much less prevalent in the upper-level language classes (at least the Japanese classes in our program), as these classes are organized around the discussions and exchange of ideas about assigned texts, not the practicing of grammar patterns.

This interactional pattern is precisely the reason why, per the Spring 2020 surveys, upper-level students described their online classroom experiences as being "very different" from in-person courses. In contrast, the lower-level students, whose answers in the survey indicated that there was "not much difference" in the regular classroom and the Zoom classroom, explained their feelings about the Zoom classroom as follows:

> Because we are still meeting together. It's synchronous and we still can see, face to face, and answer questions. So, it's like normal. And we also have breakout room[s]. So it's the same in class. (Rebecca, a 2nd year Japanese language student)

> Feel[s] like there's not a big difference; like we do talk to each other and complete the tasks, just [does] not feel so real. (Tai-Shu, a 2nd year Japanese language student)

For these students, the norm of classroom interactions is to "answer the questions" and "complete the tasks," rather than to have more organic conversations with each other. Their understanding and expectations regarding what interactions mean in the foreign language classroom was carried over from in-person space to the virtual space and were not strongly impacted in the Zoom environment.

Reflecting on the pre-COVID-19 days, many students treasured the moments before and after class when they could "just sit down next to someone and just to learn more about them" (Katy) in a classroom. In contrast, "everyone shows up for Zoom classes right on the dot" (Josephine) and "when it ends class, we leave fast. We don't really walk out with people . . . when you go into the Zoom room, you really don't talk about other things" (Cathy). Those fringe moments—spaces—that afford organic interactions in an in-person classroom are not really "fringe" but are the catalyst for nurturing the senses of familiarity, friendship, and trust that push students to be courageous to speak up and to not be afraid of making mistakes in the classroom. That being lost, students tried to figure out the new routines for class behaviors, to find ways to compensate for the lost communication cues, to renew and establish relationships with the teacher and their classmates, and, ultimately, to learn a language. In order for a space to be conducive and effective for learning—especially for a foreign language—it needs to be a place where all students feel safe and comfortable. What is fundamentally necessary to create such a space is "a sense of community" or a "feeling of comradery" shared by all who occupied the space (Rovai 2002a, 2002b).

6 Discussion

This chapter has demonstrated that a Zoom classroom is a space where a multitude of factors—technical, physical, psychological, and discursive—are intertwined in complex ways, creating an unfamiliar, uncertain learning space. When attending a class via Zoom, students are simultaneously inhabiting multiple spaces with different—often, conflicting—social meanings and significance. Even though our faces are all projected onto the same screen, that does not necessarily mean that we all are in the same space. Likewise, the performative linguistic space that was activated was interpreted differently, impacting how individual students engaged in learning and communicative practices in a Zoom classroom. Although Zoom makes it possible to mimic certain elements of a physical in-person classroom through live face-to-face interactions, many other elements that are important for encouraging and motivating students to be confident and courageous are hard to recreate in that space. Most importantly, the physical presence of other people—lively sounds of chatters, bodies sitting close enough to "nudge" or "poke," or reactions to a shared moment via the quiet exchange of a smile or a sarcastic look—does not exist in the Zoom classroom. As this study as well as other studies show (Aragon 2003; Tu and McIsaac 2002; Wut and Xu 2021; Yamada 2009), social presence of others is essential in creating successful e-learning spaces.

On the one hand, the "silent space" that is co-constructed by Zoom's features and the students' feelings and behaviors worked against producing an optimal space for learning a foreign language, especially one that emphasizes oral proficiency. If the focus of the language instruction were on writing or translation, for example, it would probably not have as much impact. On the other hand, students who perceived the Zoom classroom as a "safe space" felt secure and comfortable, ushering them to engage more in learning. Indeed, students' feelings and perceptions have an effect on the learning processes and outcomes (Wahlstedt et al. 2008; Whitelock et al. 2000). While Leimeister et al. (2006) argue that "a technically efficient platform is the most important success factors [sic] for a virtual community," as Wahlstedt, et al. (2008) remind us, the focus in designing virtual learning spaces should not be solely on technologies, but on their affordances for promoting social interactions.

In a Zoom classroom, students are not only learning the subject matter, but also learning new routines and expectations (both technical and interpersonal) in order to participate in activities and to relate to others in a novel learning space. New routines and expectations are created not only by the limitations and affordances Zoom as a technological tool presents; they are also affected by the participants' linguistic practices, which are shaped by the Zoom classroom acting as a performative linguistic space, bringing new social norms and social practices into being.

7 Conclusions

Synchronous virtual classrooms amid the COVID-19 pandemic offered a unique and peculiar learning space. Unlike online instruction during "normal" times, it was forced upon us by a deadly virus, leaving us with no other options for continuing our educational endeavors. Under the COVID-19 restrictions in place, I, as a teacher, tried to replicate the in-person classroom space with Zoom by taking advantage of features such as video, breakout rooms, screen sharing, etc. Naively, I thought being able to see each other's faces would allow everyone to feel as though they were in the same space and thus continued to rely on our previous methods of teaching and learning a language. However, moving from physical to virtual learning spaces revealed that what we previously thought of as "normal" and took for granted are the products of performative linguistic spaces. Each space shapes the ways in which people interact, relate to others, and perform communication practices.

When I was writing this chapter in the summer of 2021, one-and-half years since we shifted to fully online teaching, we were uncertain as to whether we could go back to regular in-person classes for the following academic year. The findings from this study provide us with insights into why students behave the way they do in synchronous virtual classrooms. Understanding how performative linguistic space shapes people's communication practice allows us also to change and alter the ways in which we design courses and engage in teaching practices. It prepares us to have a conversation with students about clear guidelines and expectations in order to facilitate interactions and to lessen their anxieties or insecurities about learning in a virtual space, thus allowing us to take advantage of synchronous online instruction, both during and after the age of COVID-19.

References

Aragon, Steven R. 2003. Creating social presence in online environments. *New Directions for Adult and Continuing Education* (100). 57–68.

Arbaugh, J. Ben. 2000. Virtual classroom characteristics and student satisfaction with internet-based MBA courses. *Journal of Management Education* 24 (1). 32–54.

Barab, Sasha A., James G. MaKinster & Rebecca Scheckler. 2004. Characterizing an online professional development community. In Sasha A. Barab, Rob Kling & James H. Gray (eds.), *Designing for virtual communities in the service of learning*, 53–90. Cambridge: Cambridge University Press.

Bligh, Brett & Charles Crook. 2017. Learning spaces. In Erik Duval, Mike Sharples & Rosamund Sutherland (eds.), *Technology enhanced learning*, 69–87. Springer. DOI: 10.1007/978-3-319-02600-8_7

Blum, Susan D. 2020. Why we're exhausted by Zoom. *Inside Higher Education*. https://www.insidehigh ered.com/advice/2020/04/22/professor-explores-why-Zoom-classes-deplete-her-energy-opinion (accessed 1 November 2020)

Bourdieu, Pierre. 1989. Social space and symbolic power. *Sociological Theory* 7(1). 14–25.

Chan, Chun Chuen Billy & Owen Wilson. 2020. Using Chakowa's digitally enhanced learning model to adapt face-to-face EAP materials for online teaching and learning. *International Journal of TESOL Studies 2* (1). 83–98. DOI: 10.46451/ijts.2020.06.06

Cheung, Anisa. 2021. Language teaching during a pandemic: A case study of Zoom use by a secondary ESL teacher in Hong Kong. *RELC Journal*, 1–16. DOI: 10.1177/0033688220981784

Correia, Ana-Paula, Chenxi Liu & Fan Xu (2020). Evaluating videoconferencing systems for the quality of the educational experience. *Distance Education* 41 (4). 429–452. DOI: 10.1080/01587919.2020.1821607

Cresswell, Tim. 2004. *Place: A short introduction*. Malden, MA: Blackwell Ltd.

Cresswell, Tim. 2011. Defining place. In Margaret Himley & Anne Fitzsimmons (eds.), *Critical encounters with texts: Finding a place to stand*. 7th edn., 127–136. Pearson Custom Publishing.

Ellis, Robert A. & Peter Goodyear. 2016. Models of learning space: Integrating research on space, place and learning in higher education. *Review of Education* 4 (2). 149–191.

Famularsih, Sari. 2020. Students' experiences in using online learning applications due to COVID-19 in English classroom. *Studies in Learning and Teaching* 1 (2). 112–121.

Ghazal, Samar, Zarina Samsudin & Hanan Aldowah. 2015. Students' perception of synchronous courses using Skype-based video conferencing. *Indian Journal of Science and Technology* 8 (30). 1–9.

Guillén, Gabriel, Thor Sawin & Netta Avineri. 2020. Zooming out of the crisis: Language and human collaboration. *Foreign Language Annals* 53. 320–328.

Harasim, Linda. 2000. Shift happens: Online education as a new paradigm in learning. *The Internet and Higher Education* 3 (1–2). 41–61.

Helm, Francesca & Sarah Guth. 2016. Telecollaboration and language learning. In Fiona Farr & Liam Murray (eds.), *The Routledge handbook of language learning and technology*, 267–280. New York: Routledge.

Hill, Janette R., David Wiley, Laurie Miller Nelson & Seungyeon Han. 2004. Exploring research on Internet based learning: From infrastructure to interactions. In David Jonassen & Marcy Driscoll (eds.), *Handbook of research for educational communications and technology*, 2nd edn., 437–464. New York: Routledge.

Kellerman, Susan. 1992. "I see what you mean": The role of kinesic behaviour in listening and implications for foreign and second language learning. *Applied Linguistics* 13. 239–281.

Kim, Joshua. 2020. Teaching and learning after COVID-19: Three post-pandemic predictions. *Inside Higher Education*. https://www.insidehighered.com/digital-learning/blogs/learning-innovation/teaching-and-learning-after-covid-19 (accessed 1 November 2020)

Kristóf, Zsolt. 2020. International trends of remote teaching ordered in light of the Coronavirus (COVID-19) and its most popular video conferencing applications that implement communication. *Central European Journal of Educational Research* 2 (2). 84–92. DOI: 10.37441/CEJER/2020/2/2/7917

Lave, Jean & Etienne Wenger. 1991. *Situated learning: Legitimate peripheral participation*. New York: Cambridge University Press.

Leimeister, Jan Marco, Pascal Sidiras & Helmyt Kremar. 2006. Exploring success factors of virtual communities: The perspectives of members and operators. *Journal of Organizational Computing and Electric Commerce* 16 (3/4). 277–298.

Lomicka, Lara. 2020. Creating and sustaining virtual language communities. *Foreign Language Annals* 53. 306–313.

Manegre, Marni & Kashir Ali Sabiri. 2020. Online language learning using virtual classrooms: An analysis of teacher perceptions. *Computer Assisted Language Learning*. 1–16.

Massey, Doreen. 2005. *For space*. London: SAGE publications.

Merrick, Brad. 2020. Changing mindset, perceptions, learning, and tradition: An "adaptive teaching framework" for teaching music online. *International Journal on Innovations in Online Education* 4 (2). DOI: 10.1615/IntJInnovOnlineEdu.2020035150

Moorhouse, Benjamin Luke. 2020. Adaptations to a face-to-face initial teacher education course "forced" online due to the COVID-19 pandemic. *Journal of Education for Teaching* 46 (4). 609–611.

Moorhouse, Benjamin Luke, Yenna Li & Steve Walsh. 2020. E-classroom interactional competencies: Mediating and assisting language learning during synchronous online lessons. *RELC Journal*. 1–15.

Nurieva, Guzel R. & Leila M. Garaeva. 2020. Zoom-based distance learning of English as a foreign language. *Journal of Research in Applied Linguistics* 11. 439–448.

O'Rourke, Breffni. 2007. Models of telecollaboration (1): eTandem. In Robert O'Dowd (ed.), *Online intercultural exchange: An introduction for foreign language teachers*, 41–61. Bristol, UK: Multilingual Matters.

Oblinger, Diana. 2006. Space as a change agent. In Diana Oblinger (ed.), *Learning spaces*. Brockport Bookshelf. 78. Educause. http://digitalcommons.brockport.edu/bookshelf/78 (accessed 1 November 2020)

Payne, J. Scott. 2020. Developing L2 productive language skills online and the strategic use of instructional tools. *Foreign Language Annals* 53 (2). 243–249.

Pulichino, Joe. 2005. Current trends in e-learning. *Research Report*. The Learning Guild.

Raffler-Engel, Walburga von. 1980. Kinesics and paralinguistic: A neglected factor in second-language research and teaching. *Canadian Modern Language Review* 36 (2). 225–237.

Rehn, Nicki, Dorit Maor & Andrew McConney. 2018. The specific skills required of teachers who deliver K–12 distance education courses by synchronous videoconference: Implications for training and professional development. *Technology, Pedagogy and Education* 27 (4). 417–429.

Rovai, Alfred P. 2002a. A preliminary look at structural differences in sense of classroom community between higher education traditional and ALN courses. *Journal of Asynchronous Learning Networks* 5 (3). 41–56.

Rovai, Alfred P. 2002b. Building sense of community at a distance. *International Review of Research in Open and Distance Learning* 3 (1). 1–6.

Shepherd, Clive. 2003. *E-learning's greatest hits*. Brighton, UK: Above and Beyond.

Sueyoshi, Ayano & Debra M. Hardison. 2005. The role of gestures and facial cues in second language listening comprehension. *Language Learning* 55 (4). 661–699.

Thoms, Joshua J. 2012. Classroom discourse in foreign language classrooms: A review of the literature. *Foreign Language Annals* 45 (s1). 8–27.

Tu, Chih-Hsiung & Marina McIsaac. 2002. The relationship of social presence and interaction in online classes. *The American Journal of Distance Education* 16 (3). 131–150.

Wallace, Raven M. 2003. Online learning in higher education: A review of research on interactions among teachers and students. *Education, Communication & Information* 3 (2). 241–280.

Wang, Yuping. 2004. Supporting synchronous distance language learning with desktop videoconferencing. *Language Learning and Technology* 8 (3). 90–121.

Wang, Yuping & Chengzheng Sun. 2001. Internet-based real time language education: Towards a fourth generation distance education. *CALICO Journal* 18 (3). 539–561.

Wang, Yuping, Nian-Shing Chen & Nuke Levy. 2010. Teacher training in a synchronous cyber face-to-face classroom: Characterizing and supporting the online teachers' learning process. *Computer Assisted Language Learning* 23 (4). 277–293.

Ware, Paige & Robert O'Dowd. 2008. Peer feedback on language form in telecollaboration. *Language Learning & Technology* 12 (1). 43–63.

Washlstedt, Ari, Samuli Pekkola & Marketta Niemelä. 2008. From e-learning space to e-learning place. *British Journal of Education Technology* 39 (6). 1020–1030.

White, Cynthia. 2006. Distance learning of foreign languages. *Language Teaching* 39, 247–264.

Whitelock, Denise, Daniela Romano, Anne Jelfs & Paul Brna. 2000. Perfect presence: What does this mean for the design of virtual learning environments? *Education and Information Technologies* 5 (4). 277–289.

Wut, Tai-ming & Jing Xu. 2021. Person-to-person interactions in online classroom settings under the impact of COVID-19: A social presence theory perspective. *Asia Pacific Education Review*. 1–13. DOI: 10.1007/s12564-021-09673-1 (accessed 1 June 2021)

Yamada, Masanori. 2009. The role of social presence in learner-centered communicative language learning using synchronous computer-mediated communication: Experimental study. *Computers & Education* 52 (4). 820–833.

Jennifer M. McGuire

Deaf in hearing spaces: Performative linguistic spaces shaped by audism, phonocentrism, and linguistic ideologies

1 Introduction

Whether named or not, space is intrinsic to deaf experiences. Deafness as viewed through the medical model is an audiological condition related to genetics or illness, irrespective of space. However, a shift to deaf *ways of being* reveals the processes that create and reflect deaf and hearing spaces and associated linguistic practices. Scholars in diverse fields have demonstrated how linguistic practices shape space, but "space" is not an optional subject of study when exploring the experiences of users of sign languages; it is intrinsic to the modality. For signing deaf people, "communication *is* space, and space *is* communication" (Gulliver & Fekete 2017: 125, emphasis in original). However, as I explore in this chapter, many deaf children are not signers. They are often situated in spaces (primarily, the home and the school) where spoken language communication is expected and, at times, demanded. These "hearing spaces" stand in contrast to "deaf spaces."

The opportunity to be introduced to deaf spaces in infancy and early childhood largely depends on the composition of the family. Only an estimated 4% of deaf children are born into families with a deaf parent (Mitchell & Karmcher 2004). Excluding those statistical minorities, deaf children are born into families with a "hearing culture"—a concept which eludes a clear definition (Richardson 2019)—that is likely to have an auditory orientation to the world. Since most children are born into these circumstances, their first introduction to language and social norms occurs in the home as a hearing space. Therefore, whether deaf children encounter deaf people in deaf spaces at all during their formative years becomes dependent on their educational path. Even though hearing people are the gatekeepers in deaf education—and these types of gatekeepers hold power over social bodies (Bourdieu 1977)—schools for the deaf are seen as one of the four "pillars" of deaf culture (Eickman, 2004; Lane, Hoffmeister, Bahan 1996). Schools for the deaf hold a place of nostalgia for deaf people (Ladd 2003)—despite oppressive treatment of deaf children at the hands of educators and eras of language oppression. Although ideologically one of the pillars, in reality, the deaf school experience is becoming progressively rare. Increasingly, deaf

https://doi.org/10.1515/9783110744781-005

children find themselves in hearing (spoken language) spaces until graduating from senior high school.

Globally, education through sign language is not the norm. Most deaf children are educated in spoken language settings. According to the WHO, only one to two percent of deaf people in the world are educated through sign language (WFD 2022). Sign languages' potential for production and reception through space and lack of orthography has made them vulnerable to proscription and "linguistic bigotry" (Lane 1992: 107–108). Periods of sign language bans and restrictions have occurred in schools for the deaf throughout the world, and Japan, the site of this ethnography, is no exception (see historical review in Oka and Sasaki 2020). Further, audism and phonocentrism (Bauman 2008) have resulted in a devaluation of communication which does not involve sound and speech, as I will discuss later in the chapter. At the same time, the statistics on education through sign language do not account for the deaf children who are not formally educated through sign language but may informally share sign language communication with their peers and develop a deaf habitus.

Deaf individuals traverse hearing and deaf spaces, carrying ideologies and dispositions with this movement. Habitus shapes how one enters a space and how one responds to it. The dominant habitus in society tends to be transferred to the cultural habitus of the school (Bourdieu and Passeron 1977). Since youth educated in schools for the deaf and in mainstream schools have similar experiences within the family, education becomes a point of divergence with students in schools for the deaf developing social skills and techniques in deaf spaces. Children who enter mainstream (so-called "regular") schools encounter spoken language hegemony. In these formal hearing spaces, audism (individual and institutional) is intrinsically linked to the linguistic capital associated with spoken languages. To navigate these spaces, speech is not only needed but highly valued since communicative competence in the dominant national language(s) confers symbolic capital (Bourdieu 1991). Deaf students, due to sensorial differences, do not have equal access to this capital. In this chapter, I demonstrate how situating deaf students in hearing spaces with incomplete access results in what could be considered a distinct "hybrid habitus" (Lo and Stacey 2008) and how spatial politics from hearing spaces can be brought into deaf ones. Both hearing and deaf spaces are performative linguistic spaces in that they encourage and discourage certain forms of signed and spoken linguistic practices based on linguistic ideologies.

While agreeing with Reay's argument (2004) that habitus is an overused framework in education related studies and one that is often applied to data uncritically, I maintain that Bourdieu's concept has proven illuminating in studies of deaf people's experiences by interpreting habitus as a "physiological and a sociological phenomenon" (Richardson 2019: 166). When applying habitus in this way to deaf experiences, we begin to see how "Deaf people, with qualitatively different physical and sensory experiences of their environment must develop different habitus to those of their hearing peers, even if other aspects of their social standing are, at first glance, the same" (O'Brien 2021: 8). Agreeing with O'Brien's framing of habitus as it relates to deaf people, I argue that when deaf children are educated in hearing spaces (i.e., mainstream schools), a hearing habitus cannot be acquired in the same way as it is for hearing individuals. Instead, in hearing spaces, there are conscious attempts at assimilation and the unconscious development of a hybrid habitus.

"Bottom-up accounts of deaf ontologies and epistemologies" (Kusters, O'Brien, and de Meulder 2017a: 9) are important to our understanding of deaf experiences, and, as I attempt to show in this chapter, can lead to deeper theorizing of the role of space as shaping and being shaped by linguistic practices. This bottom-up account is a close (re)inspection of data from long-term research in Japan with deaf youth ages 18–24 who were solely educated in mainstream schools.

I begin this chapter with an introduction to signing, deaf, and hearing spaces. Next, I discuss how phonocentrism (the belief that sound and speech are superior to other forms of communication) and audism (discrimination against deaf and hard-of-hearing people) (Humphries 1975) shape spaces that, in turn, are shown to shape the linguistic practices of the individuals who traverse them. I relate these two concepts to the languages and modalities used by deaf people, situating them within a linguistic hierarchy. I show how these beliefs have influenced sign language use in educational spaces. Then, I give an overview of the research methods. Following this overview, I discuss the data to demonstrate how being raised and educated in hearing spaces, which are oriented toward auditory reception, hinders sign language communication while compelling spoken language communication. I argue that the deaf youth in this research were implicitly and explicitly urged to devise mechanisms to navigate these spaces, which resulted in the development of the aforementioned assimilative hybrid habitus. In the final section, I discuss dysconscious audism (internalization and acceptance of dominant hearing norms) (Gertz 2003, 2008)[1] and examine what occurs when related spatial politics are brought into deaf spaces populated by people who have had access to visual-spatial communication (i.e., signing). Hearing spaces are shown to produce communication that has wavering cultural capital, and this assimilative habitus is not highly evaluated outside of hearing spaces.

---

1 Gertz coined this phrase based on Joyce King's work (1991) on "dysconscious racism."

2 Signed and spoken languages as shaping and being shaped by space

2.1 Signing space, deaf space, hearing space

Sign language—its absence and presence—plays a key role in creating space physically and metaphorically. Sign languages are produced in space, create deaf space, and demarcate hearing spaces. This section begins by discussing signing space before presenting research on deaf space. It concludes by briefly addressing the understudied topic of hearing space.

Sign languages are visual-spatial languages in which grammar and syntax occur in space. An area for producing language on and around the signer's body is created called the "signing space" (Klima & Bellugi 1979: 51). This three-dimensional space for articulation is used to locate people, things, places, and ideas. It is within this physical space that language is produced and received. In addition to using space for grammar and syntax, sign languages refer to and map space through spatial practices. All languages have the potential to discuss space; however, sign languages are distinct in that space itself is used to talk about space (Lane, Hoffmeister, and Bahan 1996). The spatiality of sign languages means that spaces can be described *using space* and, as such, there is less ambiguity than in spoken languages such as English (Lane 1992). Sign languages are not only distinct in how they discuss space but also in how they produce and shape it.

What exactly are deaf spaces? Their significance is noted throughout the field of Deaf Studies and related disciplines, but there is no universal definition. The concept of deaf space "moves us away from the idea that Deaf people are always a minority in a hearing world toward realizing that the world is neither Deaf nor hearing but becomes Deaf or hearing as we live in it and shape it" and can "emerge from Deaf people's visual experience of the world" (Gulliver 2015: 5). In many ways, deaf spaces are unbounded; they are local, translocal, and transnational (Breivik 2005; De Clerck 2007; Haualand 2007). Deaf people today have very few permanent "brick and mortar" places due to the declining number of deaf clubs (Padden 2008) and the global push toward mainstreaming and away from segregated education in schools for the deaf. However, deaf spaces do not need to be physical or permanent. Shared experiences of linguistic oppression, the fight for linguistic rights, encounters in sign language within institutional and non-institutional settings (Friedner and Kusters 2015) and the "common experience of living as members of a visual community in an auditory world" (Murray 2008: 100) create rich translocal, international, and transnational deaf spaces. This commonality of deaf people is signed "deaf deaf same" and celebrates "deaf similitude" across more obvious differences (Friedner 2015: 4; see also Friedner and Kusters 2015b). Dynamic interactions are also shown to occur in virtual spaces in which the format of videos and translation tools enable deaf spaces to emerge (Keating and Mirus 2003; Valentine and Skelton 2008).

Deaf spaces may be in flux. Deaf individuals themselves can alter a space's orientation through their actions. For instance, adjusting one's physical space to a signing orientation can shift it from the "default" hearing (majority) space to a deaf one (O'Brien 2020). Boundaries between supposedly disparate groups, such as hearing and deaf signers can be blurred (e.g., Groce 1985; Kusters 2015), while classifications of hearing and deaf people are interrogated when all participants, regardless of hearing status, communicate in [natural] sign languages during temporary events (Schmitt 2015). Another shift is from the temporal to the permanent. When a deaf space continues over time, it may present itself in physical form (Gulliver and Kitzel 2016).

There has also been a push toward appreciating the role of built environments in fostering communication and sociality. The concept of *DeafSpace*, defined as "an architectural pattern language comprising basic design elements and a syntax, or way of building inspired by Deaf collectivist social sensibilities" (Bauman 2014: 377), sheds light on how spaces may be customized to enable and produce different forms of communication and types of sociality, such as seating arrangements to facilitate signing. DeafSpace began as a design project at Gallaudet University in the United States (the world's first university for deaf students) in 2005 and has developed into a theoretical framework that explores aesthetics, communicative practices, and social norms. Being in a space that anticipates interactions has also been shown to create potential for sign language (Edwards 2018).

Deaf spaces can be collective or individual. Deaf spaces are often formed through communication with deaf others via a sign language. In other words, deaf spaces can be brought into existence whenever signers come together. At the same time, deaf spaces are not always socially produced; more recent research has theorized how they can be created by individual deaf bodies (O'Brien 2021). This is a departure from many works in Deaf Geography that focus on larger scale deaf spaces. Similarly, in this chapter, I attempt to build upon O'Brien's notion of individual deaf bodies by looking at how deaf individuals drag spatial politics into new spaces, adding ethnographic specificity to more abstract notions of deaf space.

While deaf spaces have been heavily theorized, hearing spaces are generally taken-for-granted and unmarked. Due to hearing hegemony, spaces are usually "hearing" by default. However, they can be seen as demarcated by the *absence* of sign languages and deaf people. Anytime someone enters a non-deaf company, shop, or other establishment, they are essentially entering a hearing space where spoken language has high linguistic capital and sign language does not. Speech—the ability to both produce and decipher it—and written language constitute a form of linguistic capital in majority hearing spaces as well as hearing-dominated deaf spaces.

2.2 Effects of phonocentrism and audism on hearing and deaf spaces

This section examines two concepts, phonocentrism and audism, to provide context for the language ideologies and practices that determine linguistic capital. It also provides a brief overview of the different forms of communication available to deaf individuals in Japan: Japanese Sign Language (JSL), signed Japanese, and Japanese (via the oral communication method and writing). The deaf Japanese youth discussed in this chapter, like their deaf peers around the world, first encounter hearing spaces. As performative linguistic spaces, these spaces indicate what types of linguistic practices can freely occur.

In hearing spaces, sign language is suppressed and spoken language is promoted because of phonocentrism, audism, and an association of signing with a stigmatized group framed as "disabled." First, I will explain phonocentrism or the belief that sound and speech are superior (to writing or other forms of communication). The most salient feature of hearing fields (spaces) is phonocentrism (Richardson 2019), which is unconsciously accepted as the norm and normal by hearing people. Spoken languages hold more linguistic capital than sign languages in majority hearing spaces because of this belief. Derrida's critique of phonocentrism has been applied in Deaf Studies to make visible and to question sound and the voice's primacy and status (Bauman 2004, 2008). Phonocentrism "begets institutional arrangements, especially in medicalized educational practices bent on normalizing deaf bodies" (Bauman 2008: 44). Practices of normalization include training in speechreading and speech, an emphasis placed on using auditory devices such as hearing aids to amplify sound, and the promotion of cochlear implantation to make deaf people more "hearing-like." Deconstructing phonocentrism in society is part of the larger exercise of analyzing how and why deaf bodies have been subject to oppression and discrimination. As I will show, the deaf Japanese youth in this study were subject to such practices of normalization, especially in schools.

Coining the term "audism" (Humphries 1975) has been a way to conceptualize the discrimination against deaf people based on one's ability to hear (Bauman 2004). Succinctly defined as "[t]he notion that one is superior based on one's ability to hear or behave in the manner of one who hears" (Humphries 1975: n.p.), audism is a way forward to make sense of individual acts of superiority along with systematic forms of oppression that disable deaf people (see Lane 1992).

Bauman extended Humphries' definition to encompass "[a] system of advantage based on hearing ability" and "[a] metaphysical orientation that links human identity with speech" (2004: 245). That is, an ability to hear and produce intelligible sound (i.e., speech) confers power in hearing spaces. Bauman (2008) applied Derrida's notion of phonocentrism to understand "hegemony of voice as presence, voice as being" (p. 50) and how it relates to valorizing oral/sound-based languages.

Audism manifests itself in a myriad of situations, such as when medical practitioners discourage parents from introducing sign language to their deaf child, when children are prohibited from signing in school, when a person's intelligence is measured by the ability to speak, and when nations do not recognize sign languages as official languages. Until the 20th century, sign languages were not even viewed as languages at all, and they continue to be poorly understood.[2] Sign languages often lack the legal backing of being recognized as official languages, as is the case in Japan today (see Mori and Sugimoto 2019 for a discussion of the legal status of JSL). Globally, 74 countries have some form of sign language legislation (WFD 2022), but this legislation does not necessarily mean that a sign language has been granted official language status. In Japan, there are sign language ordinances throughout the country that, for instance, help deaf people to secure access to sign language interpretation. However, access to sign languages in Japan is premised on disability rights via "accessibility" (i.e., "reasonable accommodations") and not on linguistic rights.

Finally, it is necessary to appreciate how the value and meaning given by dominant hearing people to spoken languages compared to sign languages is based on arbitrary power relations between so-called "able-bodied" and disabled people. While there are deaf Japanese who self-identify as being members of a cultural and linguistic minority group rather than as members of a disability group, deafness in Japan is officially classified as a disability—and the disability identity remains stigmatized. In line with this framing of deafness, JSL books are typically categorized

---

2 Sign languages gained recognition as natural languages with high-level grammatical forms (as opposed to being viewed as crude gestural systems) with Stokoe's landmark work on American Sign Language (ASL) (1960). Even with this "official" recognition from linguists, sign languages continued—and continue—to be poorly understood by people outside of sign linguistics and Deaf Studies. A common misconception, even among scholars who study linguistic practices, is that sign languages are not separate languages but variations of the spoken language of the nation. Indeed, I was asked by a linguistic anthropologist if JSL was like braille, in that it was a way to "express" and "access" the Japanese language. These types of questions are familiar to anyone working with sign languages.

in libraries and bookstores with works on "social welfare"(*fukushi*) rather than alongside other language learning material.

2.3 Sign language in educational spaces

Audism is most deeply embedded and realized in education. Dominant groups naturalize arbitrariness (Bourdieu 1977: 164), giving the impression that it is the natural order. Elite values must be accepted for a habitus to be produced (Bourdieu and Passeron 1977). The acceptance of these values can be seen in the education of deaf students in which hearing educators, policymakers, parents, and even referring doctors, often purport speech to be "legitimate." There has been pushback to this claim to legitimacy. Educating children in the dominant spoken language and/or in artificial signed forms (i.e., signed versions of the spoken language) has been framed as acts of symbolic violence and attempts to control and assimilate deaf children in inaccessible and artificial language that provides incomplete access (Branson and Miller 1993).[3]

Even when signing is introduced, it is often in the signed form of the spoken language. In the case of Japan, the signed form is known as signed Japanese (*nihongo taiou shuwa*). Signed Japanese is an artificial communication system, whereas Japanese Sign Language (JSL) is a distinct language. Signed Japanese follows the word order of Japanese and even incorporates particles, which are short words that indicate the relationship of words (e.g., *ga, ha, ni*). Signed versions of national languages were invented by educators in schools for the deaf with the aim of helping children to acquire spoken and written language. This phonocentric goal is inextricably linked to linguistic ideologies and hierarchies.

In contrast JSL was *not* created artificially; it is a natural language developed amongst groups of deaf people, especially students in residential schools. JSL is believed to be indigenous to Japan, but there is uncertainty about the exact origins (see Nakamura 2006). JSL's grammar and syntax are distinct from Japanese and include classifiers and non-manual markers expressed on the face and body (see Oka and Akahori 2011; Matsuoka 2015; Mori and Sasaki 2017). It is not enough to say that, as a sign language, JSL is embodied; the body itself produces language. There are two main groups of native JSL signers: deaf children of deaf parents

---

3 While this statement may appear limited to the polemics of academia, these concerns were raised in numerous interviews and discussions with deaf educators, researchers, and other adults, as well as hearing allies during my research in Japan.

and hearing children of deaf adults (known as "CODA").[4] Native signers follow similar language acquisition milestones as their hearing peers, develop a deaf habitus, and often go on to be linguistic and social models in deaf spaces. Despite their small numbers, native signers play an important role in deaf communities. Deaf children from deaf families have been responsible for passing on JSL in schools, even in times of sign language restriction.

As noted, institutionalized deaf spaces are on the decline due to the waning of historic deaf clubs along with declining enrollment in "separate schools" (i.e., schools for the deaf or special education institutions). Even when deaf students are educated in schools for the deaf, there is no guarantee of access to sign language. Institutional audism (Lane 1992)—a systemic advantage based on hearing abilities—is found in both schools for the deaf (where hearing people have had authority over deaf people) and mainstream schools. In the case of schools for the deaf, hearing controlled educational spaces with deaf occupants have both produced and hindered certain linguistic practices. First, these spaces produced an entirely new form of communication: the above-mentioned manual forms of spoken language in which invented signs were used to teach the spoken national language (e.g., Manually Coded English in the US, signed Japanese in Japan). As schools were often hearing-led and educators were opposed to natural signing, the deaf school as a deaf space could be one that hindered natural sign languages while promoting the use of speech and signed modalities. During times of strict oralism, communication through sign language was silenced through corporal punishment and shaming.

Deaf children are increasingly being socialized in hearing schools. The deaf Japanese youth in this research provide an example of the effects of educating deaf individuals in hearing spaces. Their experiences demonstrate how sensorial differences associated with deafness do not mean that all deaf children will develop a deaf habitus, especially when they are being socialized by and among families, educators, and peers with hearing dispositions. Moving between the hearing spaces of the home and the school can result in an assimilative, hybrid habitus because the barriers to spoken language communication and a sensorial orientation preclude deaf children from acquiring a hearing habitus in the same way as hearing children.

Studies exploring deaf epistemologies take deaf experiences of people in signing deaf families who attend deaf schools as the norm (Cue et al. 2019). For instance, children have been shown to acquire a deaf bodily habitus, deaf

---

4 The latter, CODA, as a result of acquiring the language and habitus of deaf people while also being able to negotiate and "pass" in hearing spaces, occupy a distinct positionality and act as cultural brokers between deaf and hearing people (see Shibuya 2009). The former, native deaf signers, are a minority within a minority (Saito 2014: 44).

dispositions, mannerisms, and behavior in bilingual-bicultural schools for deaf students (see Hayashi and Tobin 2015; Graham and Tobin 2020). In this chapter, I seek to address the diversity of deaf experiences by focusing on the spatial and linguistic processes of Japanese youth who were raised in hearing families and were entirely educated via the oral communication method in mainstream schools. By introducing and analyzing ethnographic research, I seek to answer the following questions: What types of linguistic practices are produced and suppressed by hearing spaces occupied by deaf individuals? What effects do the movements between spaces have on linguistic practices and their evaluation? I show how the linguistic space of the "hearing home" and "hearing school" are performative linguistic spaces that encourage and discourage certain linguistic practices. Further, I argue that linguistic practices that are highly evaluated in hearing spaces can be poorly evaluated in deaf spaces.

3 Research methods

Data gathered from ongoing multi-sited ethnographic fieldwork with deaf communities in Japan beginning in 2012 form the basis of this analysis. I primarily focus on the findings from two separate but related research projects. During the first 15-month study (2012–2014), I worked with cross-sections of deaf communities. Through participant observation, I spent extensive time in various settings including a university campus for deaf and hard-of-hearing students, sign language circles, schools for the deaf, activities and retreats with an organization for deaf university students, a "universal" camp, a sign language project, as well as symposiums and workshops (among others). I also conducted peer interviews, semi-structured one-on-one interviews, questionnaires, and social media analysis. Through the activities described above, I interacted with well over 200 deaf and hard-of-hearing (DHH) people and interviewed (both informally and formally) approximately 50 people including mainstreamed *"inte"*(explained below), youth who attended schools for the deaf, "older" DHH people of all educational backgrounds, educators, parents, deaf leaders, and deaf and hearing scholars.

Although a diverse range of individuals participated in this study, I focused my final analysis on the perspective of 18 to 24-year-old "youth" who were solely educated in mainstream schools and encountered signing peers after completing secondary education (McGuire 2020; McGuire and Tokunaga 2020). They were colloquially referred to as *inte* (in-tay), an in-group term, which is the shortened form of the loanword "integration" in Japanese (*integureshon*) used to refer specifically to academic integration. As a hearing white American adult conducting research with younger participants from what could be considered a marginalized group in Japan, I believed it was crucial to make every effort to balance power dynamics and center the participants' perspectives. Therefore, peer interviews, in which participants interviewed one another (and determined the questions, length of interview, and, in some cases, selected their interview partners), was a key research method. For the peer interview portion of the research, there were 18 participants selected through snowball sampling using emic definitions of *inte*, with 16 participants from the target 18–24-year-old group and two participants in their forties.

Participants' narratives in the first study raised questions about academic provisions in junior high school that the second 12-month study (2015–2016) sought to answer. In the second study, I visited elementary and junior high school hard-of-hearing classrooms, conducted interviews with educators and junior high school students, and volunteered as a weekly "home tutor" for a first-year female junior high school student who was enrolled in a local mainstream school in a suburb of Tokyo. Since the conclusion of this study, I have continued to reside in Japan and conduct ethnographic research with deaf communities.

4 The home and school as hearing spoken language spaces

Two questions that I often observed young deaf individuals asking one another were: 1) Is your family hearing or deaf? and 2) Did you go to a hearing or deaf school? For hearing people, majority spaces are typically unmarked and taken-for-granted (see Zerubavel 2018). A family is a family, not a *hearing* or a *deaf* family. A *hearing* school is simply a school, with the possible addition of qualifiers such as *public* or *private, single-sex* or *co-ed*. Thought is rarely—if ever—given to the auditory orientation of a space or group. However, for research participants, their difference from hearing people and their position in such spaces always appeared to be at the level of consciousness.

As I will discuss in this section, the performative linguistic spaces of the (hearing) home and the (hearing) school were shaped by phonocentrism and audism. These performative linguistic spaces discouraged deaf linguistic practices (i.e., signing) while encouraging oral forms of communication (i.e., spoken Japanese). The first section introduces the performative linguistic space of the home and explores how functional "shallow" forms of oral communication were implicitly promoted, while the second section examines how the school as a hearing space discouraged linguistic practices that would lead *inte* to "stand out" and encouraged assimilative forms of communication aimed at covering "difference."

4.1 Home as a hearing space that produces "shallow communication"

Deaf people have been referred to as "people of the eye,"[5] but the home was frequently a space focused on the ear and sound. Most homes were framed as hearing spaces occupied by a "hearing family" contrasted with a "deaf family." An orientation toward the visual-spatial develops for deaf people due to their sensory orientation (Bahan 2014), and even non-signers absorb meaning about the world through sight. However, in most cases, this visual orientation to the world is not shared by the hearing natal family. Parents' attitudes toward deafness as well as their social and linguistic capital and acceptance of professionals' guidance on raising a deaf child all influence the way language and space are understood and created in the home. Generally, a family's unconscious hearing habitus is interrupted but not entirely disrupted by the addition of a deaf child. Research has shown that hearing mothers of deaf children experience conflict between global hearing culture and their child's sensory world (Johnson 2020). Ultimately, hearing homes with one deaf child remain as hearing spaces (with the exception of families that prioritize signing) despite the presence of a deaf family member.

As noted earlier in the chapter, phonocentrism and audism are embedded in society. These notions shaped *inte's* homes because the parents brought public ideologies into the private space. Audism and phonocentrism had influenced the medical practitioners and educators who encouraged hearing parents to emphasize speech and passively—and sometimes actively—discouraged parents from introducing sign language to their deaf child. The (unsubstantiated) concern was that introducing any form of signing to a deaf child would inhibit the development of speech. Although some *inte* participants reported that their hearing parents did learn to sign to enable better communication (usually signed Japanese with the goal of teaching spoken Japanese), these parents were not the norm. *Inte* with signing parents were aware of and commented on the "specialness" of their situation.

More commonly, hearing parents, especially the mother in the role of trainer, concentrated on speech and lip-reading, coaching them to produce and interpret

---

5 "People of the eye" ignores the reality of deaf-blind people who are haptically oriented but aptly describes sighted deaf people, who were the participants in the research described in this chapter.

sounds. If JSL were perceived to have more linguistic capital, it is conceivable that parents would be more receptive to introducing this visual-spatial language into the hearing home. Instead, many parents equated "language" with speech and mastery of spoken language with academic and social success. Children were praised for speaking and deciphering speech. In the absence of sign language, communication was carried out primarily in spoken language, gestures, writing, and sometimes home signs. Based on data from participant observation and interview analysis, I have argued (McGuire 2020; McGuire and Tokunaga 2020) that the oral communication method rarely results in mutually intelligible communication. Consequently, an emphasis on spoken language creates a linguistic space that (unintentionally) precluded the deaf child from fully participating.

As a result of sign language being devalued and spoken language being valorized, deaf children (of all educational backgrounds) in hearing homes tend to have a partial grasp of the language occurring around them. This is referred to in the literature as the "dinner table syndrome," coined to describe how deaf people watch on as the hearing people around them communicate with one another (Hauser et al., 2010; Meek 2020). There are unconscious processes at work here. Hearing family members typically do not intend to exclude their deaf family member. At the same time, they have unconsciously acquired a hearing habitus, which includes overlapping (spoken) communication, rapid turn-taking, and a lack of awareness of deaf ways of attention-getting (Hauser et al., 2010; Meek 2020), making it difficult for a deaf person to follow the conversation.

The dinner table phenomenon cuts deaf people off from numerous incidental learning opportunities (Hauser et al., 2010) which can lead to language deprivation syndrome (Hall 2017; Hall, Hall, and Caselli 2019; Hall, Levin, and Anderson 2017), which will be addressed again below. Further, experiencing the dinner table syndrome prompts the first stage of developing mannerisms, communicative strategies, and a particular disposition stemming from consciously and unconsciously adapting to hearing others, including feigning comprehension.

As a result of the phenomena described above, in the home, communication is linguistically simple (due to the complexities of lip-reading), or, as *inte* explained it, "shallow." Over the course of the first 15 months of fieldwork, "shallow communication" (*asai komyunikeishon*) was spoken and signed in numerous interviews, peer interviews, and informal conversations with deaf youth from hearing families (regardless of the participant's educational background). Many deaf participants reported that these "shallow" conversations with hearing parents—and to a greater or lesser degree with siblings—tended to revolve around daily routines. Communication was utilitarian; it was need- and task-based. As one male participant explained, he mainly talked with his family about practical, day-to-day matters such as what they would be eating for dinner or what time they needed to leave the house for an appointment. He had no recollection of having content-rich conversations with his family. Language exchanges were not a means of building intimacy. It was shared activities, such as sports and games, or the use of home signs that created opportunities for bonding; a sense of connectivity was rarely achieved through spoken language communication.

4.2 School as a hearing space for assimilative communication

Inte youth moved from the home as a hearing space to the school as a hearing space, whereas their peers who attended schools for the deaf moved from the home as a hearing (or deaf) space to a school with deaf peers and sometimes deaf teachers and staff. Although most schools for the deaf remain hearing-led spaces in Japan, deaf students may socialize one another into deaf norms. In particular, students from deaf families develop a deaf habitus that can work toward socializing their classmates and peers in schools for the deaf. However, for *inte*, school was a space that compelled an assimilative form of communication.

The hearing space of the school demanded hearing ways of being. *Inte* recognized these spaces as being constructed by and for hearing people. There is not a great conceptual distance between audism and the notion of "compulsory hearing" where "passing" and behaving as a hearing person is demanded in an ableist society (Harmon 2010). As access to JSL-Japanese interpreters in educational settings is extremely limited in Japan, *inte* relied on lip-reading and the production of speech to communicate with teachers and classmates with the added support of a notetaker, in many cases. *Inte* experienced social isolation and neglect in these hearing spaces, especially after entering junior high school (McGuire 2020; McGuire and Tokunaga 2020). To offset their "difference" and deflect unwanted attention, *inte* applied strategies to appear more hearing-like.

Inte were not empty vessels of enculturation or passive observers of their own lived reality. Bondy, in his research on Burakumin youth, showed how they can "bracket" (2015) a minority identity by employing mechanisms and strategies to mitigate difference. Within the home, *inte* could ask for repetition and admit to being unable to understand, but at school pretending to understand (*wakatta furi wo suru*) was essential to maintain dignity, assimilate into the hearing space, and avoid bullying. In my research, I classified the various strategies employed by *inte* to mitigate difference as follows: concealing markers of difference (e.g., covering hearing aids and cochlear implants), rejecting classroom information support, such as notetaking (to avoid standing out), mimicking hearing peers (e.g., standing when peers stand), and performing communicative competence (e.g., lip-reading, gauging facial expressions, contextualizing conversations, guesswork, and feigning comprehension) (McGuire 2020). Here I refer to these "performances" using O'Brien's expression, "façade of competence" (2021) to avoid confusion with "performativity." Maintaining a façade of competence came at the expense of understanding the linguistic context. In other words, the dinner table syndrome continued at school.

On the one hand, employment of various communication strategies by deaf children and youth demonstrates their capabilities as agentic beings. They are multimodal multilingual communicators who engage a full range of linguistic and semiotic resources. On the other hand, there is a danger of romanticizing what are essentially coping mechanisms that do little to offset the language deprivation, mentioned above, which can occur when deaf children do not have access to direct or indirect language (Hall 2017; Hall, Levin and Anderson 2017; Hall, Hall, and Caselli 2019). Language deprivation is not caused by deafness but by restricted language access, typically in environments where the child is not exposed to sign language at an early age. Further, while multimodality and simultaneity have not been seriously considered in translanguaging studies (Kusters et al. 2017b) and it could be attractive to apply theories of translanguaging to these students' communicative practices, there is the risk of glossing over "structural and sensorial asymmetries" that lead to "unequal access to linguistic resources," especially auditory information (de Meulder et al., 2019). Unequal access to these resources in both spaces (the home and school) resulted in *inte* not developing a hearing habitus in the same way as a hearing person, despite being socialized in hearing environments. Without access to deaf spaces or opportunities to acquire a deaf habitus, they began to develop an assimilative *inte* habitus.

5 My ears are bad; your voice is good: Dysconscious audism and an assimilative *inte* habitus

5.1 Dysconscious audism in deaf spaces

Deaf spaces as performative linguistic spaces are sometimes shaped by dysconscious audism, which is an internalized belief that hearing ways are superior to deaf ones. Although deaf spaces are formed by and among deaf people, the spatial politics of hearing spaces have a profound effect on these spaces when hearing norms and values are introduced. Post-secondary deaf youth spaces in Japan—like most deaf spaces worldwide (as discussed in section two)—are usually temporary and include deaf organizations, deaf sports clubs, deaf social events, and deaf virtual spaces. When *inte* enter these deaf spaces, they tend to carry with them the notion of deafness as a deficit. Below, I introduce two brief ethnographic accounts that illustrate these internalized beliefs before analyzing their significance.

My fieldnotes were full of unfavorable adjectives, terms, and expressions employed by *inte* to describe being deaf. They frequently signed and vocalized negative ideas such as "my ears are bad" (*mimi ga warui*) and described "not being able to hear" (*kikoenai koto*) as a "nuisance" (*mendokusai*), a "burden" (*nimotsu*), and a "cause of solitude" (*hitori bocchi*). Shame about being deaf, a sense of having a stigmatized identity, and a strong desire to minimize difference and adapt to others had not been left behind in hearing spaces. An internalized stigma persisted, especially in the youngest of *inte* participants, i.e., recent senior high school graduates. Notably, *inte* who had spent several years in deaf spaces by the time we first met had been (re)shaped by those spaces and begun to develop more positive interpretations. However, even older *inte* would vacillate between positive and negative framings of deafness, speech, and signing. For instance, being able to "speak well" (*koe ga kirei*) could be evaluated positively in certain deaf spaces, indicating that *inte* had carried hearing norms and values with them, as seen in the next ethnographic example.

During one peer interview, Tatsuo (21-year-old *inte* male), who attended a "hearing university," complimented his friend Chika (20-year-old *inte* female) who also attended a "hearing university," on her clear pronunciation. She smiled broadly. He then paused before adding in signed Japanese, "Maybe . . . I don't really know if your voice is good, do I?" to which they both laughed. Tatsuo's comment raises four key points. First, when deaf people are speaking, the emphasis is often on the quality of pronunciation and intelligible speech. Second, deaf people may believe that there is value—worthy of attention and praise—in "succeeding" in acts of spoken language communication. Third, deaf people must rely on the perceptions and evaluations of hearing people when using spoken language. Tatsuo had evaluated his friend Chika's speech skills *not* based on *his* perception (as he is profoundly deaf) but on observing her "successfully" negotiating interactions with hearing people (i.e., her ability to converse with people in shops and restaurants). As someone classified as "postlingually deaf" because she became deaf after acquiring speech, Chika had "clearer" more intelligible Japanese pronunciation than most *inte*. She simultaneously took pride in her speech skills as well as her signing skills after "coming out" as a deaf person in deaf spaces. Finally, this discussion would have looked different if the performative linguistic deaf space of the peer interview had not been one formed by two *inte* whose prior movements had been exclusively in hearing spaces but by two deaf youth who had years of experience navigating deaf spaces.

The ethnographic data above relate to the concept of "dysconcious audism" (Gertz 2003, 2008, 2016). Audism encountered in both hearing and deaf spaces has a profound effect on deaf people when "relations of linguistic domination" (Bourdieu 1991: 46), here referring to spoken languages to visual-spatial ones, are internalized. Since *inte* were raised in hearing families and solely spent time in hearing spaces which demanded them to be "hearing-like," audist views were taken as common sense. As a subordinate and marginalized group, without access to power status or resources, the groundwork is set for the development of "dysconscious audism," which is the "acceptance of dominant hearing norms, privileges, and cultural values by deaf individuals, and the subsequent perception of hearing society as being more appropriate than Deaf society" (Gertz 2016: 329). This process is *not* below the threshold of consciousness. Deaf individuals are cognizant of their subjugation but do not dismiss altogether the pathologizing messages of the dominant (hearing) society (Gertz 2016).

A lack of power and access to affirmative messages of deafness contributed to the ready manifestation of dysconscious audism in *inte*. In nearly all cases, the *inte* I met had been the only deaf students in their class—and often the only deaf student in the entire school. They were surrounded by the rules, norms, and values of "hearingness" in institutionalized hearing spaces. In short, *inte* were inundated with audist messages. Many *inte* narratives revealed dysconscious audism and demonstrated that *inte* did not possess the notion of "deaf gain" (Bauman and Murray 2014), which celebrates the contributions of deaf people to humanity. The message *inte* received was that deaf ways of being, including signing and a visual orientation, held no symbolic capital. When navigating hearing spaces, there were virtually no messages to counterbalance audist views: no deaf peers or role models in the school to model a positive image of deafness or to present an inverse of the linguistic hierarchy in which sign language is valued. No one encouraged them to learn to sign. They believed Japanese speech to have value, whereas the few times they encountered signers in public spaces (e.g., observing them on the train), they found it "strange" with some *inte* even questioning *why* these people *could not speak* (see McGuire 2020; McGuire and Tokunaga 2020). Perhaps this is not surprising as JSL rarely has high linguistic capital—even at schools for the deaf.[6] The negative associations with being deaf and the high linguistic capital of speech are products of dysconscious audism that can be brought into deaf performative linguistic spaces, as seen with Tatsuo and Chika.

---

6 For instance, it was not until the first bilingual-bicultural school for the deaf, Meisei Gakuen, was founded in 2008 that JSL was ever afforded the same academic status as the Japanese language (*kokugo*) by virtue of being made an official school subject.

Dysconscious audism could be at the level of consciousness. However, at the unconscious level was an *inte* assimilative habitus, which deaf people from "deaf school" backgrounds as well as older *inte* observed. An example of the effect of introducing this assimilative *inte* habitus into deaf spaces is presented in the following section.

5.2 Introducing an assimilative *inte* habitus into deaf spaces

The hearing spaces of the home and school induced assimilative linguistic practices based on audism and phonocentrism. In spite of active attempts to behave hearing-like, as deaf individuals, their sensorial orientation resulted in a habitus that was neither deaf nor hearing. Years of linguistic exchanges focused on the production and reception of speech, rather than mutually intelligible content-rich communication, produced a distinct hybrid habitus. After graduating from senior high school and upon moving into deaf youth spaces, *inte* were able to identify and reflect on the strategies they employed during their school days. At the same time, most *inte* appeared unaware of the enduring assimilative hybrid habitus they had acquired in hearing spaces. This in-between habitus neither guaranteed belonging in hearing spaces (as most *inte* experienced "dinner table syndrome" with shallow communication at home and social isolation in schools) nor did it facilitate a smooth transition into deaf ones. On the contrary, linguistic patterns such as dominating and controlling conversations without giving others a chance to talk (because it is easier to produce speech than to perceive it) and focusing on one's own well-being (because they had been preoccupied with coping strategies) were found to be maladaptive strategies in deaf spaces, as elaborated by one signing deaf interviewee below:

> It is wonderful that "integrated people" made such great efforts. If they did not put in that effort, they could not have continued [in mainstream schools]. So much power and endurance were necessary. When they become adults and we start to do activities together, [I can look and say] ah, that person is *inte*! All by themselves, they had to fight and fight to make it. They made it by not being beaten. Myself, myself. I think [*inte*] often cannot cooperate well with others . . . Certainly, there are some people who can make friends easily if they have some sort of other association, like a local [deaf] circle or [deaf] relatives. If they were raised that way, then they can understand other people's feelings. People from deaf schools are much better at it. They could normally communicate in sign language. [For instance] if someone has an accident. They say "Are you OK? Are you alright?" . . . If deaf people have sign language they can naturally associate. [*Inte*] lack awareness and have little experience in communicating with others. —Yoshida, mid-40s, female

In her forties at the time of our one-on-one interview, Yoshida had spent over twenty years in deaf spaces. Her comments, although critical of these *inte*, also demonstrate an awareness of the effort exerted to navigate and endure a spoken language hearing school environment as a deaf person. Yoshida's opinion (that *inte* do not appreciate other people's emotions) was based on her perception that *inte* lack interest in the well-being of others. Rather than signaling self-centered dispositions, unknowingly, she was pointing to a habitus resulting from negotiating audism and the language ideologies of the hearing spaces of the home and school. An *inte* habitus is essentially a habitus acquired through attempts to assimilate and "cover" difference and focus on one's own façade of competence. Although Yoshida seemed to believe these behaviors and manners could never be transformed, engaging in deaf spaces with deaf others *could* reorient *inte* to social spaces based on sameness, shared meaning, and an acceptance of signing. This was rarely, however, a linear process.

Deaf spaces as performative linguistic spaces could promote different communication patterns: some *inte* eagerly began signing while others introduced hearing communication norms, including speech. As *inte* moved between various spaces, heterogeneous spatial politics were brought with them. For instance, I observed *inte* attempting to speak to deaf and hard-of-hearing peers with little success and much frustration. Speech can be, to some degree, effective when talking to hearing people who can monitor communication but becomes highly ineffective among deaf (and hard-of-hearing) people as neither party can decipher the sound and lipreading is highly inaccurate. The assimilative *inte* habitus may have won them praise in hearing spaces but was met with confusion and irritation in deaf ones. Deaf spaces are, on the whole, ones that expect and value sign language communication. As emerging signers and newcomers to deaf spaces, over time, *inte* discovered that their oral communication skills and the façade of communicative competence in Japanese had little cultural capital among deaf peers. Their movement (from the space of the hearing school to the space of deaf peers) threw their habitus into relief and encouraged new signed forms of communication: signed Japanese and JSL. A movement between hearing and deaf spaces worked to undo narratives of normalization.

Narratives of normalization can be undone when signing deaf people reject spoken language as having (sole) possession of cultural capital (Harmon 2010: 43). Deaf fields (here, spaces) place sign languages as holding the highest symbolic capital, although linguistic variation (such as signed and gestural forms, bilingualism with spoken languages) can also be found (Richardson 2019). There is an inverse linguistic hierarchy in deaf spaces, with native sign users holding the highest status (Hackett 2019). Confronting this inverse hierarchy in deaf spaces proves to be a type of "deaf shock" for youth known as "U-turn" students (Nakamura 2003), that is, students who were mainstreamed for a period before returning to schools for the deaf. Similarly, *inte* experienced shock upon encountering this inverse hierarchy. Usually this was associated with a period of resistance to signers and signing, which relates to dysconscious audism and an assimilative hearing habitus. However, over time, many *inte* began to accept the cultural capital of JSL in deaf spaces and in these spaces were encouraged to communicate by signing, not speaking. This acceptance was witnessed in the period of the first study as the youngest *inte* (i.e., the emerging signers) developed their signing skills—and even began to boast about their rapid improvement. It is also evidenced by the many *inte* today who play integral roles in society that require JSL proficiency, such as in deaf-led arts and education.

6 Conclusion

Although it could be assumed that deaf children will "naturally" develop a deaf habitus, this is not the case. Hearing hegemony and a global push for mainstream education results in deaf children increasingly being socialized into a type of hearing habitus. All deaf children are born into a phonocentric society with audist views in which spoken language holds the highest linguistic capital. Deaf children begin elementary school (or preschool) with different linguistic profiles and resources based on their family of origin. Children of signing deaf parents will have been exposed to deaf ways of being and communicating. However, statistically, only a small number of deaf children are raised in a visual-spatial oriented home as most deaf children are born to hearing parents. Regardless of family background, the acquisition of a deaf habitus can occur when deaf youth are introduced to deaf role models and peers in schools as native signers are able to impart their linguistic knowledge. Sign languages as fully embodied languages contribute to the acquisition of this deaf habitus, but there are many deaf people who do not have access to deaf spaces or to sign languages.

In this chapter, I showed how space and language shape—and are shaped by—audism, phonocentrism, and linguistic ideologies through an ethnographic exploration of the experiences of deaf Japanese youth, known as *inte*, who spent their earliest years in hearing spaces. All deaf youth in Japan spend time in hearing spaces as most spaces in society—including the home—are *not* deaf spaces. However, deaf children who attended schools for the deaf moved in and out of deaf spaces. In contrast, *inte* moved from the hearing space of the home where communication was shallow to the school as a hearing space shaped by institutional audism.

An *inte* habitus was developed from negotiating and minimizing difference in mainstream schools. To adapt to hearing educational spaces, *inte* had developed a communication repertoire of "covering" strategies. Mannerisms, dispositions, communication strategies, and bodily forms became deeply ingrained through years of repetition. The resulting habitus was a hybrid assimilative one. Hearing performative linguistic spaces implicitly and explicitly hindered sign language while coaxing speech and the façade of communicative competence. While *inte* expressed awareness of their coping mechanisms, after years of repetition, many of the bodily techniques and mannerisms had become fully embodied. It was only when beginning to sign and transform the habitus that *inte* were able to engage in reflexivity and evaluate their experiences and linguistic practices. At the same time, dispositions remained below the level of consciousness. *Inte* were often *not* aware that they communicated or behaved differently from non-*inte* deaf peers.

Inte dragged the spatial politics of hearing spaces into deaf ones. In select deaf spaces, particularly those where only *inte* were present, speech acts might still be highly valued. However, in many deaf spaces that encouraged signing and deaf ways, the assimilative *inte* habitus was thrown into relief and evaluated negatively. Most *inte* overcame their initial resistance to signing to acquire the signing skills expected in deaf youth spaces. The tensions and resolutions experienced by *inte* as they moved into new spaces with differing linguistic ideologies have the potential to shed light on the experiences of deaf youth in other socio-cultural contexts.

The linguistic experiences of deaf people may appear to hold little relevance or interest to those outside of Deaf Studies or sign linguistics. However, an analysis of deaf experiences can offer a unique insight into how linguistic practices produce and are produced by space. *Inte's* oppression and restriction in hegemonic audist spaces prompted assimilative communication acts to mitigate difference. Similar façades of linguistic competence are likely to occur whenever a marginalized group's linguistic habitus does not align with the dominant one (e.g., speakers of marginalized languages, children in "second language" settings). Drawing comparisons and contrasts between the communication approaches of deaf people and those of other marginalized groups has the potential to deepen our understanding of the interlocking forces of space, language, and power.

References

Bahan, Ben. 2014. Senses and culture: Exploring sensory orientations. In *Deaf gain: Raising the stakes for human diversity*. In H-Dirksen L. Bauman & Joseph J. Murray (eds.), 233–254. Minneapolis: University of Minnesota Press.

Bauman, Hansel. 2014. DeafSpace: An architecture toward a more livable and sustainable world. In Joseph J. Murray & H-Dirksen L. Baumann (eds.), *Deaf gain: Raising the stakes for human diversity*, 375–401. Minneapolis, MN. and London: University of Minneapolis Press.

Bauman, H-Dirksen L. 2004. Audism: Exploring the metaphysics of oppression. *Journal of Deaf Studies and Deaf Education* 9(2). 239–246.

Bauman, H-Dirksen L. 2008. Listening to phonocentrism with deaf eyes: Derrida's mute philosophy of (sign) language. *Essays in Philosophy* 9(1). 41–54.

Bauman, H-Dirksen L. & Joseph J. Murray (eds.). 2014. *Deaf gain: Raising the stakes for human diversity*. Minneapolis, MN: University of Minnesota Press.

Bondy, Christopher. 2015. *Voice, silence, and self: Negotiations of buraku identity in contemporary Japan*. Cambridge: Harvard University Press.

Bourdieu, Pierre. 1991. *Language and symbolic power*. Cambridge, MA: Harvard University Press.

Bourdieu, Pierre. 1977. *Outline of a theory of practice*. Cambridge, MA: Cambridge University Press.

Bourdieu, Pierre & Jean-Claude Passeron. 1990. *Reproduction in education, society and culture*. London: Sage Publications.

Branson, Jan & Don Miller. 1993. Sign language, the deaf and the epistemic violence of mainstreaming. *Language and Education* 7(1). 21–41.

Breivik, Jan-Kåre. 2005. *Deaf identities in the making: Local lives, transnational connections*. Washington D.C.: Gallaudet University Press.

Cue, Katrina R., Kimberly K. Pudans-Smith., Ju-Lee A.Wolsey, S. Jordan Wright & M. Diane Clark. 2019. The odyssey of deaf epistemology. *American Annals of the Deaf* 164(3). 395–422.

de Clerck, Goedele A. M. 2007. Meeting global deaf peers, visiting ideal deaf places: Deaf ways of education leading to empowerment, an exploratory case study. *American Annals of the Deaf* 152 (1). 5–19.

Edwards, Terra. 2018. Re-channeling language: the mutual restructuring of language and infrastructure at Gallaudet University. *Journal of Linguistic Anthropology* 28. 273–292.

Eickman, Jordan T. 2004. *The role of deaf sports in developing deaf identity*. University of Bristol, PhD thesis.

Friedner, Michele. 2015. *Valuing deaf worlds in urban India*. New Brunswick: Rutgers University Press.

Friedner, Michele & Annelies Kusters. 2015a. Introduction: DEAF-SAME and difference in international deaf spaces and encounters. In Michele Friedner & Annelies Kusters (eds.), *It's a small world: International deaf spaces and encounters*, ix-xxix. Washington D.C.: Gallaudet University Press.

Friedner, Michele & Annelies Kusters (eds). 2015b. *It's a small world: International deaf spaces and encounters*. Washington D.C.: Gallaudet University Press.

Gertz, Genie. 2003. *Dysconscious audism and critical deaf studies: Deaf crit's analysis of unconscious internalization of hegemony within the deaf community*. Los Angeles: University of California.

Gertz, Genie. 2008. Dysconscious audism: A theoretical proposition. In H-Dirksen L. Bauman (ed.), *Open your eyes: Deaf studies talking*, 219–234. Minneapolis, MN: The University of Minnesota Press.

Gertz, Genie. 2016. Dysconscious Audism. In Genie Gertz & Patrick Boudreault (eds.), *The SAGE deaf studies encyclopedia*, 330–332. Thousand Oaks: SAGE Publications.

Graham, Patrick J. & Joseph J. Tobin. 2020. The body as a canvas: Developing a deaf bodily habitus in deaf signing preschools. In Irene W. Leigh & Catherine A. O'Brien (eds.), *Deaf identities: Exploring new frontiers*, 145–161. Oxford: Oxford University Press.

Groce, Nora Ellen. 1985. *Everyone here spoke sign language: Hereditary deafness on Martha's Vineyard*. Cambridge: Harvard University Press.

Gulliver, Mike. 2015. The emergence of international deaf spaces in France from Desloges 1779 to the Paris Congress of 1900. In Michele Friedner & Annelies Kusters (eds), *It's a small world: International deaf spaces and encounters*, 3–14. Washington D.C.: Gallaudet University Press.

Gulliver, Mike & Mary Beth Kitzel. 2016. Geographies. In Genie Gertz & Patrick Boudreault (eds.), *The SAGE deaf studies encyclopedia*, 451–53. Thousand Oaks: SAGE Publications.

Gulliver, Mike & Emily Fekete. 2017. Themed section: Deaf geographies—an emerging field. *Journal of Cultural Geography* 34 (2). 121–130.

Hackett, Denise Thew. 2019. Looking through the kaleidoscope: A metaphor for convergences of identities. In Irene W. Leigh & Catherine A. O'Brien (eds.), *Deaf identities: Exploring new frontiers*, 370–394. Oxford: Oxford University Press.

Hall, Matthew L., Wyatte C. Hall & Naomi K. Caselli. 2019. Deaf children need language, Not (just) speech. *First Language* 39(4). 367–395.

Hall, Wyatte C. 2017. What you don't know can hurt you: The risk of language deprivation by impairing sign language development in deaf children. *Maternal and Child Health Journal* 21(5). 961–965.

Hall Wyatte C, Leonard L. Levin & Melissa L Anderson. 2017. Language deprivation syndrome: a possible neurodevelopmental disorder with sociocultural origins. *Social Psychiatry and Psychiatric Epidemiology* 52(6). 761–776.

Harmon, Kristen. 2010. Deaf Matters: Compulsory hearing and ability trouble. In Susan Burch & Alison Kafer (eds.), *Deaf and disability studies: Interdisciplinary perspectives*, 31–47. Washingon, D.C: Gallaudet University Press.

Haualand, Hilde. 2007. The two-week village: The significance of sacred occasions for the deaf community. In Benedicte Ingstad & Susan Reynolds Whyte (eds.), *Disability in local and global Worlds*, 33–55. Berkeley and Los Angeles: University of California Press.

Hauser, Peter C, Amanda O'Hearn, Michael McKee, Anne Steider & Denise Thew. 2010. Deaf epistemology: Deafhood and deafness. *American Annals of the Deaf* 154(5). 486–492.

Hayashi, Akiko & Joseph Tobin. 2015. *Teaching embodied: Cultural practices in Japanese preschools*. Chicago: The University of Chicago Press.

Humphries, Tom. 1975. *Audism: The making of a word*. Unpublished essay.

Johnson, Jennifer T. 2020. Participation in a global hearing culture: Hearing mothers' translations of their childrens' deafworlds. *Applied Linguistics* 41(1). 84–108.

Keating, Elizabeth & Gene Mirus. 2003. American sign language in virtual space: Interactions between deaf users of computer-mediated video communication and the impact of technology on language practices. *Language in Society* 32(5). 693–714.

King, Joyce. 1991. Dysconscious racism: Ideology, identity, and the mis-education of teachers. *Journal of Negro Education* 60(2). 133–146.

Klima, Edward S. & Ursula Bellugi. 1979. *The signs of language*. Cambridge: Harvard University Press.

Kusters, Annelies. 2015. *Deaf space in Adamorobe: An ethnographic study in a village in Ghana*. Washington D.C.: Gallaudet University Press.

Kusters, Annelies, Dai O'Brien & Maartje de Meulder. 2017a. Innovations in deaf studies: Critically mapping the field. In Annelies Kusters, Maartje de Meulder & Dai O'Brien (eds.), *Innovations in deaf studies: The role of deaf scholars*, 1–56. Oxford: Oxford University Press.

Kusters, Annelies, Massimiliano Spotti, Ruth Swanwick & Elina Tapio. 2017b. Beyond languages, beyond modalities: transforming the study of semiotic repertoires. *International Journal of Multilingualism* 14(3). 219–232.

Ladd, Paddy. 2003. *Understanding deaf culture: In search of deafhood*. Clevedon: Multilingual.

Lane, Harlan. 1992. *The mask of benevolence: Disabling the deaf community*. San Diego, CA: DawnSignPress.

Lane, Harlan, Robert Hoffmeister & Ben Bahan. 1996. *A journey into the deaf-world*. San Diego: DawnSign Press.

Lo, Ming-Cheng M. & Clare L. Stacey. 2008. Beyond cultural competency: Bourdieu, patients and clinical encounters. *Sociology of Health & Illness* 30(5). 741–755.

Matsuoka, Kazumi. 2015. *Nihon shuwa de manabu shuwa gengogaku no kiso* [Learning JSL through the fundamentals of Sign linguistics]. Tokyo: Kurosio Shuppan.

McGuire, Jennifer M. 2020. Who am I with others?: Selfhood and shuwa among mainstream educated deaf and hard-of-hearing Japanese youth. *Contemporary Japan* 32(2). 197–217.

McGuire, Jennifer M. & Tomoko Tokunaga. 2020. Co-constructing belonging: "Voluntary separation" in deaf and immigrant education in Japan. *Japanese Studies* 40(3). 291–311.

Meek, David R. 2020. Dinner table syndrome: A phenomenological study of deaf individuals' experiences with inaccessible communication. *The Qualitative Report 25*(6). 1676–1694.

de Meulder, Maartje, Annelies Kusters, Erin Moriarty & Joseph J. Murray. 2019. Describe, don't prescribe. The practice and politics of translanguaging in the context of deaf signers. *Journal of Multilingual and Multicultural Development* 40(10). 892–906.

Mitchell, Ross E. & Michaela Karchmer. 2004. Chasing the mythical ten percent: Parental hearing status of deaf and hard of hearing students in the United States. *Sign Language Studies* 4(2). 138–163.

Mori, Soya & Michiko Sasaki (eds.). 2017. *Shuwa wo gengo to iu no nara* [What does it mean to say that JSL is a language?]. Tokyo: Hitzuji Shobo.

Mori, Soya & Atsushi Sugimoto. 2019. Progress and problems in the campaign for sign language recognition in Japan. In Maartje de Meulder, Joseph J. Murray & Rachel L. McKee (eds.),The legal recognition of sign languages: Advocacy and outcomes around the world, 104–118. Bristol: Multilingual Matters.

Murray, Joseph J. 2008. Coequality and transnational studies: Understanding deaf lives. In H-Dirksen L. Bauman (ed.), *Open your eyes: Deaf studies talking*, 100–110. Minneapolis, MN: The University of Minnesota Press.

Nakamura, Karen. 2003. U-Turns, "deaf shock", and the hard of hearing: Japanese deaf identities at the borderlands. In Leila Monaghan, Constanze Schmaling, Karen Nakamura, & Graham H. Turner (eds.), *Many ways to be deaf: International variation in deaf communities*, 211–229. Washington D.C.: Gallaudet University Press.

Nakamura, Karen. 2006. *Deaf in Japan: Signing and the politics of identity*. Ithaca, NY: Cornell University Press.

O'Brien, Dai. 2020. Negotiating academic environments: using Lefebvre to conceptualise deaf spaces and disabling/enabling environments. *Journal of Cultural Geography* 37(1). 26–45.

O'Brien, Dai. 2021. Theorising the deaf body: Using Lefebvre and Bourdieu to understand deaf spatial experience. *Cultural Geographies* 28(4). 645–660.

Oka, Norie & Hitomi Akahori. 2011. *Nihon shuwa no shikumi* [Structure of Japanese Sign language]. Tokyo: Taishukan Shoten.

Oka, Norie & Michiko Sasaki. 2020. Literacy education for Japanese deaf children. In Qiuying Wang & Jean F. Andrews (eds.), *Literacy and deaf education: Toward a global understanding*, 379–401, Washington D.C., Gallaudet University Press.

Padden, Carol. 2008. The decline of deaf clubs in the US: A treatise on the problem of place. In H-Dirksen L. Bauman (ed.), *Open your eyes: Deaf studies talking*, 169–176. Minneapolis, MN: The University of Minnesota Press.

Richardson, Michael. 2019. Negotiating power and translation in a bilingual (British Sign Language/ English) rehearsal room. *New Voices in Translation Studies* 20. 163–184.

Saito, Michio. 2014. Tōjisha to hitōjisha [Central actors and non-central actors]. In Michiko Sasaki (ed.), *Minoriti no Shakai Sanka: Shōgaisha to Tayō Riterashii* [Literacies of minorities: Constructing a truly inclusive society], 88–107. Tokyo: Kurosio Shuppan.

Schmitt, Pierre. 2015. A global stage: Sign language artistic production and festivals in international contexts. In Michele Friedner & Annelies Kusters (eds.), *It's a small world: International deaf spaces and encounters*, 15–23. Washington D.C.: Gallaudet University Press.

Stokoe, William C.1960. Sign language structure: an outline of the visual communication systems of the American deaf. *Journal of Deaf Studies and Deaf Education* [Reprint 2005 Winter] 10(1). 3–37.

Shibuya, Tomoko. 2009. *Koda no sekai—Shuwa no bunka to koe no bunka* [The world of CODA: Sign language culture and orality]. Tokyo: Igaku Shoin.

Valentine, Gill & Tracey Skelton. 2008. Changing spaces: the role of the internet in shaping deaf geographies. *Social & Cultural Geography* 9(5). 469–485.

World Federation of the Deaf (WFD). 2022. "The Legal Recognition of National Sign Languages." https://wfdeaf.org/news/the-legal-recognition-of-national-sign-languages/(accessed 2022 December)

Zerubavel, Eviatar. 2018. *Taken for granted: The remarkable power of the unremarkable*. Princeton, N.J.: Princeton University Press.

Cori Jakubiak

"It's only in retrospect that I can be really critical of it": Performative linguistic "safe spaces" and becoming critical of volunteer tourism

1 Introduction

What are the conditions and "safe spaces" (e.g., The Roestone Collective 2014) that make alternative subjectivities possible? How, when, and where are individuals able to wrangle with new ways of being, question previously held convictions, and examine taken-for-granted assumptions in a fresh light? In what contexts and spaces can people voice controversial beliefs, and what leads them to do so? These are the questions with which I grapple in this chapter.

In line with this volume's attention to *performative linguistic space* (Doerr and McGuire, this volume), I examine the role of spatio-temporal contexts in 1) helping young people develop critical consciousness about volunteer tourism, a form of travel that combines voluntary service with holidaying; and 2) creating possibilities for individuals to express ideologically unpopular viewpoints. My first use of space is decidedly geographical, as corporate and non-governmental organization (NGO) sponsors frequently draw upon tropes of spatial difference, international mobility, and immersion to market volunteer tourism as an "exotic" adventure (Keese 2011).

My second use of space ties to the volume's central theme of how language use can coax, urge, or hinder the production of particular spaces. Using data collected through ethnographic interviews, I examine how two volunteer tourists, Joanne and Amanda, expressed changing views of volunteer tourism over time and in differently emplaced interview contexts. Drawing from literature on *coming-out migrations* (e.g., Gorman-Murray 2007; Puar, Rushbrook and Schein 2003), which complicates narrow understandings of sexual disclosure, I trace how the liminal, often disorienting, experience of a volunteer tourism trip generated new ideological spaces for these youths to examine volunteer tourism more critically. Coming-out migrations can be seen as "offering possibilities to make a [different] sense of self through experiences of anonymity, temporariness and displacement" (Waitt and Gorman-Murray 2011a: 1386). Similarly, the short-term, dislocating experience of a volunteer tourism trip transformed these study participants' subjectivities in unforeseen ways. By putting their volunteer tourism experiences in

https://doi.org/10.1515/9783110744781-006

dialogue with numerous temporal and spatial engagements including, but not limited to, previous and ongoing academic coursework, other international travel experiences, and ongoing reflections with family members and friends, Joanne and Amanda shifted from celebrating volunteer tourism as an exciting personal growth opportunity to expressing concerns about these programs' aims and claims. Moreover, the hesitancy with which Joanne, in particular, expressed her critique suggests that within certain ideological spaces, voicing negative views on volunteer tourism can be a risky act of disclosure.

I begin this chapter by discussing volunteer tourism and its current role in the social imaginary. I argue that despite a recent spate of academic and popular criticism, volunteer tourism remains a celebrated form of active civic engagement (Park 2018; Wearing, Beirman, and Grabowski 2020). Then, drawing theoretical support from literature on coming-out migrations, I explore how Joanne and Amanda's perspectives on volunteer tourism changed from enthusiastic to skeptical over time and through movements in and across different spaces. Literature on coming-out migrations explains individuals' narratives of sexual disclosure as slow, accretive processes that involve a spatial tacking back-and-forth between different material and psychological sites across the life course (Gorman-Murray 2011). Similarly, Joanne and Amanda's revised, cautious stances toward volunteer tourism developed as they traversed different physical and ideological terrains before, during, and after their service trips.

This chapter concludes with a discussion of the relations between performative linguistic "safe spaces" and ethnographic interview contexts. When I first interviewed Joanne and Amanda during their service tenure in Costa Rica, they assumed the practice's dominant discourses uncritically. Eighteen months later, however, in US-based *return interviews* (Tobin and Hayashi 2017), Joanne and Amanda both shared new concerns about volunteer tourism and its aims. These two distinct interview contexts thus produced qualitatively different performative linguistic spaces—spaces in which it was more or less possible to speak cautiously about volunteer tourism.[1] I discuss this observation and its links to performative linguistic space in the final sections of the chapter.

---

1 My use of the term, context, here indexes the temporality of my interviews, some of which were conducted in Costa Rica and others retrospectively in the US. I argue that these two different temporal interview contexts helped to produce different performative linguistic spaces; thanks to an anonymous reviewer for helping me to make this more explicit.

1.1 Volunteer tourism: Always seemingly benevolent

Volunteer tourism is defined as short-term, alternative travel that combines voluntary service with holidaying, generally in the Global South (Wearing 2001). The practice has received widespread public acclaim as a form of global citizenship education for volunteers (United Planet 2020) and as a community-based approach to development work (Lyons and Wearing 2008). US government advisors have characterized volunteer tourism as a form of diplomatic "smart power" (Brookings Institution 2006), and the benefits associated with participating in volunteer tourism have shifted the practice from being considered a "fringe," or hippy-like, activity to a mainstream, family-friendly one (Germann Molz 2016).

It is difficult to overstate the extent to which positive discourses adhere to volunteer tourism. College[2] admissions boards often look favorably upon volunteer tourism experiences, which are taken as evidence of an applicant's public service commitment (Vrasti 2013). Many US universities and colleges have in-house volunteer tourism programs that operate in the name of "service-learning" (Bodinger de Uriarte and Jacobson 2018; Park 2018). Also, many private firms with corporate social responsibility initiatives grant their employees leave to be volunteer tourists, as doing so can augment a corporation's humanitarian brand (see Richey and Ponte 2011, for a discussion of corporate humanitarianism).

What volunteer tourists actually *do* in their service placements varies widely. While some volunteers may engage in construction work or visit orphanages (Guiney 2018), teaching English is a popular program option (Guttentag 2012). Like volunteer tourism more generally, what I have elsewhere called "English-language voluntourism" (cf. Jakubiak 2020) occupies a virtuous place in the public imaginary. Teaching English to speakers of other languages (TESOL) is frequently associated with charity, immigrant integration, and general helpfulness (Spack 1996), and TESOL has long been associated with generosity and Christian missionary work (Snow 2001).

Linked to the perceived benevolence of TESOL, then, as well as volunteer tourism, English-language voluntourism is widely seen as a righteous development intervention and beyond critique (Jakubiak 2012, 2020). Like other forms of volunteer tourism, which "have come to occupy a (suspiciously) firm moral grounding that *demands* applause" (Vrasti 2013: 4 [emphasis in original]), English-language voluntourism operates as a form of institutional and discursive "common sense" (Sedgwick 1990) about what it means to do good and well in the

---

2 I use the term, college, here to refer specifically to undergraduate, postsecondary education in the US context.

world. To criticize English-language voluntourism—to ask, for example, about the role of English in community language shift or whether short-term, inexperienced volunteers should be intervening in Global South classrooms—risks framing oneself as a rabble rouser or someone who is "not nice."[3] As my study participant, Joanne, reflected during her return interview:

> [I]f you are critical of [dominant formations such as volunteer tourism], that necessarily means that you have some sort of destructive tendency towards them in that, in the sense that you want to change them. And the way that you want to change them is that you don't agree with those structures, meaning you want to break them down, and that's really scary to people [. . .]. [The volunteer tourism program sponsor, a non-governmental organization] doesn't want me to come out thinking this way [. . .]. I often feel like somewhat of an outsider.

As this interview excerpt reveals, to be critical of volunteer tourism in certain contexts can put one in a metaphorical closet: at odds with normative values, a social deviant.

Joanne, however, is not alone in her critique of volunteer tourism. Both she and Amanda, whom I interviewed as a part of a larger research project and whose voices I highlight in this chapter, expressed discomfort with volunteer tourism's normative assumptions and goals. However, their critical stances developed not immediately but as a consequence of their physical and psychological movements in and out of various spaces over time. Their changed perspectives thus illustrate the "situated spatialit[ies] of subjectivity" (Waitt and Gorman-Murray 2011b: 1239) that scholars of coming-out migrations have long detailed. I now turn to a discussion of this literature.

1.2 Coming out migrations and the temporal/spatial contingencies of new subjectivities

My use of literature on coming-out migrations as a theoretical frame for examining volunteer tourists' changed perspectives is not to equate developing a critical perspective on a topic or concept such as volunteer tourism with the material violence, social stigma, and dispossession faced by people who have publicly disclosed

---

3 See Angelina E. Castagno's (2019) edited volume on how discourses and practices of "Niceness" uphold economic and racial inequality. Scholar Wanda Vrasti (2013) also reports having some friends say that her "thesis was mean" when they learned that she was critiquing volunteer tourism. Relatedly, Ji Hoon Park's (2018) critical analysis of a university-sponsored volunteer tourism program in Cameroon was met by supervising faculty with "strong concern[s] that this research could hurt [their] future funding" of similar volunteer projects (p. 159).

LGBTQIA+ identities[4] (see Scott 2018, for commentary on how "coming out" metaphors have been depoliticized). Rather, I use theoretical insights from work on coming-out migrations as a lens for highlighting the temporal-spatial nature of individuals' subjectivities.

Situated at the intersection of queer theory, human geography, and mobilities studies (e.g., Hannam, Sheller, and Urry 2006), scholarship on coming-out migrations complicates simplistic understandings of sexual disclosure. Rather than conceptualizing the coming out process as a one-time, life course event in which a person moves permanently from "closeted to open" by publicly disclosing their sexual extra-normativity (Sedgwick 1990), work on coming-out migrations suggests that coming out is a fluid, accretive process contingent upon spatial and temporal arrangements (Gorman-Murray 2007; Puar, Rushbrook, and Schein 2003). In their case study of one Australian teenager's coming-out migration, for example, Gordon Waitt and Andrew Gorman-Murray (2011a) note that this teenager credited his ability to live as an openly gay man in a small, rural town to a prior experience of having lived temporarily in a large, urban, gay center. Although the teenager had originally migrated from a different rural hometown to the city in order to come out, his urban experience was not the one-way "queer homecoming" that is frequently suggested in the literature (e.g., Fortier 2001). Instead, tempted by drug use in the urban club scene and feeling overwhelmed by unwanted sexual attention, the teenager migrated to a new, small rural town to make a permanent gay home. As Waitt and Gorman-Murray (2011a: 1399) explain, "[S]elf-understandings arise, and can change or become irrelevant, via the intersection of different subject positions through a process of oscillating between 'here' and 'elsewhere,' as well as between 'present' and 'past' places." In other words, segments of mobility at various temporal junctions can facilitate new subjectivities.

Nathaniel Lewis' investigation of 48 gay men's coming-out migrations also highlights how individuals' subjectivities are spatially and temporally constructed. Focusing on "the discontinuous, segmented, and ongoing nature of queer coming-out *journeys*" (2012: 216 [emphasis in original]), Lewis argues that sexual disclosure is fluid and space/time dependent. Many of his study participants, for example, "re-closeted" themselves upon career-related relocations over the lifespan despite having lived as openly gay men in the past. Additionally, study participants' unforeseen migration experiences sometimes prompted new sexual disclosures. One of Lewis' study participants came out as a gay man due to the pressure of an impending move with his girlfriend; he felt he could not continue to live in a heterosexual

---

4 Thank you to my student, Greta Schmidt, for stressing this important point.

partnership while also adjusting to life in a new town. Space and time are inextricably intertwined in and with the coming out process. As Waitt and Gorman-Murray (2011a: 1386) point out, "[W]ork on the spatiality of subjectivity has emphasized how movement can enhance an awareness of the self."

These theoretical findings on coming-out migrations provide a useful framework for the analysis that I present here. Larry Knopp and Michael Brown write that "a certain spatial tacking back and forth between different scales and environments is very common in the ongoing process of constructing queer subjectivities, cultures, and forms of resistance" (2003: 417) to dominant political and social norms. Similarly, I offer that participating in volunteer tourism—a hegemonic, spatially dislocating, liminal practice also grounded in dramatic movements between "here" and "there"— allows some youths' subjectivities to shift in unexpected directions. A volunteer tourist's experiences abroad and at home—their "spatial tacking back and forth between different scales and environments"—can complicate their previous understandings of such issues as the role of Northern, unskilled volunteers in international development work; the necessity of broad-scale policy reforms to address social problems; and the ways in which peoples' best intentions can nevertheless cause harm. In that sense, youths' "spatial tacking back and forth" can help to engender new, performative linguistic spaces in which volunteer tourism can be discussed more critically.

2 Research methods

Data for this study were collected as part of a larger, multi-sited ethnography of volunteer tourism that took place between 2007 and 2014. During that time, I conducted and collected approximately seventy qualitative interviews with fifty-five different stakeholders: current and former volunteers; staff workers in the offices of a US-based non-governmental organization (NGO) that sponsored English-language voluntourism programs; and NGO staff workers abroad. I also conducted participant observation in three different contexts: I taught English as a volunteer tourist in Costa Rica for six weeks; volunteered at an intentional community in Romania for two weeks; and worked for a month as a volunteer program assistant in the US home offices of my NGO Costa Rica program sponsor. This multi-sited methodology allowed me to trace volunteer tourism's contours across various contexts over time (Marcus 1995).

This chapter focuses specifically on interview data that I collected from two study participants: Joanne and Amanda. Both in their early twenties and students at a prestigious Ivy League college at the time of our interviews, Joanne and Amanda were unique in my data set. I interviewed each of them multiple times: Joanne once and Amanda twice in Costa Rica, where they were members of my own volunteer tourism cohort, and eighteen months later, in the US city where their college is located.[5] My analysis of interview data reveals that Joanne and Amanda's respective stances toward volunteer tourism became more critical as they moved in and out of different physical and ideological spaces over time. Furthermore, the ways in which Joanne, in particular, spoke in her return interview suggest that some volunteers may feel discomfort with volunteer tourism while they are still in the field. However, there seem to be few spaces within volunteer tourism programs for expressing concerns about the practice.

2.1 Joanne: "It's only in retrospect that I can be really critical of it"

Noting the ways in which coming-out migrations are partial and subject to deferment, Nathaniel Lewis writes that "Coming out [. . .] is not just the fulfillment of a short-term appetite for self-declaration, but rather an ongoing, dialectical journey in which someone comes to know themselves as gay" (2012: 213). Borrowing from Lewis' thickening of the coming out journey, I suggest that making sense of volunteer tourism is also an ongoing, dialectical journey for many volunteers. This was indeed the case for Joanne.

Joanne was a White, female, anthropology major from a large, northeastern US city. When we first sat down to talk after an evening of salsa dancing in Costa Rica during our program's orientation, Joanne conveyed excitement about volunteer tourism. She expressed admiration for other people who had been volunteer tourists in the past, and she hoped that volunteer English teaching abroad would give her insight on education as a career. Joanne said:

> I knew at least five friends who had done it [volunteer tourism] last year and heard really good things about it. [. . .] I also like teaching in general. I've taught before, although not in front of a classroom, but—I thought it would be a good experience, because I might want to

---

5 I had the chance to conduct return interviews with three members of my own Costa Rica volunteer cohort, as all of them attended the same college in the northeastern U.S. city where I conducted a broader set of retrospective interviews. Because the NGO's volunteer summer cohorts are typically comprised of 10–20 people from across the United States, it was difficult to conduct return interviews—at that time—with other cohort members. The wider accessibility of video-conferencing since the Covid-19 pandemic, however, could make return interviews more possible in future volunteer tourism studies. Still, this would involve new methodological quandaries associated with virtual interviews.

go into teaching after college. So, I wanted to see if I could actually do it, in front of a whole classroom—what that would be like, every day, for two months. To see how tired I would be at the end of the day—if I thought I could handle it for another ten years. Just the adventure of it—going off. I've never been away from home for so long by myself or traveled alone [. . .]. So, it's all a big adventure. I just think it [will] help me grow as a person. Whenever I talk to other kids at school who have done these sorts of things over the summer or taken time off and done all of these things, they just seem to have a better perspective on everything, and they're just more interesting people.

Here, Joanne takes up the dominant discourses of volunteer tourism marketing literature. She frames short-term, volunteer English teaching abroad as adventurous and life-defining. Her words reflect the language used by volunteer tourism sponsors, who often make similar claims on their promotional websites. To wit: "A volunteer trip abroad with Cross-Cultural Solutions will change you. Change the way you see other cultures. Maybe even change how you live your life" (Cross-Cultural Solutions 2016).

Interviewed eighteen months later in the US, Joanne had indeed changed. However, the changes wrought to her person by volunteer tourism were not the ones that she had earlier discussed. In contrast to the enthusiasm toward volunteer tourism that Joanne had expressed in Costa Rica, she was strikingly critical toward the practice when interviewed retrospectively. Putting her volunteer tourism experience in dialogue with recollections of a prior Habitat for Humanity trip to Botswana,[6] Joanne now castigated volunteer tourism for being wasteful and undertheorized. She said:

I had done Habitat for Humanity the year before [my Costa Rica volunteer tourism trip], and going into [Habitat], I was excited about it, but [. . .] I had no idea what I was getting into. And so we ended up going to Africa for two weeks. And the amount of money that we spent in getting ourselves to Africa could've built ten billion houses in this village and fed everyone [there] for ten years. It was just astronomical. And so it seemed like we were benefitting far more than we were actually, like, supposedly helping people. So, I became quite critical of the notion of going somewhere to help people.

Joanne's revised, cautious stance toward volunteer tourism comes through clearly in this interview excerpt. It is a dramatically different orientation toward the

---

6 During both of our interviews—in Costa Rica and later, in the return interview context— Joanne referred to her Habitat for Humanity experience as having occurred "in Africa" rather than naming a specific country. I was able to discern that she had gone to Botswana because she mentioned having learned about Botswanans' daily wages during our first interview. However, Joanne homogenized the African continent frequently in her discussions of her Habitat for Humanity experience, using expressions like "going to Africa" rather than "going to Botswana." This tendency to reduce the African continent to one specific place reflects an Orientalizing discourse (cf. Keyl 2016).

practice than that she had expressed to me in Costa Rica. Literature on coming-out migrations reminds us, however, that a person's decision to take up a particular subjectivity is not a one-off event. As Nathaniel Lewis reports about gay men's segmented coming-out journeys, those "who moved out and 'went back in' [. . .] did not merely interrupt a predetermined process of opening the closet door; they were often negotiating 'in-between' worlds that multiple subjectivities had rendered more complex than imagined or anticipated" (2012: 219). Joanne's journey toward skepticism concerning volunteer tourism was also fuzzy and circuitous. Her narrative suggests that she had previously felt uncomfortable with Habitat for Humanity's aims; yet, her discomfort at the time was not severe enough to prevent her from volunteering abroad again. It wasn't until *after* her trip to Costa Rica—her second volunteer tourism experience—that Joanne's expressed stance toward volunteer tourism shifted from supportive to critical.

In one sense, Joanne's ongoing participation in international voluntary service trips must be understood in the context of the current historical moment. Like a person who identifies as gay who goes back into the closet due to relocation or work contingencies, Joanne may have set aside her disdain for volunteer tourism in order to accrue a valued form of cultural capital. As aforementioned, many groups view volunteer tourism as evidence of worldliness and active civic engagement and reward it accordingly (Vrasti 2013). Costa Rica's location as a tourist destination may have also accentuated the trip's allure (Keese 2011).

Later in the same return interview, however, Joanne highlighted an incident from Costa Rica that had prompted extended reflection. Although she, herself, had previously built houses with Habitat for Humanity, she was angered by the presence of a US youth group that had come to build a school in her host site. Joanne's frustration toward these visiting volunteers led her to reevaluate her own role in Costa Rica. She explained:

> While I was there [in Costa Rica], a high school group from the US came to build the new high school. And so this group of, maybe, like thirty American thirteen-year-olds who were the same age as my kids [students]—came and were building, brick by brick, this [school]—and, they only came, I think they came four days—like, once a week for four weeks. And I said to my [Costa Rican] kids, "Why aren't *you* building this school?" And they said, "Ohh, uhh"—they didn't really have an answer [. . .]. I was like, "Why, why should these kids from however many thousands of miles away pay thousands of dollars to come and build the school that my kids who are healthy, young teenagers can totally build with their own two hands—and should be building with their own two hands—because it's their school! Why should these, like, rich White people come and build the school *for* them?" And I just— it made me so mad, and I was probably, like, so rude to them. But in the same way, I could be as critical of my place. Like, why should I come and teach English rather than funnel the money into improving the entire national educational system so that the English teachers actually can teach English? Like, all the thousands of dollars and time and energy that the

volunteers spend going to have their own experience—if the goal is really to improve the
education of international development, whatever it is, you would funnel it into actually
improving the structures of education.

Here, Joanne sees a parallel between her own position and that of the visiting
youth group. Although she was frustrated that US outsiders were building her
Costa Rican students' new school, Joanne saw the youth group's presence in her
host site as a lens for (re)examining her own role there.

Gordon Waitt and Andrew Gorman-Murray note that *displacement* can be "a
mechanism or trigger for self-transformation" (2011a: 1398). For Joanne, the dislocating, temporary experience of participating in English-language voluntourism—
informed by a previous trip with Habitat for Humanity—advanced her concerns
about volunteer tourism's interventions and political engagements. Joanne's experiences of tacking back-and-forth between her US home and international service
trips complicated an earlier, simplistic view of volunteer tourism and its goals.
When asked if there had been space or time in Costa Rica for her to explore these
conflicting feelings, Joanne remarked:

> I'm not sure, because at the time, I wasn't thinking like this [. . .]. If I was thinking like this
> two years ago, I probably wouldn't have gone and done it [volunteer tourism], because I
> currently wouldn't go and do it again. It's only in retrospect that I can be really critical of it
> [. . .]. Even my brother [also a former volunteer]—we've had long arguments about this,
> and he's certainly not as critical as I am at all, and [he] has a tinge of the Orientalist-type
> view—but then again, he was five and a half years older than I am. So, I think he had a
> better framework to enter, at least, like, an academic sort of framework. Whereas I was
> like, "I don't know what I'm doing here. Let's teach some English."

Joanne's growing discomfort with volunteer tourism can be seen here in her description of her own brother, also a former volunteer, whom she describes as pos-
sessing an Orientalist viewpoint. Precisely *because* her brother held this view,
Joanne suggests, he was able to more fully enjoy being a volunteer tourist.
Joanne's observations accord with related scholarship on volunteer tourism,
which suggests that most volunteer tourism programs lack a social justice educational component and draw heavily on Orientalist tropes (Henry 2019; Keyl 2016).

Nathaniel Lewis notes that "both coming out and the journeys that mediate it
are nonlinear, with uneven and discontinuous trajectories" (2012: 225). Joanne's
journey toward skepticism concerning volunteer tourism was also peripatetic. It
was mediated by a wide array of personal and dislocating experiences, including
international volunteering across multiple sites. Joanne's further admission that
she "wouldn't go and do [volunteer tourism] again" suggests that being publicly
critical of volunteer tourism was less possible before her trip to Costa Rica. That
is, Joanne had to *be* a volunteer tourist multiple times—and put these experiences
in dialogue with prior discomfort as well as sustained reflection—to come to a

new subjectivity vis-à-vis volunteer tourism.[7] "What, then, might be the spatialities of contingent, dialectical journeys through which coming out transpires?" Lewis (2012: 214) asks. In order for youth to push back against the rhetoric of popular humanitarianism in both their speech and actions, moving back-and-forth between a Global South volunteer service trip and one's Global North home— even multiple times—may be a necessary and powerful spatiality. Joanne's peripatetic journey helped to produce a new performative linguistic "safe" space in which her critique of volunteer tourism could come to light.

2.2 Amanda: "I didn't do something villainous; I just also didn't do something perfect"

Amanda was another member of the same volunteer tourist cohort that included me and Joanne. Prior to being sent to different host sites around Costa Rica, Amanda and I got to know each other socially during the NGO's volunteer orientation and, later, during the NGO's mid-service conference. A White woman in her early twenties from the US West Coast,[8] Amanda self-identified as an evangelical Christian and was a Latin American Studies major at an Ivy League college. When I asked Amanda what had motivated her to participate in volunteer tourism, she spoke about these program's educational benefits for volunteers. Amanda explained that she wanted to practice living outside of the United States, and that volunteer tourism provided structure. She said:

> This past January, I had a chance to visit the Philippines with my mom as a short vacation, and we visited friends of ours who are missionaries, and it allowed me to see—a little bit— how different people and groups developed and how some interaction with, like, really developed countries like the US could do positive things. And it made me realize that there was just so much more of the world that I wanted to see. And I wanted to see it in a way that wasn't just, you know, seeing what other White people saw [. . .]. Like everyone else, I'm looking for a little bit of direction. I feel like this program attracts a lot of people who are, like, a little gypsy,[9] a little bit of, of wanderers and drifters [. . .]. And so, I'm looking for some sort of amazing inspiration for work in the future. But, in actuality, I think I just wanted to see if

---

7 Joanne specifically noted in our return interview that her brother's volunteer tourism experience was the only time that he'd ever travelled or volunteered abroad, unlike her. "It was like the [recruitment] poster to him," she explained, describing her brother's positive stance toward volunteer tourism.

8 Scholars have noted that most participants in volunteer tourism programs identify as White women (cf. Vrasti 2013), and my pool of study participants reflected these same demographics.

9 Numerous volunteers in my study used this term—a derogatory reference to Roma people— unselfconsciously and in discussions of their own travel desires.

living abroad could be something that I could do, like baby steps. I was two weeks abroad in the Philippines; now, I'll be two months abroad, and maybe after, you know, after college is done, I could do two years abroad, you know, with the Peace Corps [. . .] [or] another kind of organized adventure like this. So, it was part of my baby step plan on, you know, having larger adventures and [. . .] perspective on life.

Like Joanne, Amanda appropriates the dominant language of volunteer tourism sponsors.[10] Marketing materials routinely suggest that participating in volunteer tourism will help youth revise their current priorities, absorb local wisdom, and gain life direction for the future. In illustration, a website describing Global Volunteers' Cook Islands program tells prospective volunteers that "[Y]ou learn to appreciate 'island time' and a life style that is safer, slower and friendlier than what you might have been used to. You come home more relaxed and more aware of what really matters" (Destination NOW 2013).

When I met her again for coffee a year and a half later on a blustery January day in the US northeast, Amanda had indeed become more aware of many things. While she expressed appreciation for Costa Rica's *pura vida*—a philosophy of slowness and simplicity in daily life—our conversation centered on Amanda's new questioning of volunteer tourism as development. Over the course of eighteen months and as a consequence of moving in and out of different physical and ideological spaces including, but not limited to, her Costa Rican host site; academic classrooms; campus dining halls; and recollections of her family trip to the Philippines, Amanda's stance toward volunteer tourism had shifted from celebratory to cautionary. Her altered perspective captures how changes in subjectivity "are ongoing, relational, and often discontinuous journeys influenced by both [. . .] individuals' intersectional subjectivities (e.g., age, race, and class) and the social contexts of the places they encounter" (Lewis 2012: 211).

A central feature of Amanda's volunteer tourism trip had been her supplementary service project. All of the volunteers in our cohort had been charged with designing and implementing an extracurricular service project; most projects—mine included—were small initiatives such as offering extra English tutoring. By contrast, Amanda raised over $3000.00 to help her host school complete a half-built classroom. Amanda wrote a series of colorful newsletters describing her host community's financial difficulties, and she emailed these newsletters home to her parents and their American friends. The result was an outpouring of financial support from Christians who belonged to her family's home church;

---

10 Amanda's positionality as an evangelical Christian may be salient here. She implicitly takes up the benevolence of missionary interventions (i.e., by not critiquing her friends in the Philippines or their intentions).

consequently, Amanda's Costa Rican host community was able to finish construction of the school.

Amanda's service project far surpassed the NGO's and many other stakeholders' expectations. She received widespread praise for her fundraising efforts and was later featured prominently on an NGO recruitment poster. We looked at a copy of this poster together during our stateside return interview. Skimming it, Amanda remarked:

> [The NGO staff] were so impressed. You've met [the head of admissions at the NGO]. [He] was *so* stoked. He was like, "This is the coolest thing ever. I'm going to put you on our posters if I can [. . .]. You are a notable person; this is a really phenomenal project." These sorts of things. Because it's the idea of connecting [host] community resources with American resources. But it's also reaffirming that community resources are things like labor and support and American resources are things like money.

Here, Amanda expresses a growing awareness of her project's political dimensions. She regretted that her project exacerbated her host community's financial dependency. While Amanda was in Costa Rica, she explained, she hadn't considered the broader implications of giving money to her town. However, eighteen months later and after academic study as well as multiple conversations with a trusted advisor, Amanda had developed a cautious stance toward her service project and its entailments. Her revised thinking prompted a broader critique of volunteer tourism as a whole. Amanda explained:

> [My service project] definitely probably reinforced the idea that the United States is rich—I mean, the "United States can help us." Which is something that I understand now is not positive. I mean, although what has been left there, the building itself, will be very useful to [my host community], it's still possibly a bad policy to come in with American money and just give, because it's not a sustainable way of developing. The country's not working for itself. The same with being a volunteer abroad; the country isn't paying for you. And it's not encouraging a country [. . .] to foster education in such a way that it's raising its own teachers. Or fostering, even building development so that it's raising its own—you know, building financiers [. . .]. So that is the debate that has been presented to me by different classes here [in college] or people who have done international development stuff here. A friend of mine is a—she did Peace Corps in Niger—and she is an advisor of mine; she's a very close friend and advisor. She goes to [Ivy League graduate school] now, and she's probably the one who gave me the closest statement of why it's not—what I did wasn't a bad thing, but it also wasn't necessarily, like, the best thing.

Here, Amanda credits academic study and conversations with a respected advisor for changing her point of view. She contrasts the NGO's response to her service project—"[He] was *so* stoked"—with a more nuanced approach to international development that aligns with critical scholarship (e.g., Sen: 1999).[11] Curious to hear more about her shift in thinking, I asked Amanda how she interpreted these different reactions to her service project. She explained:

> My advisor, who's not involved with [the NGO] was looking at it from a slightly more universal international development perspective and [the NGO] is maybe looking at it from a good-for-[NGO] international development perspective. Like, [building a school] is something you tell other people about and they say, "Wow! [NGO] is really doing things. We should donate so that they can do more programs and continue and grow." It's a good PR piece [. . .]. The fact that there is international development sticky-places in it can get smoothed over for being a PR piece. And so, [the NGO's director of recruitment], who I think was even in charge of PR at that time, was really excited, because he could take this story and use it to sort of better [the NGO]. And it still is good things. It's not all bad; I didn't do something villainous. I just also didn't do something perfect.

Here, Amanda shows a growing awareness of how various actors' goals can shift the purposes and meanings of development. Although the NGO lauded her fundraising efforts, Amanda resists their framing of her project as straightforwardly good and uncomplicated. Larry Knopp and Michael Brown call for increased attention to how participants in heterosexist, normative projects "seize upon [these projects'] discontinuities, contingencies, and contradictions to live lives that are more of their own choosing than ones scripted for them (even though they unwittingly reproduce those scripts at the same time)" (2003: 413). Similarly, even though Amanda reproduced a particular "script" about normative civic engagement by participating in volunteer tourism, she ultimately became more critical of these programs and their ancillary features, like philanthropic giving, by being a volunteer.

A key factor that had complicated volunteer tourism for Amanda was the role that religion had played in her service project's success. Alluding to the historical links between Christian missionary work and humanitarianism, Amanda noted that many of her donors had been motivated by religious zeal. She explained:

> Again, with the very generous donors—like, that's the only reason that it [the service project] worked out. Like, people that sort of I didn't realize were that interested just sort of—I mean, my parents sent [my newsletters] to a lot of their Christian friends, so the people that I didn't even know were that interested prayed about it and gave us a lot of money. So, and that's another complicating factor for me in international relations is that I'm from an evangelical Christian home—that is, the people who say [we] should go out and, like, are interested in

---

11 My own experience when doing fieldwork in the NGO's home offices aligns with Amanda's perceptions. There was a general lack of criticality toward volunteer tourism among office staff; instead, the prevailing ideology in the NGO was one of modernist, Western-led development (see Kapoor 2004).

The Great Commission[12] and going out and preaching gospel to all peoples. And, I feel a tension in that. Because I'm interested in all this cultural relativity and cultural respect—what's the word? You know what I'm trying to say. Like, coming in and not being a dominant, colonial, whatever, you know? So, that's why it was also funny, because I wasn't doing missions work.[13] But these people still felt somehow religiously driven to give me money to just developmental, humanitarian work—is maybe some way we can classify what that building was or what my presence there was.

Amanda's ongoing, relational, and dialogic thinking about volunteer tourism comes through clearly here in this interview excerpt. It is a vastly more complex stance toward volunteer tourism than the one that she voiced in Costa Rica. Literature on coming-out migrations is useful here for making sense of Amanda's changed perspective. As Andrew Gorman-Murray points out in regard to traditional treatments of coming-out as a singular, life course event that takes place in cities, "[T]here seems to be an assumption that moving from the country to the city is a one-off event which facilitates coming out, suggesting a teleological and ontological finality with respect to relocation and identity-formation. This is contrary to current ideas of fluid, contingent identities" (2007: 110).

Amanda's stances toward volunteer tourism are also fluid and time-space dependent. Within community spaces like her family's home church, Amanda is perceived as doing God's work and receives material support for her efforts. Similarly, the NGO sponsor of her Costa Rica program placed Amanda on recruitment posters as a "model" volunteer tourist. Yet, in academic spaces like her campus dining hall and in Latin American Studies classes, Amanda is developing a critical orientation toward Global North-South interventions. Rather than fostering a "teleological and ontological finality with respect to [. . .] identity formation," a volunteer tourist trip to Costa Rica resulted in a new and more fluid subjectivity for Amanda. Amanda's volunteer tourism experience—situated at the nexus of her home community's support of Christian missionaries, coursework in Latin American Studies, and conversations with knowledgeable others—complicated her earlier, simplistic assumptions about volunteer tourism and generated a new, productive space in which Amanda could wrangle with the complexities of international development.

---

12 The Great Commission is an expression used to refer to biblical passages that are interpreted by some as authorizing and encouraging the Christian conversion work of missionaries.

13 Amanda's remark suggests an awareness of differences between the secular orientation of the NGO and the kinds of Christian missionary work sponsored by her home church. My own experiences with the NGO affirm that the NGO assiduously avoided any references to Christian missionary work, despite discursive and ideological parallels between Western development apparatuses and missionary work (see, for example, Bornstein 2005).

3 Performative linguistic "safe space" and return interview contexts

As Neriko Musha Doerr and Jennifer M. McGuire note in this volume's introduction, the "movement of individuals between spaces creates contours of specific performative linguistic space" (Introduction: 17). That is, performative linguistic spaces are produced not only because of who is present in a particular space at a certain moment in time, but also through the prior movements and experiences of those who are also present in the space.

The return interviews that I conducted with Joanne and Amanda produced distinct performative linguistic spaces in which certain speech acts were made possible. In these spaces, it was safe to critique volunteer tourism in a way that was less possible in Costa Rica. As Joanne and Amanda had traversed different physical and ideological terrains over the course of eighteen months, they took on new subjectivities that were influenced by their mobilities. Yet, as we saw in the case of Joanne, discomfort with volunteer tourism may have existed prior to the Costa Rica trip. Why, then, did skepticism not come through in the first interview(s) that I conducted?

I suggest that the return interview context produced a performative linguistic "safe space" for expressing concerns about volunteer tourism. Originally referring to physical sites in which people with marginalized identities are free from physical and psychological harm (The Roestone Collective 2014), the term, "safe space," is now used more broadly to refer to any context in which contentious social issues can be discussed without personal risk or injury (Verduzco-Baker 2018). For Joanne and Amanda, the return interview context generated a performative linguistic "safe space" in which they could freely discuss their growing hesitation toward volunteer tourism's political engagements. As noted in the introduction, a performative linguistic space "space is not performative on its own; rather the space becomes performative as a result of the specific intersections of linguistic politics carried from the various spaces that individuals have traversed" (Introduction: 9). Return interviews, I offer, may usher in distinct performative linguistic spaces, as "return interviews allow the [researcher] to ask better questions, the informants to give better answers, and the researcher/researched dyad to achieve greater levels of trust and a deeper level of intersubjectivity" (Tobin and Hayashi 2017: 320). In other words, more trust and increased intersubjectivity between me and my study participants helped to *produce* a unique performative linguistic space—a space in which richer, more nuanced discussions of volunteer tourism were possible. This idea harkens back to theoretical work on coming-out migrations, which demonstrates the spatio-temporal nature of peoples' subjectivities. Here, Joseph Tobin and Akiko Hayashi speak to the role of return interviews in capturing such changes in subjectivity—including those changes that have occurred in researchers themselves:

> Return interviewing facilitates not just intersubjectivity between researchers and informants but also possibilities for understanding change over time in individuals, cultures, and communities [. . .]. When we conduct a return interview, we have changed but so have our informants. We have been changed by time we have spent back in our offices pouring over transcripts of earlier interviews, reading new theory, and writing, and also by events that have transpired in our professional and personal lives, as well as by changes in our society. (2017: 325)

The performative linguistic spaces that my return interviews produced, then, were also reflective of changes in me as a researcher. When I conducted my first interviews with Joanne and Amanda in Costa Rica as a doctoral student, I was keen to understand volunteer tourists' motivations and was, myself, a volunteer. By contrast, my positionality in the return interviews was clearly that of a researcher: I had scheduled these interviews well in advance, and I interviewed Joanne and Amanda on their "home turf," in coffee shops that they chose near their campus. The questions I asked in the return interviews were informed by my own extended reading, as I, too, had been changed by my time in the field. As Natalie Djohari and her colleagues write, "Safe spaces are co-created, co-imagined and co-experienced, born out of ongoing, renewing and ever-evolving relationships with others. These relationships are shaped by prior histories and memories, both personal and collective, within a changing socio-political landscape" (Djohari, Pyndiah, and Arnone 2018: 354). Performative linguistic "safe spaces" similarly emerge from fluid and changing contexts. Joanne, Amanda, and I all brought our Costa Rica memories, shared trust in one another, and new subjectivities to the return interview settings, and in so doing, we co-produced a performative linguistic "safe space."

4 Conclusion

My aim in this chapter has been to highlight how two youths' movements in and across different spaces over time led to new and unexpected changes in their subjectivities. I drew upon work on coming-on migrations to explain how certain stances and disclosures are time-space dependent. For Joanne and Amanda, volunteer tourism was not a containerized space in which Orientalist discourses ran rampant and White saviorist tropes went uncontested (cf. Park 2018). Rather, the dislocating, liminal experience of a volunteer tourism trip—mediated by other spatially-emplaced social relations such as academic study, other voluntary service experiences, and conversations with knowledgeable others—led Joanne and Amanda to question volunteer tourism and its engagements.[14]

Critics have lamented the "White Savior Industrial Complex" that undergirds volunteer tourism (Cole 2016), and some scholars have suggested that volunteer tourism might end in the near future (Henry 2019). However, because powerful groups continue to reward participation in volunteer tourism, it may be unrealistic to suggest that youth will reject these programs entirely. Volunteer tourism continues to structure opportunities for youth to engage with global problems; to be sure, even Covid-19 didn't stop it, as the industry simply moved online (see United Planet 2020). A better approach might be to recognize the discontinuities and contradictions that influence volunteers' perceptions of their service over time. Like Joanne and Amanda, some youth may participate in volunteer tourism only to later become its most ardent critics and revisionists. Larry Knopp and Michael Brown observe this contradiction about metaphorical closets, noting that, "Closets are simultaneously sites of oppression and empowerment. Even as they stigmatize and disempower by denying people resources and even language by which to understand their own experience, closets at the same time *create* spaces for the expression of desire, resistance to oppression, and the transformation of society" (2003: 422). In other words, sites of disempowerment[15] and dislocation can also be powerful sites of change. "It's only in retrospect that I can be really critical of it," Joanne said in her return interview. Her comment highlights the spatio-temporal nature of developing a new subjectivity.

In regard to debates around safe spaces, Malte Philipp Gembus urges us to reject "static physical and geographic readings [and instead] embrace a fluid view of 'safe spaces' that are momentarily and spontaneously created through performative interactions" (2018: 433). Talk is one of those performances, as speech act theory reminds us (Austin 1962). I close by suggesting that it is *through* participation in volunteer tourism—and having the chance to reflect on one's experience in a return interview—that former volunteers and researchers can together generate

---

14 The only other return interview that I conducted—with a male, college-aged student who attended the same higher education institution as Joanne and Amanda—also showed new skepticism toward volunteer tourism over time and in the return interview context.
15 My sense of volunteer tourism as a site of disempowerment for participating youth is heavily influenced by Wanda Vrasti's (2013) critical analysis of these programs. Using a Marxian framework, Vrasti argues that volunteer tourism programs interpellate youth as neoliberal, enterprising, self-regulating subjects who must treat every aspect of their lives—including their leisure time—as an opportunity for cultural capital accumulation. Whether volunteers, themselves, perceive this interpellation as disempowering is open to debate. However, Joanne's comment at the beginning of this chapter—"The organization doesn't want me to come out thinking this way"—suggests that becoming critical of volunteer tourism is at odds with program sponsors' goals and discourses.

new performative linguistic "safe spaces." Such spaces make critiquing dominant forms of social action—like volunteer tourism—not only possible, but more likely.

References

Austin, John L. 1962. *How to do things with words*. Cambridge, MA: Harvard University Press.

Bornstein, Erica. 2005. *The spirit of development: Protestant NGOs, morality, and economic in Zimbabwe*. Palo Alto, CA: Stanford University Press.

Bodinger de Uriarte, John J. & Shari Jacobson. 2018. Dirty work: The carnival of service. In Bonnie Urciuoli (ed.), *The Experience of Neoliberal Education*, 73–105. New York: Berghahn Books.

Brookings Institution. June, 2006. *International volunteering: Smart power*. (Policy Brief No. 155). Washington, DC: L. Rieffel and S. Zalud.

Castagno, Angelica E. (ed.). 2019. *The price of nice: How good intentions maintain educational inequity*. Minneapolis, MN: University of Minnesota Press.

Cole, Teju. 2016. *Known and strange things: Essays*. New York, NY: Random House.

Cross-Cultural Solutions. 2016. *Why volunteer abroad with CCS*. New Rochelle, NY. www.crossculturalso lutions.org (accessed 28 December 2016).

Destination NOW. 2013. Tag: Cook Islands. https://destinationnow.me/category/south-pacific-cook-islands (updated 5 January 2014).

Djohari, Natalie, Gitanjali Pyndiah & Anna Arnone. 2018. Rethinking 'safe spaces' in children's geographies. *Children's Geographies* 16(4). 351–355.

Fortier, Anne-Marie. 2001. "Coming home": Queer migrations and multiple evocations of home. *European Journal of Lesbian and Gay Studies* 4(4). 405–424.

Gembus, Malte Phillip. 2018. The safe spaces "in-between": Plays, performance and identity among young "second generation" Somalis in London. *Children's Geographies* 16(4). 432–443.

Germann Molz, Jennie. 2016. Making a difference together: Discourses of transformation in volunteer tourism. *Journal of Sustainable Tourism* 24(6). 805–23.

Global Volunteers. 2002-Present. *Be the change in the world: Volunteer abroad*. Global Volunteers. St. Paul, MN: http://www.globalvolunteers.org. (accessed 19 October 2019).

Gorman-Murray, Andrew. 2007. Rethinking queer migration through the body. *Social and Cultural Geography* 8(1). 105–121.

Guiney, Tess. 2018. "Hug-an-orphan vacations": "Love" and emotion in orphanage tourism. *The Geographical Journal* 184(2). 125–137.

Guttentag, Daniel. 2012. Volunteer tourism: As good as it seems? In Tej Vir Singh (ed.), *Critical studies in tourism*, 152–159. Bristol, UK: Channel View Publications.

Hannam, Kevin, Mimi Sheller & John Urry. 2006. Editorial: Mobilities, immobilities, and moorings. *Mobilities* 1(1). 1–22.

Henry, Jacob. 2019. Pedagogy, possibility, and pipe dreams: Opportunities and challenges for radicalizing international volunteering. *Journal of Tourism and Cultural Change* 17(6). 663–675.

Jakubiak, Cori. 2012. "English for the global": Discourses in/of English-language voluntourism. *International Journal of Qualitative Studies in Education* 25(4). 435–451.

Jakubiak, Cori. 2020. "English is out there—you have to get with the program": Linguistic instrumentalism, global citizenship education, and English-language voluntourism. *Anthropology and Education Quarterly* 51(2). 212–232.

Kapoor, Ilan. 2004. Hyper-self-reflective development? Spivak on representing the Third World "Other." *Third World Quarterly* 4. 627–647.

Keese, James R. 2011. The geography of volunteer tourism: Place matters. *Tourism Geographies* 13(2). 257–279.

Keyl, Shireen. 2017. Learning English in the margins: Migrant worker knowledge production in Beirut's NGO spaces. In Jose Aldemar Álvarez V., Cathy Amanti, Shireen Keyl & Erin Mackinney (eds.), *Critical views on teaching and learning English around the globe: Qualitative research approaches*, 157–176. Charlotte, NC: Information Age Publishing, Inc.

Knopp, Larry & Michael Brown. 2003. Queer diffusions. *Environment and Planning D: Society and Space* 21. 409–424.

Lewis, Nathaniel M. 2012. Remapping disclosure: Gay men's segmented journeys of moving out and coming out. *Social and Cultural Geography* 13(3). 211–231.

Lyons, Kevin & Stephen Wearing (eds.). 2008. *Journeys of discovery in volunteer tourism: International case study perspectives*. Wallingford, CT: CABI.

Marcus, George E. 1995. Ethnography in/of the world system: The emergence of multi-sited ethnography. *Annual Review of Anthropology* 24. 95–117.

Park, Ji Hoon. 2018. Cultural implications of international volunteer tourism: US students' experiences in Cameroon. *Tourism Geographies* 20(1). 144–162.

Puar, Jasbir Kaur, Dereka Rushbrook & Louisa Schein. 2003. Sexuality and space: Queering geographies of globalization. *Environment and Planning D: Society and Space* 21. 383–387.

Richey, Lisa Ann & Stefano Ponte. 2011. *Brand aid: Shopping well to save the world*. Minneapolis, MN: University of Minnesota Press.

Scott, D. Travers. 2018. "Coming out of the closet": Examining a metaphor. *Annals of the International Communication Association* 42(3). 145–154.

Sedgwick, Eve K. 1990. *Epistemology of the closet*. Berkeley, CA: University of California Press.

Sen, Amartya. 1999. *Development as freedom*. New York, NY: Alfred A Knopf.

Snow, Donald B. 2001. *English teaching as Christian mission: An applied theology*. Scottdale, PA: Herald Press.

Spack, Ruth. 2006. English lessons. *TESOL Quarterly* 40(3). 595–604.

The Roestone Collective. 2014. Safe space: Toward a reconceptualization. *Antipode* 46(5). 1346–1365.

Tobin, Joseph & Akiko Hayashi. 2017. Return interviews and long engagements with ethnographic informants. *Anthropology and Education Quarterly* 48(3). 318–327.

United Planet. 2020. *Virtual internship and virtual volunteer opportunities*. Boston, MA: Author. https://www.unitedplanet.org/virtual-internships-virtual-volunteering. (accessed 15 May 2020).

Verduzco-Baker, Lynn. 2018. Modified brave spaces: Calling in brave instructors. *Sociology of Race and Ethnicity* (4)4. 585–592.

Vrasti, Wanda. 2013. *Volunteer tourism: Giving back in neoliberal times*. New York: Routledge.

Waitt, Gordon & Andrew Gorman-Murray. 2011a. "It's about time you came out": Sexualities, mobility and home. *Antipode* 43(4). 1380–1403.

Waitt, Gordon & Andrew Gorman-Murray. 2011b. Journeys and returns: Home, life narratives, and remapping sexuality in a regional city. *International Journal of Urban and Regional Research* 35(6). 1239–1255.

Wearing, Stephen. 2001. *Volunteer tourism: Experiences that make a difference*. Wallingford, CT: CABI Publishing.

Wearing, Stephen, David Beirman & Simone Grabowski. 2020. Engaging volunteer tourism in post-disaster recovery in Nepal. *Annals of Tourism Research* 80. Article 102802.

Laura Miller
Afterword: Japanese loanwords in performative linguistic spaces

Most scholars recognize that the common understanding of languages as uniform and monolithic entities is an artifact of state ideology. All entities that carry a specified language name, whether it is English, Spanish, Japanese, or any other named language, entail magnificent diversity and variation in who, where, and how people write or speak them. However, when we talk about specific lexical items that travel between linguistic spaces (rather than the users of languages), we must acknowledge that the word often originated in a known codified named linguistic system. Even though it is slightly divergent from this book's stated goals, I would like to use a few examples of word borrowing to explore the complexity of an issue raised in this collection. Although in the past I examined loanwords and pseudo loanwords found in Japanese (Miller 1997), the ideas in this volume led me to think about aspects of linguistic contact in a new manner. My essay is not an ethnographic study but is merely a musing on the life of a few words. As a starting point, I was struck by the proposal to think in terms of "performative linguistic space":

> Every space can be a performative linguistic space because space gives cues as to what kind of utterance or sign can occur . . . space is not performative on its own; rather the space becomes performative as a result of the specific intersections of linguistic politics carried from the various spaces that individuals have traversed (Doerr and McGuire, Introduction this volume).

It is the last part of this proposal about how participants in interactions carry their own linguistic politics into these spaces that held the greatest interest for me.

Even though this volume does not endorse the common assumption that languages are discrete bounded units, in my discussion of loanwords I use the categories of "English" (usually American English) and "Japanese" (including all varieties and dialects) because I am talking about loanwords that are borrowed from one linguistic system into another. The idea of considering the performative linguistic space, however, was productive in helping me understand how two Japanese words, *kawaii* (cute) and *otaku* (nerd), are used or understood in English language contexts. Each word has various meanings and understandings in different performative linguistic spaces in which participants are using English but are not members of a shared nationality or community of practice. This innovative edited volume inspired me to re-evaluate some initial reactions I had to the use of one of the loanwords and to a debate that the other loanword generated. In particular, when the editors say that

https://doi.org/10.1515/9783110744781-007

locating an analysis in a performative linguistic space will demonstrate that "practices are shaped by the language politics 'dragged' from various spaces" (Doerr and McGuire, Introduction this volume) by participating individuals, the two Japanese loanwords I discuss fit this model quite well.

The kawaii loanword debate

In 2021, a black Instagram and TikTok media personality known for cosplaying and dressing in Japan-derived cute fashions created a firestorm because of her outfit and because of her use of the Japanese word kawaii. Mia Angelina uploaded a video to TikTok in which she wore a costume from a Japanese anime series, along with the hashtag #Kawaii. Apparently, not everyone appreciated her perfect rendition of an anime character, nor her use of the word kawaii. Among the flood of comments below the video were claims such as these:

> Kawaii culture is Japanese, so when foreigners use the word 'kawaii,' it's cultural appropriation. Kawaii is a slur!!

Angelina received an avalanche of negative reaction, and as a result, TikTok temporarily suspended her account. She also felt obligated to issue an apology. On her Instagram account she wrote:

> I apologize to any Japanese people I harmed by using the word k***ii to describe an american artist that isn't k***ii while presenting as hyperfemme. I understand that it can be used as a slur and that using the word while presenting as hyperfemme using pastel colors and pink can be harmful to Japanese people and will fetishize them especially if im using it to describe something that isn't k***ii or unanimously considered k***ii. From now on I will never use that word again. (Angelina 2021)

In related spaces others self-censured by using k@wåii or k***ii, as if the word is truly taboo. Angelina was not the only target of censure for using the term kawaii and for cosplaying a Japanese character. The black cosplayer Mia Rios was similarly accused of fetishizing a Japanese anime character (Montgomery 2021). Rios, too, was banned from TikTok and attacked for appropriation of Japanese culture.

Meanwhile, the majority of Japanese people who were interviewed or who wrote about foreigners' use of the word kawaii were perplexed. The YouTube channel named Ask Japanese, which conducts random interviews with Japanese people on the street in Tokyo, asked some young people about non-Japanese people using the word kawaii, and no one objected to it (Ask Japanese 2021). A major figure in the Japanese Harajuku fashion landscape and now a published academic author named Haruka Kurebayashi posted responses on several social media platforms defending anyone's right to use the word kawaii. For example, she tweeted that *"Kawaii ga kaigai de aisareru koto wa zenzen tabū de wa arimasen"* (It is not at all taboo for kawaii to be loved overseas, Kurebayashi 2021). The dustup even made it into national news sites in Japan. In one article, Kurebayashi is put forward as a defender of the use of kawaii by non-Japanese. She also expressed concern that eventually kawaii might evolve into *sabetsu yōgo* or a "discriminatory term" (Ogawa 2021). A writer named Kilara Sen (2021) similarly wondered how kawaii could legitimately be criticized as cultural appropriation. She points out that kawaii does not fit the definition of cultural appropriation she found in an online article: "the use of objects or elements of a non-dominant culture in a way that doesn't respect their original meaning, give credit to their source, or reinforces stereotypes or contributes to oppression" (Cuncic 2020). She notes that not one person in the scenario was part of the dominant US culture, and that the term kawaii is not commonly viewed as a name for a separate subculture in Japan as it is outside Japan.

Like many other scholars of Japan, my first response to the "Kawaii is a slur!!" claim was that it is an extreme form of American social justice surveillance unrelated to the meaning of the term. It seemed a stretch to view an aesthetic term with polysemic meanings and positive interactional functions as a type of cultural/linguistic appropriation, particularly when the Japanese government itself actively promotes global consumption of kawaii (Miller 2011). Yet, thinking about this volume's insistence that space shapes linguistic practices, I began to reconsider the motivations for condemnation of a black or white person's use of the word. Although ultimately such censure might be off the mark, it is still good to acknowledge that in the TikTok space where the kawaii debate occurred, the participants brought with them to that space legitimate concerns about appropriation and anti-Asian racism (even while demonstrating their own racism against African Americans). The space allowed the voicing of frustrations with cultural appropriation and mockery of Asians, described by Bow (2018) in her analysis of anthropomorphized kawaii objects circulating in the US. Bow suggests that consumption of kawaii commodities reproduces infantilization and racist framings of Asian Americans. Unpacking the kawaii loanword debate requires some background and some diversion into a related example, that of otaku, but ultimately, I think aspects of the case illustrate at least one theme of the volume.

The other Japanese loanword, otaku, is used in a similar fashion as kawaii to mark a specific urban youth subculture in the US. The term otaku originally described a type of person in Japan during the 1980s, and it did not have a positive meaning. It was often used pejoratively to refer to a man who is creepily obsessed, verging on perverted. After 2000, otaku started to be used in a general way to mean someone with an obsessive interest in something, similar to English nerd or geek. It is no longer pejorative yet remains slightly denigrating depending on the speaker and the context. One change in the meaning of otaku in Japan is that it is not restricted to someone, female or male, who loves anime or manga as in the American English loanword context. Rather, it can be used for any obsessive interest or hobby, including trains, history, and sports. Otaku as a loanword used by English speakers does not carry the same tainted historical weight and is generally limited in scope to fandom of Japanese manga, games, and anime. It functions as an open display of membership in a subculture of fans. There is even the American magazine named *Otaku USA*, and several books with otaku in the title written by the prolific anthropologist Galbraith (2014, 2019). My detour from kawaii to otaku as a loanword is meant to drive home the complexity of understanding the meanings and uses of words when they are deployed in different linguistic settings (i.e., performative linguistic space), especially when used as loanwords. Kawaii also might be accomplishing a type of social marking when used in an otherwise English language context. It will let the reader or hearer know that the user is a participant in Japanese popular culture fandom. In that sense, it is no different than a wine enthusiast friend who calls our wine an "oak monster." I understand that it signals that they are a connoisseur with access to insider terminology. When a young American person who is not Japanese and does not know the Japanese language uses kawaii in an otherwise English context, I understand the function of the word as marking their affiliation with a subculture of fans.

There is an important difference between otaku and kawaii even when used as markers of membership in a subculture. When American students introduce themselves to me by saying "I'm an otaku!" it continues to be a little jarring or uncomfortable to hear. I first lived in Japan when this term was introduced as a descriptor for an abnormal man. For older people it still carries the whiff of the stigmatized. Kawaii, in contrast, never had a pejorative meaning. In addition, it does not have the restricted meanings many writers attribute to it. For example, Ngai (2012:42) analyzes kawaii as an "aestheticization of powerlessness," with meanings of smallness, helplessness, and deformity. However, her understanding is based on a small range of the meanings and functions of kawaii, because the term is much broader and can encompass almost any other aesthetic to yield vibrant and new connotations. Furthermore, kawaii is not the sole province of children and young women. Japan's kawaii aesthetic spread beyond the expected domains of girl culture into politics, conduct literature, history textbooks, and elsewhere, and is appreciated by all age groups and genders (Miller and Stevens 2021). Kawaii serves legitimate and important social and cultural functions—it is a clever way to do the work of informing us, admonishing us, and convincing us. There is a spectrum of kawaii imagery found in diverse cultural domains and with a history that predates the 1970s (many writers cite an article that dates kawaii to the 1970s). Kawaii is polysemic, with a broad range of meanings not captured by the translation "cute," including meanings of sweet, adorable, awesome, interesting, pretty, and wonderful. Kawaii is also used in social interaction as a response similar to American English "cool," to simply serve as acknowledgement or ratification.

Returning to the statement "Kawaii is a slur," in order to understand the sentiment behind this claim, it is important to step away from the normal meanings of kawaii in a Japanese context to be able to consider issues of appropriation and racism that participants in the performative linguistic space carried with them to the scene.

Linguistic and cultural appropriation

Discourse about cultural appropriation extends beyond the harmful practices normally associated with the concept, such as white college students who once dressed up in a Sioux costume during football halftime performances (Farnell 2004). Also included is the adoption of language elements, slang, or speech styles from other groups of speakers. This has led some writers to consider adoption or use of specific lexical items or expressions in English as appropriative or deeply steeped in racism. For example, one writer calls out the everyday expression "No can do" as a mocking imitation of Chinese immigrants to the US during the 19th century (Bleyle 2020). These studies of contaminated lexical borrowing or coinage are somewhat different from my understanding of English loanwords in Japanese. I strongly make the case that once an English word is adopted into Japanese it is no longer an English word and is thus open for extreme modification in its semantic and phonological traits. Those many websites about "bad" English in Japan always bewilder me because the writers apparently want English words to eternally retain the pronunciations and meanings that they are familiar with. Yet, I realized that my own first reaction to the "kawaii is a slur" debate was no different, as I felt resistance to the possibility that the word might be used in a negative manner as a loanword in English.

Scholars such as Reyes (2005) have documented adoption of linguistics features and style from one ethnic group to another, tracking how it is intertwined with the larger social setting of racialization of language and cultural appropriation. As she writes "While non-African Americans may gain local social prestige through peppering their speech with African American slang terms, they do so without suffering the daily experiences with discrimination that plague the lives of many African Americans" (Reyes 2005: 509–510). At the same time, her study of the use of African American slang by a group of Asian Americans showed that speakers were using the borrowed lexical items as a method for creating their own identities separate from other Asian Americans, as well as to signal participation in urban youth subculture (Reyes 2005: 527). When I hear people who are not Asian Americans use the words otaku or kawaii, it is this later social function that seems most fitting.

Many of the Twitter, Instagram, TikTok, and other social media writers who weighed in on the "kawaii is a slur" debate had seemingly been nourished on a body of literature that enabled them to be sensitive and aware of how language encodes racism and sexism. One of the most vocal critics was "Sam," a writer on Tumbl (Sad-queer 2013). In a scathing blog post Sam shared many points but here are a few that are worth attending to:

> I am Japanese and I find the usage of the word "kawaii" by non-Japanese people to be extremely appropriative and damaging. I'll tell you why:
>
> "Kawaii" as an aesthetic contributes to the commodification and exotification of Japanese people. Japanese pop culture and style is not for your consumption. It is not for you to steal and make money off of. It is not for you to exploit. There is a very thin line between "appreciating" things from other cultures and appropriation. You are allowed to engage in Japanese pop culture, but chances are that your desire to consume it is rooted in some really deep exotification, which also ties into . . .
>
> Japanese people are not your prop or your costume, we are not here to be cute for you. "Kawaii" and its implications contribute to stereotypes about Asian people. We are not cute, quiet, submissive playthings for your enjoyment. The stereotype that all asian people are just docile is really damaging. I am not your asian bitch. . . . .
>
> So basically, if you're not Japanese, don't say "kawaii." Just call it fucking cute. That way your words won't carry racist implications and I won't think you're an asshole.

Sam's anger is understandable, considering the US cultural and linguistic landscape. The kawaii loanword debate became a focal point for expression of frustrations with orientalism, anti-Asian sentiment, and cultural appropriation. It was the vehicle for processing legitimate concerns, although often overlooking some of the social and linguistic aspects of the actual use of kawaii. Those who were upset by non-Asians using the term appeared to be primarily from the US (Although Sam claims Japanese identity, he is half Japanese and lives in the US). Racism continues to be embedded in the language of Americans, often used unconsciously in seemingly innocuous idioms and catch phrases. Hill (2008) for example, exposed the underlying racism that allows the introduction of Spanish lexical items into English monolingual discourse to lend pejorative or low-brow nuances, such as "Hasta la vista, Baby," which takes an elegant parting expression and turns it into a nasty kiss-off. Another example was discussed by Bright (2000), who tracked the controversy over use of the word "squaw" in US placenames and argued that both the fictive etymology as well as the linguistically verified benign origin of the word are irrelevant—all that matters is that Native Americans today find the term offensive. If subjective associations are intensely negative for the majority of Native Americans, we should stop using it for placenames. Perhaps the critics of non-Asians using kawaii were making a flawed analogy in assuming that kawaii is only used to index or point to negative meanings, or as Sam and others do, to limited meanings of abject docility and submissiveness. Yet, if I take the goal of this volume seriously, and consider the spaces of debate about kawaii that emerge when people bring different language politics with them, then it allows for linguistic actions such as condemnation. Similar to the squaw debate, the actual meanings or etymology of a term are irrelevant if enough people find it offensive. Even if I would not like to see kawaii become a taboo word in American English, it is ultimately something that will not be solved by using the facts of linguistic science.

Cosplay spread from Japan to neighboring Korea, Taiwan, Hong Kong and China, where people similarly dress up as anime characters in the same manner as Mia Angelina. It joined many other Japanese popular culture forms such as print club photos and Boys Love manga as youth subcultural activities (Miller 2017). A difference is that the bodies involved are Asian and not black or white. This is a key feature that underscores the debate. US commentators viewed the cosplay of Angelina and Rios as gross cultural appropriation no different than the white celebrity Katy Perry wearing a weird kimono-like outfit, which was widely condemned. Kawaii became a touchpoint for a larger issue in interethnic relations and identity marking. The word became the putative focal point, where it functioned as a substitute for a different complaint. Even so, the idea that doing cosplay as a Japanese anime character should be restricted to Asian-coded bodies is odd. King (2019), an academic scholar who studies Japanese and global cosplay, notes that global communities have created welcoming spaces for those who cosplay beloved characters regardless of their race, age or gender (King 2019). Cosplay in foreign countries is much appreciated by people in Japan, not just the bureaucrats at the Ministry of Foreign Affairs. For decades, its global spread has been celebrated by Japanese cosplayers themselves. For example, one of the many specialized cosplay publications in 2006 featured hundreds of photos spread over several pages with descriptions of anime and cosplay conventions in the US, Paris, and Singapore (Cosmode 2006). I am not aware of any people living in Japan who consider cosplaying of anime characters by black or white fans as cultural appropriation.

The Japanese subcultures of Lolita and Decora have similarly spread around the globe from Japan to other parts of Asia, Europe, Australia, US, and elsewhere. There is one famous Muslim Lolita who has thousands of followers on her Tumblr website named The Hijabi Lolita (Herwees 2019). These subcultures of multiethnic members use kawaii as a core unifying concept. The limited abject meanings attributed to kawaii by theorists such as Ngai (2012), are ones that members of Lolita and Decora subcultures themselves vehemently reject (Rose, Kurebayashi, and Saionji 2022). Based on qualitative data that reflects the worldview of participants themselves, the authors strongly object to the view that love of kawaii is a type of infantile regression such as that proposed by many scholars.

Although there is pushback in accepting it because of political tensions and nationalist impulse, it is clear that the Japanese word kawaii also became a loanword in Korean and Mandarin. In Korean it is kawai 카와이. Although Chinese characters were imported into Japan, their use in an entirely different language resulted in new word formations, and many of those new formations as Chinese characters were borrowed back into Mandarin. These are known as *wasei-kango* (Japan-made Chinese words) and are those words composed of Chinese characters but invented in Japan rather than borrowed from China. The word kěài 可爱 (lovely, cute) is normally considered to be a Japan-made Chinese word and is listed as such in new dictionaries. It was also at one time straightforwardly transliterated as 卡哇伊 kāwāyi (Zhou 2015). In Taiwan, the kawaii aesthetic has had an enormous impact on consumer goods and even religious commodities. Silvio (2019) tracks the explosion of interest in Buddhist and Daoist deity figurines that encode the kawaii aesthetic, especially among male and female urban office workers, small business owners, and toy designers. One would find it hard to imagine any of them thinking that "kawaii is a slur." These examples make it clear that the US debate is not really about the loanword kawaii itself.

Outside the TikTok community space, scholars normally think about loanwords in ways that reflect descriptive linguistics, but we also need to acknowledge the right of others to contest or problematize the use of any words, including loanwords. The kawaii loanword debate is interesting because unlike other "slurs" it was never a stigmatized or taboo word in the donor language. There are many cases of speakers using loanwords to replace possibly offensive words, or of loanwords acquiring a taboo status in the recipient language (Miller 2022). Kawaii has the potential to become a negative word among any group of speakers. Once a word is borrowed, it ceases to be subject to the phonological and semantic rules of the donor language. It is a new word in a new space. If enough people who are English speakers decide that kawaii is a stigmatized word, it will acquire that status regardless of its prior life in Japanese.

I am avoiding some of the theoretical stances and the impetus of this volume because I continue to treat space as a place where linguistic practices occur. Yet, using the notion of performative linguistic space explained why kawaii was negatively sanctioned in the manner discussed above. As this volume's editors noted, "The result is a specific performative linguistic space that encourages or discourages certain linguistic practices, temporally and contextually" (Doerr and McGuire,

Introduction to this volume). The studies collected here are ambitious, asking us to theorize space, performance, language, identity, and more. Scholars across different disciplines will find provocative and stimulating ideas, and hopefully, some will think about old research topics in a different way.

References

Angelina, Mia. 2021. "The use of the word k@wåii as a Japanese slur." Instagram account @sincerely nymphie. https://www.instagram.com/p/CTiZ9vSre7d/ (accessed 7 September 2021)

Ask Japanese. 2021. "Is 'kawaii' cultural appropriation? We asked Japanese girls and boys in Tokyo." YouTube Channel. https://www.youtube.com/watch?v=B_g2zpFxkKs (updated 18 November 2021)

Bleyle, Lydia. 2020. "Give me back my language! The harmful nature of language appropriation for American minorities." Literature and Social Change: The State University of New York at Fredonia English 400 Senior Seminar Capstone Project. *Medium*. https://medium.com/literature-and-social-change/give-me-back-my-language-d8244c817067 (updated 5 May 2020)

Bow, Leslie. 2018. Racist cute: Caricature, kawaii-style, and the Asian thing. *American Quarterly* 71(1). 29–58.

Bright, William. 2000. The sociolinguistics of the "s–word": Squaw in American placenames. *Names: A Journal of Onomastics* 48 (3–4).207–216.

Cuncic, Arlin. 2020. "What is cultural appropriation?" *Very Well Mind*, Dotdash Meredith Publishing. Originally published May 11, 2018. https://www.verywellmind.com/what-is-cultural-appropriation-5070458 (updated 13 August 2022)

Cosmode. 2006 "Kaigai snap dai tokushū" [Major special report photos from overseas]. *Cosmode*.14. 82–89.

Farnell, Brenda. 2004. The fancy dance of racializing discourse. *Journal of Sport and Social Issues* 28 (1) 30–55.

Galbraith, Patrick W. 2014. *The otaku encyclopedia: An insider's guide to the subculture of Cool Japan*. Tokyo: Kodansha International.

Galbraith, Patrick W. 2019. *Otaku and the struggle for imagination in Japan*. Durham: Duke University Press.

Herwees, Tasbeeh. 2019. "Meet the Hijabi Lolita." Vice. https://www.vice.com/en/article/dp5pm7/meet-the-hijabi-lolita-968 (28 June 2019)

Hill, Jane H. 2008. *The everyday language of white racism*. Hoboken, NJ: Wiley-Blackwell.

King, Emerald. 2019. Performing gender: Cosplay and otaku cultures and spaces. In Lucy Fraser, Mark Pendleton & Jennifer Coates (eds.), *Routledge companion to gender and Japanese culture*, 279–288. London and New York: Routledge.

Kurebayashi, Haruka. 2021. "Nihongo to eigo no dōga na node" [Since the video is in Japanese and English]. Twitter post. https://twitter.com/90884/status/1443964623531569153 (1 October 2021).

Miller, Laura. 1997. Wasei eigo: English "loanwords" coined in Japan. In Jane Hill, P.J. Mistry & Lyle Campbell, *The life of language: Papers in linguistics in honor of William Bright*, 123–139. Mouton/De Gruyter: The Hague.

Miller, Laura. 2011. Cute masquerade and the pimping of Japan. *International Journal of Japanese Sociology* 20(1). 18–29.

Miller, Laura. 2017. Girl culture in East Asia. *Transnational Asia: An online interdisciplinary journal* 1(2). https://doi.org/10.25613/7z4f-g488

Miller, Laura. 2022. Bad mouths: Taboo and transgressive language. *Annual Review of Anthropology* 51. 17–30.

Miller, Laura & Carolyn Stevens. 2021. From beautiful to cute: Shifting meanings in Japanese language and culture. *International Journal of Language and Culture* 8(1). 62–83.

Montgomery, Hanako. 2021. "A black TikToker was accused of appropriating a Japanese character. Then she was banned." *VICE World News*. https://www.vice.com/en/article/epxn3j/black-cosplay-japanese-anime-tiktok (24 November 2021).

Ngai, Sianne. 2012. *Our aesthetic categories: Zany, cute, interesting*. Cambridge: Harvard University Press.

Ogawa, Takahiro. 2021. "Kawaii bunka no tōyōna no ka, kokujin no kosupure o jishō nihonjin ga hihan, Kurebayashi Haruka-san wa yōgo" [Is kawaii appropriation of culture? Self-proclaimed Japanese criticize black cosplay, Ms. Haruka Kurebayashi defends]. *Asahi Shimbun Globe*. https://globe.asahi.com/article/14471641 (31 October 2021)

Reyes, Angela. 2005. Appropriation of African American slang by Asian American youth. *Journal of Sociolinguistics* 9(4). 509–532.

Rose, Megan Catherine, Haruka Kurebayashi & Rei Saionji. 2022. Kawaii affective assemblages: Cute new materialism in decora fashion, Harajuku. *M/C Journal*, 25(4). https://doi.org/10.5204/mcj.2926

Sad-queer. 2013. "On 'kawaii' and appropriation." Posted by Sam on the Sad-queer blog on Tumblr. https://sad-queer.tumblr.com/post/48182159965/on-kawaii-and-appropriation (16 April 2013)

Sen, Kilara. 2021. "Is kawaii a slur? Reaction of a Japanese HBCU alum." *Medium*. https://kilaracomedy.medium.com/day-7-is-kawaii-a-slur-thoughts-of-a-japanese-attending-at-hbcu-a2653b096d56 (8 November 2021)

Silvio, Teri. 2019. *Puppets, gods, and brands: Theorizing the age of animation from Taiwan*. Honolulu: University of Hawai'i Press.

Tucker, Lindsay. 2021. Culturally appropriative words and phrases to stop using today. *Yoga Journal*. Outside Interactive, Inc. https://www.yogajournal.com/lifestyle/cultural-appropriation/ (3 February 2021)

Zhou, Albert R. 2015. Hybridity of hanyu: Classification and characteristics of loanwords in Mandarin Chinese. *Tokoha Diagaku Keiei Gakubu Kiyō* [Bulletin of the Faculty of Business Administration, Tokoha University] 3(1). 57–67.

Notes on contributors

Ngoc Anh Do received a master's degree from the Graduate School of International Culture and Communication Studies at Waseda University. She is interested in the concept of translanguaging, and how it can be applied in exploring the realities of multilingual students in higher education settings. In the chapter "Translanguaging practices within an ideology of monolingualism: Two ethnographic perspectives" in *The global education effect and Japan: Constructing new borders and identification practices* (edited by Neriko Musha Doerr, 2020), she made a collaborative attempt to employ translanguaging and autoethnography to reflect on her language practices and ideology as a university student at an English-medium-instruction program in Japan.

Neriko Musha Doerr received a Ph.D. in cultural anthropology from Cornell University. Her research interests include politics of difference, language and power, civic engagement, and education in Japan, Aotearoa/New Zealand, and the United States, as well as study abroad. Her publications include *Meaningful Inconsistencies: Bicultural Nationhood, Free Market, and Schooling in Aotearoa/New Zealand* (Berghahn), *The Native Speaker Concept: Ethnographic Investigations of "Native Speaker Effects"* (Mouton de Gruyter), *Constructing the Heritage Language Learner: Knowledge, Power, and New Subjectivities* (Mouton de Gruyter), *Rethinking Language and Culture in Japanese Education* (Multilingual Matters; as the co-editor with Shinji Sato), *Transforming Study Abroad: A Handbook* (Berghahn), *The Global Education Effect and Japan: Constructing New Borders and Identification Practices* (Routledge), and *Fairies, Ghosts, and Santa Claus: Tinted Glasses, Fetishes, and the Politics of Seeing* (Berghahn) and articles in various peer-reviewed journals. She currently teaches at Ramapo College in New Jersey, U.S.A.

Cori Jakubiak is an associate professor of education and Director of the Center for Prairie Studies at Grinnell College in Grinnell, Iowa, USA, where she teaches courses on the Cultural Politics of Language Teaching, world language and ESOL methods, and Differentiating Instruction for All Learners. Her research program centers on the intersections among language education, tourism, and global citizenship, and she has published numerous studies of English-language voluntourism, or short-term, volunteer English language teaching in the Global South. Cori's newest scholarly project examines the language and other ideologies that circulate within a language-based tourism program in Florence, Italy.

Yuri Kumagai received Ed.D. in Language, Literacy, and Culture from University of Massachusetts, Amherst. She is a senior lecturer of Japanese at Smith College, USA. Her specializations are critical literacy and multiliteracies in world language education. Her research interests include language ideologies, semiotic landscapes, and translingual practices. She publishes journal articles and book chapters in English and Japanese. Her publications include *Multiliteracies in World Language Education* (co-edited, 2015, Routledge), *Tomo ni Ikiru Tameni* [For Living Together] (co-edited, 2022, Shunpū-sha), *Critical Literacies in East Asian Languages: Examples form Japanese in Foreign Language Education* (2023, *in International Encyclopedia of Japanese*, vol. 10, Elsevier). Her articles appear in journals such as *Critical Inquiry in Language Studies*, *Japanese Language and Literature*, *Journal of Bilingual Education and Bilingualism*, *Writing Systems Research*, and *L2 Journal*.

Jennifer M. McGuire is currently an associate professor at the Institute for the Liberal Arts at Doshisha University in Kyoto, Japan. She received a doctorate in social anthropology from the University of Oxford. Her research interests include deaf education, sign language acquisition and

https://doi.org/10.1515/9783110744781-008

communication, and inclusive practices in educational spaces. She has published on emerging signers, research ethics with deaf children, academic and social inclusion, and sign language co-enrollment programs. Jennifer's most recent project examines sign language interpreter training and professional practices in Japan.

Laura Miller is the Ei'ichi Shibusawa-Seigo Arai Endowed Professor of Japanese Studies and Professor of History at the University of Missouri St. Louis. She is an internationally prominent scholar of Japan Studies, cultural history, and linguistic anthropology who has authored or co-edited five books in addition to more than ninety articles and book chapters. Research topics have included buzzword and kanji contests, gyaru moji (girl characters), the third century shaman ruler Himiko, purikura (print club photos), Abe no Seimei, and elevator girls. "Bad mouths: Taboo and transgressive language" appeared in the Annual Review of Anthropology 51, 2022. Her forthcoming book is *Occult Hunting and Supernatural Play in Japan* (University of Hawai'i Press).

Gregory S. Poole received a doctorate in social anthropology from the University of Oxford. His area of research focuses mostly on the anthropology of education and his books include *Foreign Language Education in Japan: Exploring Qualitative Approaches* (2015, co-edited with Sachiko Horiguchi and Yuki Imoto), *Reframing Diversity in the Anthropology of Japan* (2015, co-edited with John Ertl, John Mock, and John McCreery), *The Japanese Professor: An Ethnography of a University Faculty* (2010), and *Higher Education in East Asia: Neoliberalism and the Professoriate* (2009, co-edited with Ya-chen Chen). Greg is currently a professor at the Institute for the Liberal Arts, Doshisha University, Kyoto.

Index

https://doi.org/10.1515/9783110744781-009

www.ingramcontent.com/pod-product-compliance
Lightning Source LLC
Chambersburg PA
CBHW030829090426
42737CB00009B/938